Homelessness Prevention in Treatment of Substance Abuse and Mental Illness: Logic Models and Implementation of Eight American Projects

Homelessness Prevention in Treatment of Substance Abuse and Mental Illness: Logic Models and Implementation of Eight American Projects has been co-published simultaneously as *Alcoholism Treatment Quarterly*, Volume 17, Numbers 1/2 1999.

Homelessness Prevention in Treatment of Substance Abuse and Mental Illness: Logic Models and Implementation of Eight American Projects

Kendon J. Conrad, PhD
Michael D. Matters, PhD
Patricia Hanrahan, PhD
Daniel J. Luchins, MD
Editors

Homelessness Prevention in Treatment of Substance Abuse and Mental Illness: Logic Models and Implementation of Eight American Projects has been co-published simultaneously as *Alcoholism Treatment Quarterly*, Volume 17, Numbers 1/2 1999.

LONDON AND NEW YORK

Homelessness Prevention in Treatment of Substance Abuse and Mental Illness: Logic Models and Implementation of Eight American Projects has been co-published simultaneously as *Alcoholism Treatment Quarterly*, Volume 17, Numbers 1/2 1999.

First published 1999 by
The Haworth Press, Inc.
10 Alice Street, Binghamton, NY 13904-1580 USA

Published 2014 by Routledge
711 Third Avenue, New York, NY 10017
2 Park Square, Milton Park, Abingdon, Oxfordshire OX14 4RN

First issued in paperback 2014

Routledge is an imprint of the Taylor & Francis Group, an informa business

© 1999 by The Haworth Press, Inc. All rights reserved. No part of this work may be reproduced or utilized in any form or by any means, electronic or mechanical, including photocopying, microfilm and recording, or by any information storage and retrieval system, without permission in writing from the publisher.

Cover design by Thomas J. Mayshock Jr.

Library of Congress Cataloging-in-Publication Data

Homelessness prevention in treatment of substance abuse and mental illness: logic models and implementation of eight American projects/Kendon J. Conrad . . . [et al.] editors.
    p. cm.
Includes bibliographical references and index.
    ISBN 978-0-789-00750-6 (hbk)
    ISBN 978-1-138-00239-5 (pbk)

    1. Homelessness–United States–Prevention. 2. Substance abuse–Treatment–United States. 3. Alcoholism–Treatment–United States. 4. Mental illness–Treatment–United States. I Conrad, Kendon J.
HV4505.H6577 1999
363.5'7'0973–dc21   99-32742
                                                                                                                               CIP

Homelessness Prevention in Treatment of Substance Abuse and Mental Illness: Logic Models and Implementation of Eight American Projects

CONTENTS

Preface   xvii
   Kendon J. Conrad
   Michael D. Matters
   Patricia Hanrahan
   Daniel J. Luchins

Cooperative Agreements for CMHS/CSAT Collaborative Program to Prevent Homelessness: An Overview   1
   Lawrence D. Rickards
   Walter Leginski
   Frances L. Randolph
   Deirdre Oakley
   James M. Herrell
   Cheryl Gallagher

Creating and Using Logic Models: Four Perspectives   17
   Kendon J. Conrad
   Frances L. Randolph
   Michael W. Kirby, Jr.
   Richard R. Bebout

Homelessness Prevention Therapeutic Community (TC) for Addicted Mothers   33
   JoAnn Y. Sacks
   Stanley Sacks
   Michael Harle
   George De Leon

Dyadic Case Management as a Strategy for Prevention of Homelessness Among Chronically Debilitated Men and Women with Alcohol and Drug Dependence 53
> *Michael W. Kirby, Jr.*
> *G. Nicholas Braucht*
> *Ellen Brown*
> *Sigmund Krane*
> *Mary McCann*
> *Nancy VanDeMark*

Preventing Homelessness in Florida 73
> *Colleen Clark*
> *Gregory B. Teague*
> *Robert M. Henry*

Housing Solutions: The Community Connections Housing Program: Preventing Homelessness by Integrating Housing and Supports 93
> *Richard R. Bebout*

From Streets to Homes: The Pathways to Housing Consumer Preference Supported Housing Model 113
> *Sam Tsemberis*
> *Sara Asmussen*

Project H.O.M.E.: A Comprehensive Program for Homeless Individuals with Mental Illness and Substance Use Disorders 133
> *Kathleen Coughey*
> *Kelly Feighan*
> *Karlene Lavelle*
> *Kristen Olson*
> *Maureen DeCarlo*
> *Monica Medina*

A Home-Based Family Intervention for Ethnic Minorities
   with a Mentally Ill Member   149
       Linda Connery
       John Brekke

Representative Payee for Individuals with Severe Mental
   Illness at Community Counseling Centers of Chicago   169
       Kendon J. Conrad
       Michael D. Matters
       Patricia Hanrahan
       Daniel J. Luchins
       Courtenay Savage
       Betty Daugherty
       Marc Shinderman

Cross-Site Issues in the Collaborative Program to Prevent
   Homelessness: Conclusion   187
       Patricia Hanrahan
       Deidre Oakley
       Lawrence D. Rickards
       Daniel J. Luchins
       James M. Herrell
       Kendon J. Conrad
       Michael D. Matters
       Cheryl Gallagher

Index   209

ABOUT THE EDITORS

Kendon J. Conrad, PhD, is Professor in Health Policy and Administration at the School of Public Health of the University of Illinois at Chicago and Associate Research Career Scientist of the Midwest Center for Health Services and Policy Research at Hines Hospital, Department of Veterans Affairs. He is the principal investigator on the representative payee project described in this volume and has published principally in the areas of substance abuse treatment, long term care, and evaluation research methodology.

Michael D. Matters, PhD, is Research Assistant Professor in Health Policy and Administration at the University of Illinois at Chicago and a co-investigator on the representative payee project. He received his doctorate in sociology from the College of Liberal Arts and Sciences at the University of Illinois at Chicago specializing in the study of organizations and in linguistics in December of 1994. He has worked on studies of programs for substance abuse and mental illness.

Patricia Hanrahan, PhD, is Associate Professor in the Department of Psychiatry at The University of Chicago, the Director of Clinical Program Evaluation for the Illinois Department of Human Services (IDHS), and a co-principal investigator on the representative payee project. Her research interests include evaluation research in social work, adult day care, and more recently, hospice care for dementia patients, supportive housing for severely mentally ill individuals, and the provision of a novel anti-psychotic drug, risperidone, through a retrospective analysis using the IDHS pharmacy database.

Daniel J. Luchins, MD, is Associate Professor in the Department of Psychiatry at The University of Chicago and Associate Director of Clinical Services at IDHS. He is a co-principal investigator on the representative payee project and has published principally in the areas of the significance of structural brain abnormalities in schizophrenics. He has also developed a strong interest in polydipsia and other repetitive behaviors in chronic schizophrenia. The more recent of his over 100 publications include examinations of rehospitalization rates, factors influencing rehospitalization rates, and the assessment of substance abuse or dependence among individuals with severe mental illness.

Preface

In 1996 the Substance Abuse and Mental Health Services Administration (SAMHSA) funded eight, three-year knowledge development projects designed to prevent homelessness in high risk populations with problems of alcoholism, drug abuse, and/or mental illness. These projects were selected because they are state-of-the-art representations of four types of homelessness prevention: (1) supportive housing, (2) residential treatment, (3) family support and respite, and (4) representative payee and money management.

The primary goals for the first year of the homelessness prevention projects were: first, to develop logic models of each project's theory, implementation, and intended outcomes; and second, to develop program manuals that would enable replication of the models to promote best practice and scientific generalizability. The second and third years were devoted to evaluating the interventions described in the program manuals and logic models. The purpose of this volume is to present the theory or logic guiding each program including an up-to-date review of the literature supporting each theory. These program theories will include a logic model which is a graphic depiction of the context, population, theoretical foundations, activities and intended outcomes of each program. This will be followed by a description of the implementation of the program including its history, the practical issues involved in delivering services, the pitfalls, lessons learned and recommendations for the future. As much as possible, the articles will include data on the characteristics of clients, types and amounts of services as well as existing data on the effectiveness of program implementation. Project outcomes, even preliminary outcomes, are not included since the evaluations are ongoing at the time of this writing, and it would be premature and potentially misleading to present preliminary findings.

As was the case in an earlier volume, *Treatment of the Chemically Dependent Homeless* (Conrad, Hultman, and Lyons, 1993), there was some concern over whether to describe the projects before we knew how successful they were. The consensus of the participating sites, however, was to present these descriptions based on the rationale that follows.

The projects were selected through a rigorous merit review process. Each program was based on some prior experience and a theoretical rationale that had to be articulated and defended before an expert peer-review panel and a subsequent site visit by SAMHSA project staff.

A description of this theoretical rationale with an up-to-date review of the literature could be helpful to others considering program design and might offer new ideas and variations to those with existing programs. In many cases, given the current state-of-the-art, these are our best guesses of what types of programming are likely to be successful. Unfortunately, the overwhelming majority of social programs lack thorough, well-articulated program descriptions. Those having program manuals do not make them readily available for general use. Additionally, the manuals that we have seen are usually daunting to read in terms of their length, style, and organization. The advantage of the proposed articles is that they will present refined descriptions resulting from a year of careful study by each project. Most of these projects include qualitative and quantitative studies by experienced research teams that describe program implementation using case studies, focus groups, and analyses of existing data.

The principal scientific rationale for presenting the program descriptions was based on the fact that all of the programs would be studied in a rigorous way. Therefore, whether they were found to be effective or not, the program descriptions would form templates on which replication could be based for those found to be successful or on which improvements could be made for those found to be unsuccessful. Thus, the program description is analogous to the formula for a drug in a drug trial. Whether or not the drug is found to work, it is important to document what the formula was.

Therefore, a volume that presented an array of homelessness prevention strategies for alcoholism, drug abuse, and mental illness in a brief readable form would be very useful to the field because information on this topic is not commonly available. The program descriptions serve as state-of-the-art models that can inform new program development as well as existing program improvement.

Our previous volume was well-reviewed and well-received and serves as a useful companion to the present volume. After publication as a journal issue, it was published in hard cover and, subsequently, in soft cover. Whereas the prior volume dealt with treatment of those with established histories of homelessness, this one addresses prevention of homelessness for those most at risk. We believe that the presentation of each project in a one page, graphic logic model will be a useful improvement over the prior volume since the logic model summarizes each program concisely but with sufficient detail to describe the program well. This should make the volume very easy to use and accessible to clinicians, administrators, policy-makers, and researchers alike.

Finally, given the inherent difficulties involved in obtaining valid results in program evaluation and health services research (see Conrad, 1994, for a thorough discussion with examples), it is often the case that a good explanation is as powerful as an effect finding. This is a corollary to the truism credited to Kurt Lewin that there is nothing as practical as a good theory–or, in program evaluation, a good logic model.

OVERVIEW

Following this introduction describing the purpose and content of the volume, the first article provides an overview of the SAMHSA cooperative agreement by the project officer and staff who are directing this innovative collaborative approach to research and service provision. This paper presents important background information and a description of the ground rules that form a foundation for understanding the subsequent articles. The second article discusses the rationale and methods used in developing logic models from the points of view of a SAMHSA staff person, an external evaluator, an internal evaluator, and a program manager.

The next eight articles describe the homelessness prevention projects. Each of these papers, like the projects themselves, is unique. However, they are organized to cover a common set of themes that all of the projects share. In addition to the literature review and logic model, each article has a discussion of the setting of the program including descriptions of the political, economic, and social context in each city. The specific target population is described including its special needs. All of the target populations have substantial alcoholism and drug abuse issues, and each program is designed to deal with these issues as they increase the risk of homelessness. Along with a detailed description of the innovative program, the customary services are described and compared with the innovative treatment. Then the objectives of the innovations are linked with the needs of the target population and the presumed gaps in customary services. This forms the theoretical rationale for believing that the program will be more effective than previously existing services.

The articles discuss some of the major issues that arose during implementation. Many of the projects share common themes such as: overcoming political, economic, and environmental barriers; selecting the most appropriate clients for scarce resources and matching the clients to the most appropriate treatments; preventing relapse; case management; training in independent living skills and money management; and acquiring and maintaining housing, benefits and employment.

The final article is a summary and synthesis of the major themes including both the commonalities and the interesting or controversial divergences of the individual projects in the volume. It includes a section on issues to be addressed in future program development and research. It serves as an attempt to digest the contents of the entire volume for those who would like such a synthesis or for those who were only directly interested in a few chapters but still wanted to have a workable understanding of the volume as a whole. The following section presents brief descriptions of the projects which are each fully described in a paper.

HOUSING LOSS-RESIDENTIAL TREATMENT

National Development and Research Institutes, Inc., Center for Therapeutic Community Research, New York, NY. This organization is documenting interventions provided by Gaudenzia, Inc., located in West Chester, Pennsylvania, using a modified therapeutic community (TC) intervention targeting mothers recovering from substance abuse living with their children. Clients move from residential to transitional to permanent housing through a continuum of treatment, preparatory, and homelessness prevention activities. Five major goal areas are included: (1) housing stabilization; (2) entering the workforce; (3) family preservation; (4) building a supportive community; and (5) social reintegration. Services for the children are also incorporated.

HOUSING LOSS-PROVIDING SUPPORTS IN HOUSING

Arapahoe House, Inc., Thornton, CO. Arapahoe House's PROUD (Project to Reduce Overutilization of Detoxification Services) program uses a dyadic intensive case management approach for women with co-occurring mental health and substance use disorders. Teams of case managers (one trained in the provision of mental health services; the other in substance abuse services) work together to provide an array of client services, including: outreach, needs assessment, housing location, living skills building, service coordination and linkages and education and job training.

Boley Center for Behavioral Healthcare, Inc., St. Petersburg, FL. Collaborating with the Florida Mental Health Institute of the University of South Florida, the Boley Center has implemented a model consisting of a cluster of housing-related support services for persons with serious mental illnesses and those with co-occurring substance use disorders. The services include: in-home skills training and counseling, vocational training and placement, landlord and management negotiation, orientation to the neighborhood and community, and linkages to additional services.

Community Connections, Washington, DC. Targeting persons with serious mental illness and those with co-occurring substance use disorders, a clinically-managed Housing Continuum (HC) model maintains stable residential status. The HC model features a broad range of housing options supported by a team of clinical housing specialists. Central themes of specialists include: goal planning with the client and case manager to assess housing preferences; ongoing monitoring and support through group meetings and planned events; development of social supports; crisis stabilization; planned use of respite beds or detox facilities during progressive crisis; coordination of housing moves; and advocacy with property managers.

Pathways to Housing, Inc., New York, NY. The Consumer Preference Independent Living (CPIL) model allows clients with serious mental illnesses and those with co-occurring substance use disorders to select their own independent apartments. Clients receive assistance in apartment living, training in housing maintenance, and locating community resources. Other services include: case management, skills building, assistance with entitlements, medical services and vocations and recreational programs.

Philadelphia Health Management Corporation, Philadelphia, PA. Project H.O.M.E. (Housing Opportunities, Medical care, and Education) is a multi-faceted housing intervention with support services. Clients are primarily those with serious mental illnesses, but some have co-occurring substance use disorders. The intervention operates as a continuum from street outreach, to emergency/low-demand residences, to highly supportive housing, to permanent housing. The intervention consists of three components: (1) support services that include food, medical care, mental health and substance abuse services and case management; (2) an employment program that includes job training and educational skills, job readiness training, literacy, and sheltered work experience; and (3) education for the community and advocacy.

FAMILY SUPPORT AND RESPITE

Barbour and Floyd Medical Associates, Lynwood, CA. This intervention targets families caring for family members with serious mental illnesses as well as those with co-occurring substance use disorders. Components of the support and respite model include: (1) home visits for relationship building and *in vivo* skill building and education; (2) case management; (3) family education addressing conflict, medication management, budgeting and use of resources as well as decision making skills; (4) family support groups; and (5) respite care through day rehabilitation services or short-term board-and-care type facilities used by consumers in the program.

REPRESENTATIVE PAYEE AND MONEY MANAGEMENT

Illinois Department of Human Services (IDHS), Chicago, IL. The Community Counseling Centers of Chicago (C4) is a representative payee program which operates a client "bank." Clients include those with serious mental illnesses and those with co-occurring substance use disorders. Enrollment is usually mandated by the Social Security Administration, but many clients enroll voluntarily. The bank, located at C4, is operated like a regular commercial bank, with the exception of the profit motive. Case managers, who are the gatekeepers for funds, develop budgets and issue vouchers to clients which are redeemable at the bank for cash. The budget usually includes direct payment of rent and other recurring bills by the bank. The ultimate goal of the intervention is to help clients develop skills to manage their financial affairs independently.

Kendon J. Conrad, PhD
Michael D. Matters, PhD
Patricia Hanrahan, PhD
Daniel J. Luchins, MD

REFERENCES

Conrad, K.J. (ed.) (1994). *Critically Evaluating the Role of Experiments. New Directions for Program Evaluation*, no. 63. San Francisco: Jossey-Bass.

Conrad, K.J., Hultman, C.I., & Lyons, J.S. (eds.) (1993). *Treatment of the Chemically Dependent Homeless: Theory and Implementation in Fourteen American Projects*. New York: The Haworth Press, Inc. Also issued by the Haworth Press, Inc., under the title *Treatment of the Chemically Dependent Homeless: Theory and Implementation in Fourteen American Projects*, as a special issue of *Alcoholism Treatment Quarterly*, T.F. McGovern (ed.) (1993) vol. 10, nos. 3/4

Cooperative Agreements for CMHS/CSAT Collaborative Program to Prevent Homelessness: An Overview

Lawrence D. Rickards, PhD
Walter Leginski, PhD
Frances L. Randolph, DrPH
Deirdre Oakley, MA
James M. Herrell, PhD, MPH
Cheryl Gallagher, MA

SUMMARY. Although there has been a considerable investment in housing, treatment, and support services over the past decade, homelessness continues to be a risk for individuals with serious mental illnesses and particularly those with co-occurring alcohol and other drug disorders. In 1996, the Center for Mental Health Services and the Center for Substance Abuse Treatment launched a two-phased, three-year initiative to document and evaluate the effectiveness of homelessness prevention interventions that focus on persons with psychiatric and/or substance use disorders who are formerly homeless or at-risk for home-

---

Lawrence D. Rickards, Walter Leginski, and Frances L. Randolph are affiliated with the Homeless Programs Branch, Center for Mental Health Services, 5600 Fishers Lane, Room 11C-05, Rockville, MD 20857. Deirdre Oakley is Technical Assistance Coordinator, National Resource Center on Homelessness and Mental Illness, Policy Research Associates, Inc., Delmar, NY. James M. Herrell is affiliated with the Division of Practice and Systems Development at CSAT, and Cheryl Gallagher is affiliated with the Organization of Services Branch, Division of Practice and Systems Development, both at the Center for Substance Abuse Treatment, Rockville, MD.

[Haworth co-indexing entry note]: "Cooperative Agreements for CMHS/CSAT Collaborative Program to Prevent Homelessness: An Overview." Rickards, Lawrence D. et al. Co-published simultaneously in *Alcoholism Treatment Quarterly* (The Haworth Press, Inc.) Vol. 17, No. 1/2, 1999, pp. 1-15; and: *Homelessness Prevention in Treatment of Substance Abuse and Mental Illness: Logic Models and Implementation of Eight American Projects* (ed: Kendon J. Conrad et al.) The Haworth Press, Inc., 1999, pp. 1-15. Single or multiple copies of this article are available for a fee from The Haworth Document Delivery Service [1-800-342-9678, 9:00 a.m. - 5:00 p.m. (EST). E-mail address: getinfo@haworthpressinc.com].

© 1999 by The Haworth Press, Inc. All rights reserved.

lessness, and who are engaged with the mental health and/or substance abuse treatment system(s). This article describes the background, logic model, goals, and structure of the CMHS/CSAT Collaborative Program to Prevent Homelessness. *[Article copies available for a fee from The Haworth Document Delivery Service: 1-800-342-9678. E-mail address: getinfo@haworthpressinc.com]*

KEYWORDS. Dual diagnosis, cooperative agreements, logic models, program manual

INTRODUCTION

On any given night, about 600,000 individuals are homeless in the United States (Burt & Cohen, 1989). Of these, approximately one-third, or about 200,000 individuals, have serious mental illnesses (Tessler & Dennis, 1989). In addition, a large percentage of homeless adults with serious mental illnesses, between 50% to 70%, have a co-occurring alcohol or other drug disorder of varied duration and severity (Ross, Glaser, & Germanson, 1988; Center for Mental Health Services, 1994; Kessler, Nelson, McGonagle, Edlund, Frank, & Leaf, 1996).

Although most persons with serious mental illnesses do not become homeless, the symptoms of mental illnesses are risk factors for housing instability and for homelessness (Lezak & Edgar, in press). Homeless persons with co-occurring psychiatric and substance use disorders often experience a level of disability that makes it extremely difficult for them to access the fragmented treatment, services, benefits, and housing systems (Devine & Wright, 1997). Thus, those with the greatest need are frequently the least served.

In 1987, the Stewart B. McKinney Homeless Assistance Act (P.L. 100-77) provided the first significant federal funding directed specifically to the needs of homeless persons. Initially, the McKinney act primarily funded short-term help designed as stop-gap measures until people could return to the mainstream. McKinney funding provided important new resources to local programs for shelter, food, medical care, case management, and other services, and set the stage for several generations of service demonstration, systems integration, and evaluation research studies. Although the levels of services and research funding have increased over the past decade, the number of individuals with serious mental illnesses, substance use disorders, or co-occurring disorders continues to eclipse the total of those being helped into treatment, housing, and stability (Lezak & Edgar, in press). During this period the composition of those becoming homeless has evolved from a predominantly adult population to one comprising families, often single parents with their young children (Bassuk, Weinreb, Buckner, Browne, Solomon, & Bassuk, 1996). Clearly the time has arrived to explore approaches to homelessness that are not only service-based but that address causes and risk factors, yielding interventions that effectively reduce the number of those entering homelessness.

THE HOMELESS PROGRAMS BRANCH, CENTER FOR MENTAL HEALTH SERVICES

The Homeless Programs Branch (HPB) of the Center for Mental Health Services (CMHS) serves as the lead unit within the U.S. Department of Health and Human Services (DHHS) and its Substance Abuse and Mental Health Services Administration (SAMHSA) for initiating and administering programs that address the treatment, housing, and support service needs of homeless persons with serious mental illnesses and programs to prevent homelessness in at-risk populations. The Branch has initiated a broad array of service delivery, demonstration, technical assistance, and national leadership projects to assist states and localities in meeting the needs of this population. These activities have provided HPB with the perspective and experience needed for addressing the issue of homelessness prevention.

Prior Federally Supported Demonstrations, Programs, and Activities

The HPB, and its predecessor the NIMH Office of Programs for the Homeless Mentally Ill, has funded several generations of knowledge development demonstration and evaluation studies, as well as administering a service delivery program. HPB administered three programs supported under provisions of the McKinney Act. First, the McKinney Research Demonstration Program for Homeless Mentally Ill Adults, originally awarded in fiscal year (FY) 1990 in collaboration with the Department of Housing and Urban Development (HUD), supported the provision of comprehensive community mental health services coordinated with housing services (Center for Mental Health Services, 1994). Second, CMHS awarded "Access to Community Care and Effective Services and Supports" (ACCESS) cooperative agreements to nine states in FY 1993. This interdepartmental effort–with input from components of DHHS, and the Departments of Labor, Education, Veterans Affairs, Agriculture, and HUD–is testing whether integration of fragmented services: (1) can be accomplished, and (2) will substantially contribute to ending homelessness among persons with serious mental illnesses (Randolph, Blasinsky, Leginski, Parker, & Goldman, 1997; Morrissey, Calloway, Johnsen, & Ullman, 1997; Rosenheck & Lam, 1997a & 1997b). Third, the ongoing "Projects for Assistance in Transition from Homelessness" (PATH) formula grant program provides funds to each state and U.S. territory to support service delivery to individuals with serious mental illnesses, and those with co-occurring substance use disorders, who are homeless or at-risk for homelessness. PATH funds may be used for such activities as outreach services, community mental health and substance abuse services, rehabilitation services, case management, staff training, supportive and supervisory services in residential settings, and other defined services.

In addition, CMHS and the Center for Substance Abuse Treatment (CSAT) collaborated in the funding and administration of a three-year, non-McKinney, demonstration program to document and evaluate treatment interventions designed to address co-occurring substance abuse and serious mental illness in homeless adults. Begun in FY 1993, six projects not only documented their approaches via treatment manuals, but also evaluated their interventions over a twenty-four month period. Among the results from the cross-site evaluation was strong support for an integrated approach to providing mental health and substance abuse treatment services as an effective intervention for homeless individuals with co-occurring disorders.

HPB represents CMHS on the Federal Interagency Council on the Homeless, where it provides leadership in implementing the 1994 Federal plan to break the cycle of homelessness (Interagency Council on the Homeless, 1994). Specifically, the Branch is focusing on improving discharge planning for persons who are homeless or at-risk of homelessness and who are in transition from institutional settings to community-based services. The Interagency Workgroup on Improving Discharge Planning convened, in June 1997, to identify key elements and "best practices" in discharge planning. Attention was targeted to optimizing a community-based continuum of care that includes treatment, housing, support services, income, and case management services that promote community reintegration and the prevention of homelessness.

Conceptualization of Prevention

The results, experience, and perspective derived from these knowledge development, service programs, and interagency activities enabled the HPB to construct a model of the risk and protective factors related to homelessness.

Of particular significance is a recurring finding that emerges in these initiatives: most individuals who are homeless and have serious mental illnesses have prior treatment histories with the formal service system (Center for Mental Health Services, 1994). This finding inspired the Branch to propose that interventions targeted to persons at-risk for homelessness while they are actively engaged with the service system would offer hope for reducing the number of individuals who subsequently experience homelessness.

Figure 1 provides a logic model for the activities of the HPB pertaining to homelessness prevention. A logic model is a heuristic device that helps

FIGURE 1. Homelessness Programs Branch: Prevention Logic Model

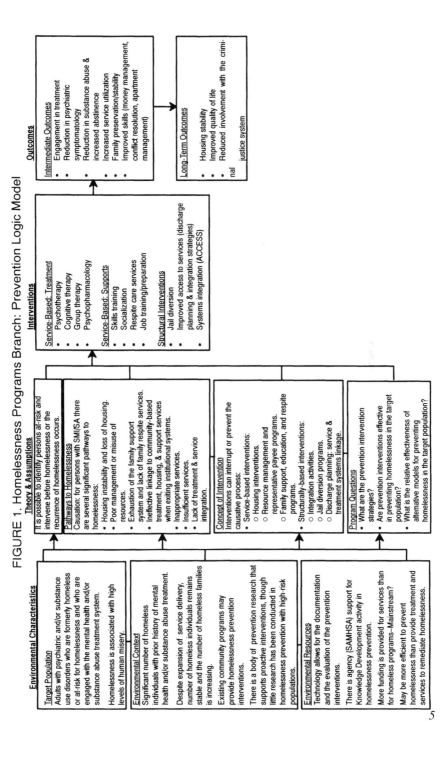

organize independent and dependent variables into a format that shows their relationships and helps to make hypotheses evident. Some have described it as a pictorial representation of "program theory" (Bickman, Guthrie, Foster, Lambert, Summerfelt, Breda, & Heflinger, 1995; Julian, Jones, & Deyo, 1995; Julian, 1997; Conrad, Randolph, Kirby, & Bebout, 1999). The HPB prevention logic model is a representation of the interaction between the focus population, assumptions about pathways to homelessness, ways of leveraging these pathways, specific intervention strategies that are proposed, and the anticipated intermediate and long-term outcomes. Thus, for the homelessness prevention program, HPB focuses on adults with serious mental illnesses and/or substance use disorders who are formerly homeless or at-risk for homelessness and who are engaged with the mental health or substance abuse treatment system(s). This population focus is within an environmental context where there is a large number of homeless individuals with prior histories of psychiatric and/or substance abuse treatment, and where the number of such homeless individuals has remained constant or has increased. The focus is within a resource environment where advances in technology allow for the documentation and the evaluation of prevention interventions. Finally, there are also signs within the national environment, particularly with the shift towards managed care, suggesting that service expansion may be approaching its apogee and that it may become more efficient to prevent homelessness than provide treatment and services to remediate homelessness. A fuller picture of the population and context issues is presented in Figure 1.

The assumptions central to the program state that it is possible to identify persons at-risk and to intervene prior to homelessness or the recurrence of homelessness. The risk and protective factors theory (Pransky, 1991) defines *risk factors* as those conditions, characteristics, or variables that make it more likely for an individual to develop a particular disorder or experience a condition. Countering risk factors are *protective factors,* those characteristics or conditions that minimize the likelihood that a person will develop a particular disorder or condition, even with risk factors present (Lezak & Edgar, in press).

For persons with psychiatric and/or substance use disorders, several significant risk factors have been identified as pathways to homelessness, including: (1) housing instability or eviction from housing precipitated by their illness; (2) poor management or misuse of financial resources; (3) exhaustion of the family support system and the lack of family respite services; (4) when exiting institutional systems, ineffective linkage to community-based treatment, housing, and support services; (5) inappropriate services; (6) insufficient services; and (7) lack of systems integration. Identification of the pathways to homelessness has led to the development of conceptual strategies to address causes and risks. Service-based intervention strategies include: interventions based in and on housing; resource management and representative payee programs; and family support, education, and respite programs. Structurally-based intervention strategies have also been developed, including: systems integration strategies, jail diversion programs, and discharge planning that links service, housing, and treatment systems.

The intervention approaches listed in the third column of the logic model, derive from the theory and assumptions of the causes and risk factors for homelessness. Protective factor interventions can be categorized as service-based treatment or support approaches and structural interventions.

- Service-based treatment approaches include such interventions as: psychotherapy, cognitive therapy, group therapy, assertive community treatment (ACT) case management approaches, and psychopharmacologic agents.
- Service-based support approaches include: skills training, respite care services, representative payee programs, socialization programs, and job training and preparation.
- Structural interventions include: jail diversion programs, improved access to services (improved discharge planning or service integration activities), and housing and support services.

Lastly, the logic model addresses the anticipated consequences. As a result of receiving these protective interventions, it is anticipated that clients will improve in predictable ways and that these changes can be measured on outcome scales. Predicted intermediate client outcomes include: (1) engagement or maintenance in mental health and/or substance abuse treatment; (2) reduction in psychiatric symptomatology; (3) reduction in substance abuse and increased abstinence; (4) increased service utilization and improved access to other services; (5) family preservation and stability; and (6) improvement in such skills as money management, conflict resolution, and apartment management. As clients engage in and accrue intermediate benefits, long-term outcomes can be derived, including: housing stability, improved quality of life, and reduced involvement with the criminal justice system.

The structure and content of the HPB homelessness prevention logic model explicitly shaped the nature of the knowledge development projects discussed later. Not every aspect of the model is addressed by the projects. It is hoped that the model itself, as well as unexplored relationships covered by it, will stimulate additional service delivery, research, and dialogue concerning homelessness prevention.

CMHS/CSAT COLLABORATIVE PROGRAM TO PREVENT HOMELESSNESS

To evaluate the theory, assumptions, and hypothesized intervention strategies contained in the logic model, the Center for Mental Health Services and the Center for Substance Abuse Treatment signed an Interagency Agreement, in 1996, to jointly initiate, fund, and administer a homelessness prevention knowledge development program, titled "Cooperative Agreements for CMHS/CSAT Collaborative Program to Prevent Homelessness." CMHS assumed the lead responsibility for preparing the guidance for applicants (GFA), managing the technical assistance contract, and preparing fiscal documentation. The program management team, consisting of the government project officers (GPOs) and evaluation officers from CMHS and CSAT, oversee day to day operation of the collaborative agreement program.

Program Structure

CMHS and CSAT agreed to jointly fund and administer a two-phased, three-year program to document and evaluate the effectiveness of homelessness prevention interventions. Consistent with the logic model, the interventions focus on individuals with serious mental illnesses and/or substance use disorders who are formerly homeless or at-risk for homelessness, and who are engaged with the mental health and/or substance abuse treatment system(s).

The Phase One guidance for applicants (GFA), issued in April 1996, announced the availability of support to organizations to document their currently existing and operating interventions to prevent homelessness in the target population and to develop a plan for evaluating the prevention approach in the second program phase. The GFA called for awardees to articulate their intervention in the form of a manual and to develop a plan, using an experimental or quasi-experimental design, to evaluate the documented intervention. The manuals paralleled the HPB logic model in linking population, environment, and program assumptions with the described intervention and anticipated outcomes. The manuals codified and explicitly described the prevention interventions. This first phase lasted one year.

The Phase Two GFA, issued in May 1997, announced the availability of support, through a competitive renewal process, for the evaluation of homelessness prevention interventions documented in Phase One of the CMHS/CSAT collaborative program. Eligibility to apply for Phase Two awards was limited to Phase One grantees. The twenty-four month evaluation phase began in October 1997.

SAMHSA approved the use of the cooperative agreement mechanism to fund the homelessness prevention program as it allowed for substantial government involvement in the two phases of the program. In Phase One, the

GPOs from CMHS and CSAT conducted site visits to their assigned projects, provided technical assistance and consultation on the development of the manuals and evaluation plan designs, and arranged grantee meetings and telephone conference calls for the discussion of relevant issues. The CMHS GPO is a member of the program steering committee comprised of the project directors from each of the project sites. In Phase Two, the GPOs are conducting monitoring and consultation site visits to each of their assigned projects, providing technical assistance on individual project and cross-site evaluation issues, and training on the collection and analysis of cross-site data.

The two-phased collaborative program was designed to respond to three central questions regarding the prevention of homelessness that are noted in the logic model:

1. What are prevention intervention strategies?
2. Are prevention interventions effective in preventing homelessness in the target population?
3. What is the relative effectiveness of alternative models for preventing homelessness in the target population?

Summary of the Cooperative Agreement Projects

The eight projects engaged in Phase Two of the program can be categorized into three broad prevention approaches: the prevention of housing loss, resource management and representative payee interventions, and family education and respite care. A project may provide more than one prevention intervention. As can be seen from Table 1, the projects in the homelessness prevention program reflect diversity in their specific intervention settings, target population(s), types of intervention, and evaluation designs.

The prevention of housing loss is the focus of three-fourths of the projects. However, there is considerable variation between sites regarding their theories and approaches to this issue. Community Connections (CC) and Pathways to Housing (PH), for example, are both evaluating fundamental structures for providing housing to homeless individuals with psychiatric and/or substance use disorders. CC's theory and model are geared towards a continuum of care approach that integrates treatment and housing, and address stabilization in housing as a long-term goal, while PH's theory and model provides for immediate client access to an independent apartment, without housing readiness or treatment requirements, and offers support services on the tenant's own terms. Although Arapahoe House is also intervening to prevent housing loss, their project is evaluating the effectiveness of dyadic case management in enhancing stability. The Boley Centers utilize a psychosocial rehabilitation theory and approach that integrates housing, housing-related support services, and access to independent treatment and rehabilitation

TABLE 1. Description of Projects in the CMS/SAT Collaborative Program to Prevent Homelessness

Project Name/City	Intervention Setting	Target Population	Intervention and Evaluation Design
Arapahoe House, Thornton, CO	Community-based substance abuse treatment facility	Adults with substance abuse and/or co-occurring disorders.	Dyadic case management, housing, and treatment. Random assignment to study or control condition. Except for case management, both groups have access to all other services provided by the agency.
Barbour and Floyd Medical Associates, Los Angeles, CA	Integrated family service agency	Families of adult clients with serious mental illnesses.	*In vivo* family services assessed with two design components: documented intervention compared to other existing services within the agency; documented intervention compared to a second agency which does not offer in-home family services.
Boley Centers for Behavioral Healthcare, St. Petersburg, FL	Psychosocial rehabilitation agency	Adults with serious mental illnesses and/or substance use disorders.	Intervention provides housing, housing-related support services, and linkage to psychosocial, clinical, and medical services. Outcome evaluation: repeated measures non-equivalent comparison group design utilizing a local CMHC as the comparison intervention.
Center for Therapeutic Community Research, Philadelphia, PA	Therapeutic community	Women who are pregnant or with their children who have extensive substance use histories; high percentage of co-occurring disorders.	Study and comparison group will receive services in a TC environment; study group will receive distinctive prevention interventions. Repeated measures non-equivalent comparison group.
Community Connections, Washington, DC	Clinical housing specialists and case managers	Adults with serious mental illnesses; high percentage of co-occurring disorders.	Random assignment of adults to either housing continuum or supported housing (comparison group) conditions. Baseline and one-year follow-up of all participants.
Illinois Department of Human Services	Community mental health center	Adults with serious mental illnesses; high percentage of co-occurring disorders.	Representative payee intervention. Non-equivalent control group design of eligible clients who receive or do not receive the intervention.
Pathways to Housing, New York, NY	Supported housing provider	Adults with serious mental illnesses; high percentage of co-occurring disorders.	Random assignment of adults to either supported housing or continuum of care (comparison group) housing conditions. Baseline and repeated measures at 6 and 12 months post-baseline.
Philadelphia Health Management Corp., Philadelphia, PA	Housing and support services provider	Adults with serious mental illnesses and/or co-occurring disorders.	Quasi-experimental, two group design to compare Project H.O.M.E. residents to a match sample who are in treatment at a local CMHC. Comparison group resides in supportive housing, boarding homes, shelters, independently, or with their families.

services. The Center for Therapeutic Community Research provides a highly structured therapeutic environment with homeless prevention services to substance abusing women who have their children. The Philadelphia Health Management Corporation takes a continuum of care approach that includes outreach, housing, case management, education, and employment, as well as addressing prevention on three levels: individual, neighborhood, and societal. Each of these projects relies on some form of case management, whether Assertive Community Treatment, dyadic, or more standard model, to help maintain engagement with their service population.

The Illinois Department of Human Services is unique as the only project focused exclusively on evaluating a representative payee/money management homelessness prevention approach. Pathways to Housing also has a representative payee component in their intervention that will be evaluated.

The Barbour and Floyd Medical Associates is the sole family-focused homelessness prevention intervention. Their comprehensive model includes in-home services and utilization of the home environment to provide family psychoeducation, support, skills development, and facilitating community engagement. Respite care is provided outside of the home.

Unique and Cross-Site Evaluations

CMHS and CSAT developed the GFA to focus on both project-specific and cross-site program evaluation questions. Each project applicant, as part of its GFA submission for continued funding, presented its unique evaluation hypotheses, key domains to be studied, and proposed instruments to measure outcomes. Each applicant was also required to include a process that would measure and ensure continued fidelity to its intervention. The following chapters will provide additional project descriptions, including the site-specific domains and measures.

Role and Process of the Steering Committee in Determining the Cross-Site Evaluation

The mechanism used to address issues and make decisions regarding the cross-site evaluation was the steering committee. The following steering committee structure was included in the GFA: (1) Composition: to include the project directors from each of the project sites, CMHS and CSAT GPOs, and CMHS and CSAT evaluation officers; (2) Chair: to be appointed by SAMHSA from among the grantees; (3) Limits on SAMHSA: SAMHSA staff participates, but constitutes less than one-half of the committee, collectively has only one vote, and does not have veto power; (4) Responsibility: for the development of the common data measures, design of the cross site analysis, and policies on data sharing, access to data and materials, and publications and conference presentations; (5) Decisions: by consensus on most decisions, majority vote otherwise; decisions of the steering committee are binding.

During Phase One, the steering committee formed three subcommittees to deliberate on cross-site baseline, program/fidelity, and outcome questions, domains, and measures. Grantees self-selected to participate on the subcommittees. Subcommittee work was conducted primarily through conference calls supported through a parallel contract for a Technical Assistance Coordinator (TAC).[1] Prior to each conference call, the TAC collected proposed instruments and information on their psychometric properties and distributed them for review by subcommittee participants. A three-day grantee meeting was convened four months prior to the Phase Two application deadline to allow projects to achieve consensus on baseline domains, cross-site evaluation questions, instruments, procedures for implementation and data submission, and timelines. To be included in the cross-site protocol, measures were examined on three primary criteria: ability to measure the domain; relevance across multiple sites, questions, and populations; and appropriateness of use with individuals with psychiatric and/or substance use disorders who are formerly homeless or at-risk for homelessness. Several instruments were ultimately rejected because they implied a stably housed population or were otherwise not appropriate for persons with a history of homelessness. Consensus was reached on a tentative cross-site protocol for pilot testing, with the baseline interview of about 40 minutes in length and the two follow-up interviews, to be conducted at 6- and 12-month intervals post-baseline, estimated to take about 20 minutes each.

Table 2 presents the domains, questions, and measures that were selected by the steering committee as the baseline protocol for the cross-site evaluation. The protocol was pilot tested regarding: (1) the average time and range of administration time; (2) thoroughness of administration instructions, procedures, and definitions; (3) appropriateness of the measures across sites; (4) ways to improve formatting; (5) need to deviate from standard administration procedures; and (6) how best to include site-specific questions with the cross-site protocol. Pilot testing revealed variations in protocol administration time, minor coding and formatting issues, and lack of clarity in interviewer administration of some instruments. Additional conference calls and a grantee meeting were devoted to addressing problems in instrument administration. To better achieve uniformity in the administration of the final protocol, CSAT sponsored a two-day training session at the New Hampshire-Dartmouth Psychiatric Research Center on administering the cross-site instruments that was attended by interviewers from project sites.

The steering committee also achieved consensus on the coding process to be used for project and cross-site data entry and quality assurance. A central-

TABLE 2. Cross Site Domains, Questions, and Measures

Domain	Cross-Site Evaluation Question	Measure
Client Demographics and History	Who are the clients receiving the prevention intervention?	• Personal History Form • ACCESS Evaluation Form
Physical Health	What are the client's physical health problems?	• ACCESS Evaluation Form
Mental Health Symptomatology	Do the interventions reduce psychiatric symptomatology?	• Colorado Symptom Index
Substance Abuse	Do the interventions reduce the level of substance abuse and promote abstinence?	• Drug/Alcohol Six Month Follow-Back Calendar
Housing Stability	Do the interventions increase housing stability and reduce homelessness?	• Six Month Residential Follow-Back Calendar • Personal History Form
Quality of Life	Do the interventions improve clients' quality of life?	• Quality of Life Interview (subjective measure–one question)
Service Utilization	• Do the interventions increase mental health and substance abuse treatment and services utilization? • Are units of services utilized comparable across sites?	• Treatment Services Review (*modified*)

ized core data set is being hosted and managed by the TAC. The contractor will be able to assist grantees in both their site-specific and cross-site data analysis and with their interim and final reports. Additionally, the TAC has provided client tracking software to sites that will assist them in maintaining records on client relocations and will alert interviewers to their upcoming schedules for follow-up contact with study participants.

LESSONS LEARNED

The cooperative agreement has already generated detailed information on approaches to addressing homelessness in the study population. The project intervention manuals from the eight Phase Two sites will be disseminated through the SAMHSA website (www.mentalhealth.org) and the Knowledge Exchange Network (KEN; 1-800-700-2647). These documents can assist communities and programs in developing interventions to address the prevention of homelessness at the local level.

Important lessons have been learned about program management and initiating cross-site evaluations. These lessons may be valuable for future planning of cross- and multi-site initiatives. The lessons will be detailed in the program's interim report, which will be disseminated through the SAMHSA website and KEN.

In addition, as the baseline information is collected, using the cross-site protocol, and merged into the common database, a clearer demographic picture of those at-risk for homelessness should emerge. Analysis of this information will allow both a collective view of the population, as well as local variations in each of the eight project sites. The similarities and differences on variables across sites and localities may eventually allow for better targeting of populations and approaches to prevention, treatment, housing, and support services.

Although program results will not be available for approximately two years, it is hoped that the answers to cross-site and program hypotheses will help address the fundamental question: "Are we able to prevent at-risk individuals from experiencing homelessness by intervening while they are in treatment?" We anticipate this knowledge will serve not only to reduce the human misery associated with homelessness, but offer significant promise for the role that mainstream programs can play in helping reduce the numbers of homeless individuals with serious mental illnesses and/or substance use disorders.

NOTE

1. Coordination was provided by the National Resource Center on Homelessness and Mental Illness, Policy Research Associates, Inc., Delmar, NY, under contract CMHS 280-94-0008.

REFERENCES

Bassuk, E.L., Weinreb, L.F., Buckner, J.C., Browne, A., Solomon, A., & Bassuk, S.S. (1996, August 28). The characteristics and needs of sheltered homeless and low-income housed mothers. *Journal of the American Medical Association*, 276(8), 640-646.

Bickman, L., Guthrie, P.R., Foster, E.M., Lambert, E.W., Summerfelt, W.T., Breda, C.S., & Heflinger, C.A. (1995). *Evaluating managed mental health services*. New York: Plenum.

Burt, M. & Cohen, B. (1989). *America's homeless: Numbers, characteristics, and the programs that serve them*. Washington, DC: Urban Institute Press.

Center for Mental Health Services. (1994). *Making a difference: Interim status report of the McKinney demonstration program for homeless adults with serious mental illnesses*. DHHS Publication No. (SMA) 94-3014.

Conrad, K.J., Randolph, F., Kirby, M.W., & Bebout, R.R. (1999). Creating and Using Logic Models: Four Perspectives. *Alcoholism Treatment Quarterly,* 17(1/2), 17-31.

Devine, J.A. & Wright, J.D. (1997, October). Losing the housing game: The leveling effects of substance abuse. *American Journal of Orthopsychiatry,* 67(4), 618-631.

Interagency Council on the Homeless. (1994, March). *Priority: Home!-The federal plan to break the cycle of homelessness* (HUD Publication No. HUD-1454-CPD). Washington, DC: U.S. Government Printing Office.

Julian, D.A. (1997). The utilization of the logic model as a system level planning and evaluation device. *Evaluation and Program Planning,* 20(3), 251-257.

Julian, D.A., Jones, A., & Deyo, D. (1995). Open systems evaluation and the logic model: Program planning and evaluation tools. *Evaluation and Program Planning,* 18(4), 333-341.

Kessler, R.C., Nelson, C.B., McGonagle, K.A., Edlund, M.J., Frank, R.G., & Leaf, P.J. (1996, January). The epidemiology of co-occurring addictive and mental disorders: Implications for prevention and service utilization. *American Journal of Orthopsychiatry,* 66(1), 17-31.

Lezak, A.D. & Edgar, E. (In press). *Preventing homelessness among people with serious mental illnesses: A guide for states.* Rockville, MD: Center for Mental Health Services.

Morrissey, J., Calloway, M., Johnsen, M., & Ullman, M. (1997, March). Service system performance and integration: A baseline profile of the ACCESS demonstration sites. *Psychiatric Services,* 48(3), 374-380.

Pransky, J. (1991). *The critical need.* Springfield, MO: Burrell Foundation.

Randolph, F., Blasinsky, M., Leginski, W., Parker, L.B., & Goldman, H.H. (1997, March). Creating integrated service systems for homeless persons with mental illness: The ACCESS program. *Psychiatric Services,* 48(3), 369-373.

Rosenheck, R. & Lam, J.A. (1997a, March). Client and site characteristics as barriers to service use by homeless persons with serious mental illness. *Psychiatric Services,* 48(3), 387-390.

Rosenheck, R. & Lam, J.A. (1997b, March). Homeless mentally ill clients' and providers' perception of service needs and clients' use of services. *Psychiatric Services,* 48(3), 381-386.

Ross, H.E., Glaser, F.B., & Germanson, T. (1988, November). The prevalence of psychiatric disorders in patients with alcohol and other drug problems. *Archives of General Psychiatry,* 45(11), 1023-1031.

Tessler, R.C. & Dennis, D.L. (1989). *A synthesis of NIMH-funded research concerning persons who are homeless and mentally ill.* Rockville, MD: National Institute of Mental Health.

Creating and Using Logic Models: Four Perspectives

Kendon J. Conrad, PhD
Frances L. Randolph, DrPH
Michael W. Kirby, Jr., PhD
Richard R. Bebout, PhD

SUMMARY. The use of logic models in program development, evaluation, and dissemination is becoming more commonly accepted as a means of facilitating communication, replication, quality improvement, and assessment. Each of the following chapters in this book includes a logic model of the program being described. The purpose of this chapter is to describe what logic models are, and to convey to a diverse field the role and functioning of logic models in the conceptualization, delivery, management, and evaluation of programs. Since this volume is intended for a wide audience including service providers, program administrators, and researchers, we will attempt to provide information on logic models that is broadly useful. Therefore, this chapter is structured so that each of the four authors presents her/his unique perspective based principally on their own experience using logic models. *[Article copies available for a fee from The Haworth Document Delivery Service: 1-800-342-9678. E-mail address: getinfo@haworthpressinc.com]*

Kendon J. Conrad is Professor, University of Illinois at Chicago, School of Public Health and Research Career Scientist in the Department of Veterans Affairs. Frances L. Randolph is the project officer at SAMHSA who designed the logic model section of the guidance for applications (GFA) for the Homelessness Prevention projects presented in this book. Michael W. Kirby, Jr. is Chief Executive Officer of Arapahoe House, a substance abuse and behavioral health treatment agency. Richard R. Bebout is the Research Director of Community Connections, a mental health agency that provides housing and supports to people with serious mental illness.

[Haworth co-indexing entry note]: "Creating and Using Logic Models: Four Perspectives." Conrad, Kendon, J. et al. Co-published simultaneously in *Alcoholism Treatment Quarterly* (The Haworth Press, Inc.) Vol. 17, No. 1/2, 1999, pp. 17-31; and: *Homelessness Prevention in Treatment of Substance Abuse and Mental Illness: Logic Models and Implementation of Eight American Projects* (ed: Kendon J. Conrad et al.) The Haworth Press, Inc., 1999, pp. 17-31. Single or multiple copies of this article are available for a fee from The Haworth Document Delivery Service [1-800-342-9678, 9:00 a.m. - 5:00 p.m. (EST). E-mail address: getinfo@haworthpressinc.com].

KEYWORDS. Logic models, program development, program evaluation

WHAT IS A LOGIC MODEL?

A logic model is a graphic representation of a program that describes the program's essential components and expected accomplishments and conveys the logical relationship between these components and their outcomes. It is usually limited to one page. A useful reference on logic modeling is *Evaluation: Promise and Performance* by Joseph Wholey (1979), although Wholey uses the term "program plan" rather than logic model. His other useful works on the topic include Wholey, 1987 and Wholey, 1994.

There is no one way to represent a logic model; however, most logic models describe a program in terms of four properties. These include (1) the context; (2) the theory and assumptions that underlie the program's intervention, (3) the intervention, and (4) the outcomes. Context refers to the background conditions in which the program operates and which could have moderating effects on the program's success. These include the geographic, economic, demographic, and political characteristics of the community where the program resides, regulations and policies that govern the program's operations, fiscal resources that finance the program, and community resources that the program might access. The context may also include the target population who are served by the program.

The theory or assumptions that underlie the program's intervention refers to the theoretical construct that guides the design and development of the intervention that addresses the problems. The key activities are those components of the intervention that are assumed to be essential to achieve the intended outcomes. Finally, the outcomes are the effects of the intervention and are defined as short-, intermediate- or long-term.

A logic model also represents the probable relationships among the various components. In other words, it provides directional assumptions about the factors that cause mediating, moderating and direct effects on the outcomes. A template for designing a logic model is shown in Figure 1.

USING LOGIC MODELS IN PROGRAM EVALUATION

For the grantees of a knowledge development program such as the Homelessness Prevention Program, logic modeling accomplishes several things for evaluators: it clarifies the goals and expectations of a project; identifies underlying theories; provides a framework for doing a process evaluation; determines whether a program is ready to be evaluated; and helps to focus the design of its outcome evaluation.

FIGURE 1. A Logic Model Template

POPULATION AND ENVIRONMENT	THEORY AND ASSUMPTIONS	INTERVENTION	OUTCOMES
Patient Population Describes the characteristics of the clients in the program.	**Concept of Problem** The nature of the problem that the program is designed to address. May include the inclusion and exclusion criteria for clients to be admitted.	**The Program** Provides the details of the intervention, such as the functions of key personnel, the flow of activities from initial services such as outreach to intermediate components, to the final stages leading to completion.	**The Intended Effects of the Program** These are the key, plausible outcomes that can logically be ascribed to the intervention.
Environmental Context Describes the setting of the program, may include the characteristics of the service area in terms of population, geography, history, and other things of relevance.			
Program Resources Describes the funding, staffing, and facilities needed to run the program. May include characteristics of the umbrella agency or service network of which the program is a part.	**Concept of Intervention** The purpose/goals of the program and how it will go about achieving them. May be expressed as statements of what the program intends to do in order to achieve the desired outcomes. These statements comprise the program theory.		

Clarification of Program Goals. Most programs have multiple goals. Some of them are clearly stated while others are less obvious. Logic models can identify the goals that are most important to the evaluation and for which there are reasonable ways to measure their success. When evaluators and program staff work collaboratively to clarify the program's goals and outcomes, the modeling process also becomes an important consensus building process.

Identification of Underlying Program Theory. Many programs are developed from experience or ideas and not from a strong theoretical foundation. However, every program has an underlying theory with implicit hypotheses about the nature of the of the population, problem, and how it can be addressed (Bickman, 1987). In order to determine what should be evaluated and how each concept should be measured, an evaluator must understand or develop the theory underlying the program. A logic model can be a valuable tool for elucidating the theory behind a program because it defines the assumptions and the line of reasoning among the assumptions, activities and outcomes (Weiss, 1997).

Framework for Organizing Process Evaluations. A logic model provides a blueprint that delineates all of the elements of the program that need to be documented in order to fully understand the program. When fully developed, a logic model will describe the program in such detail that it will clarify the evaluator's task of determining what data should and should not be collected as a part of a process evaluation.

Process for Determining Readiness to be Evaluated. According to Wholey, logic models are useful in assessing the evaluability of programs. An evaluability assessment is a study that is done before the actual evaluation to determine whether it is possible and desirable to conduct an evaluation. During an evaluability assessment, the evaluator examines the context of the program and the evaluation to see if it will permit a rigorous, objective study. It determines the availability and willingness of clients and staff to conduct an evaluation. It determines whether an evaluation is really needed versus a literature review or a meta-analysis or an analysis of existing data. It determines the political context and intended role of the evaluation, such as facilitating change, supporting someone's position, or postponing a decision.

Guiding the Outcome Evaluation. A logic model also guides the evaluator in designing the program's outcome evaluation. By clarifying the relevant goals, identifying the measurable outcomes (dependent variables), delineating the target population and the intervention (independent variables), the evaluator can determine how best to evaluate the program. When a customary condition is used for a comparison group, a logic model of the customary condition is helpful in illustrating and clarifying the differences between the experimental and comparison treatments in the evaluation. These differences in treatment form the basis for the expectation of differences in outcomes.

Structure for Assessing Program Fidelity. A logic model represents a theory of how the program is intended to be implemented. Then researchers or managers assess implementation and resolve any discrepancies that are found between the ideal and the real. Sometimes the real informs the ideal which results in beneficial changes to the model. Other times implementation falls short of the intentions and staff must strive to modify the program to achieve model fidelity. Thus, there is an interactive process where the discovery of discrepancies between the theory and the implementation may result in changes in the theory or changes in the implementation.

The logic model is a living document that changes as the program changes or as perceptions of the program change. For example, an evaluator will view the program in one way and a program manager will view it another way. Neither perspective may be consistent with the way the program is actually implemented. Understanding the extent to which there is consistency (fidelity) between the logic model and the program as implemented is critical for both evaluator and program manager. From a program manager's perspective, the logic model becomes a management tool that helps the program manager keep the program from deviating from its ideal implementation. For the evaluator, the logic model provides a framework for understanding the extent to which the program as implemented is consistent with the program as intended.

THE FEDERAL AGENCY PERSPECTIVE

The Substance Abuse and Mental Health Services Administration (SAMHSA) has long regarded logic modeling as an important tool for grantees as well as federal staff. SAMHSA uses logic models within its agency in order to enhance the review of grant applications, to monitor projects by project officers and to design and implement an evaluation of a Federal grant program. As a review tool, when included in a grant application, logic models of the project and of the evaluation design can facilitate the technical assessment of the application by reviewers to determine the appropriateness of the study. As a project monitoring tool, a logic model of a grant project can be used to determine the extent to which the implementation of the project over time remains faithful to its design. Finally, as an evaluation tool, logic models of projects within a grant program can be used to understand the similarities and differences across projects so that a common protocol for a minimum database can be developed for evaluating the grant program as a whole.

As a part of the requirements for participating in the SAMHSA Cooperative Agreement Homelessness Prevention Program, grantees were required to develop logic models of their interventions during Phase One. Grantees were given latitude in the methods used to develop the logic models. Some grantees did documentation reviews; others interviewed program staff and program recipients; and others used focus groups and concept mapping, a quantitative method for visually summarizing group input (Trochim, 1989; 1993).

Many of the grantees used a combination of different methods. Three of the grantees present their perspectives on the development and usefulness of logic models below.

THE EXTERNAL EVALUATOR'S PERSPECTIVE

The first task of an external evaluator is to understand the program to be evaluated. Social programs are complex, and to describe them well is no easy task. One can rely on the descriptions provided by the program administrator, but experience informs us that such reports may have little relationship to what is actually happening in the program. There may also be differences among various stakeholders, such as managers, staff, clients, and staff of other programs, regarding their perceptions of the program. Over the years we have relied on logic modeling in order to include the various perspectives, reconcile them, and achieve consensus on how programs work.

The first logic model that an external evaluator develops of a program is usually very rudimentary and provides program staff the opportunity to "set the evaluator straight" about the program. Subsequently, the refined model often brings the program to light to the diverse parties involved and enables each different perspective to see the whole picture, understand it differently or better, and provide their own point of view in reaction. Comments arise such as, "I never looked at it that way," or "I never saw the whole picture before." Having the program depicted on one page facilitates consensus as well as learning about differences of opinion. The following is an example of how a logic model was developed and an evaluation study was designed for a representative payee program.

The representative payee (RP) program at Community Counseling Centers of Chicago (C4) is an agency-based representative payee and money management service for persons with severe mental illness. After an initial examination when it was decided that the RP program was probably worth studying, we met with program staff to begin constructing the logic model. Preliminary discussions about their RP program provided ideas about where to look in the literature to see what had been written or researched on the subject. Conducting a literature review was a crucial first step in developing the logic model. It provided us with the best available theory or assumptions to connect with the RP program. It also provided a context for better understanding how RP should work.

In order to understand the C4 RP program and how it interacts with the rest of the agency and the community, we decided it was important to understand the entire agency. So a logic model of the agency and the community context in which the agency operates was developed. This logic model is presented in Conrad et al. (1999). Since the entire agency was not to be the focus of evaluation, the development of this logic model simply relied on documentation and interviews with a few key informants who were very knowledgeable about the agency.

In order to understand how the RP program was set up, we toured the program and met the staff. This first-hand experience provided important information about the physical setting in which the program operates, including the waiting room for the banking facility, the registration desk, teller windows, and the safe. When RP staff said they had a "bank" within the agency, we realized that this was not a figure of speech. We also had a chance to learn about the qualifications and experience of the staff.

We still lacked information about how providers and clients experienced the program. This information can be obtained by communicating with staff and clients through face-to-face interviews, surveys and other written methods, telephone conversations, or focus groups. In developing logic models, we have found that focus groups are probably the most effective and efficient method for collecting this information (see Krueger, 1988). We conducted a series of focus groups: two with clinical staff, one with administrative staff, one with clients, and one with staff from outside agencies including Social Security, Department of Human Services, other mental health agencies, and a consumer advocate. These free-flowing discussions provided a lot of detail and established major areas of consensus on the components of the program, how they worked together and how they influenced each other. However, we soon realized we had too much information for a one-page graph.

Mostly our information was too detailed for understanding the core resources, activities, and outcomes of the program and we needed to refine our thinking. To do so we began an iterative, consensus-building process. We presented a draft of the logic model to all of the program's stakeholders for their review and input, i.e., administrators, staff, and clients. We also asked outside experts and staff from other RP programs to review the logic model. The feedback from these different sources helped us identify the most essential elements of the C4 RP program. The resulting logic model is found in Conrad et al. (1999). The iterative process served several purposes. It clarified the logic model, but also informed the stakeholders about the study and enabled them to provide their input. This process reassured us that the program was evaluable and that all key parties were on board.

Planning the Evaluation. After developing a relatively thorough understanding of the program, we were ready to begin planning the evaluation. Our understanding of resources, activities and outcomes enabled us to define the measurements that would be needed. In other words, the logic model described the constructs to be measured, i.e., the measurement model. For the evaluation, it was necessary to find or create at least one good measure of each construct. In the process of doing this, we learned that no measures existed to define or target the subject population. In other words, there were no inclusion/exclusion criteria or measures of who should go into RP. To address this issue, we performed a retrospective study of RP vs. non-RP clients to describe the major discriminating characteristics of the two groups. This led to a measure we called the Determination of Need for Representative Payeeship (Conrad et al., 1998). To assess the implementation of program activities and apply standards by which to judge fidelity and change, we adapted the Adult Day Care Assessment Procedure (Conrad et al., 1989). To assess the intended outcomes, we worked with the cooperative agreement group to choose and develop measures of outcomes that we had in common with the other homelessness prevention projects. However, since no other projects were assessing financial outcomes specific to RP, we developed new measures called the Money Management Outcome Measure (MMOM) and the Financial Victimization Questionnaire (FVQ). Additionally, our understanding of the agency and its other programs helped us to clarify the research design that would be possible within this context. Finally, the logic model provided us with an outline for a program manual that would present, in detail, the nature and functioning of the C4 RP program (Conrad et al., 1998). The program manual could then serve to explain to other providers the fine points of implementing and maintaining an RP program.

THE INTERNAL EVALUATOR'S PERSPECTIVE

The Washington Homelessness Prevention Project is comparing two different models of housing: a continuum housing model that is provided by Community Connections versus a supported housing model that is provided by the District of Columbia's three Mobile Community Outreach Treatment Teams (MCOTT). The evaluation uses a randomized experimental design. The internal evaluator serves in a liaison role between the lead service provider, i.e., Community Connections and several external parties, including co-investigators and consultants in university settings, other collaborators from the local community, and the federal funding agency. Additionally, the internal evaluator had previously held a leadership role in Community Connections and so had intimate knowledge of the structure and operation of the continuum housing model.

Both the task of developing the logic model and the logic model itself served a variety of important functions. First, the process of gathering information from current providers and other stakeholders helped to lay a foundation for the evaluation to be a genuinely participatory process. Eliciting input from various parties at the outset facilitated later cooperation with the evaluation and increased the likelihood that the findings from the evaluation will have some meaningful impact on reshaping the program at the conclusion of the evaluation.

Second, we quickly recognized the need to narrow the focus of the evaluation because of the great complexity of the housing program itself and the service agency in which it was nested. The logic model helped us to select a particular "focal depth" for our evaluation lens. Evaluations of multi-component programs like the housing continuum at Community Connections often fail because of the long list of uncontrolled variables.

Third, the logic model required us to clarify our conceptual framework and to articulate a rationale for various practices. Sometimes we discovered that our practices had lost their connection to the overall program goals or perhaps were even at odds with the stated philosophy and beliefs of the program staff. The discipline imposed by the logic model helped program staff to make explicit what often remains implicit. One program change that resulted was the development of a revised statement on substance abuse and relapse in the residential program.

Those who participated in the development of the logic model experienced a number of benefits. Framing the program around the overarching goal of preventing homelessness lent a degree of coherence and a sense of purpose that helped staff who were in the trenches day-to-day to remember why they do what they do. Doing this exercise aloud also helped to surface and resolve inconsistencies among program staff in how they viewed the overall mission of the program and the role their specific program responsibilities played into the larger whole.

Reducing the statement of the problem, the theory of the intervention, its goals and practices to a one-page schematic representation also serves to provide service providers with a framework for policy and decision-making. It is very easy to lose sight of the forest if you are too close to the trees. The logic model IS the BIG PICTURE and people can return over and over to it.

From the evaluation standpoint, development of the logic model was useful in several specific ways, including: (1) the selection of a comparison group; (2) choice or development of appropriate process measures; and (3) highlighting short-term and intermediate changes expected to mediate achievement of long-term stable housing. First, it helped to confirm our choice of an appropriate comparison group for our randomized design. We were not interested in comparing a high intensity case management model plus mental health housing (continuum housing) against a low intensity or standard services model. Such a comparison would not have validly addressed the core questions of interest to us and to the field. The continuum housing approach at Community Connections features a range of agency-controlled housing opportunities explicitly linked to treatment participation. In contrast, the Assertive Community Treatment approach practiced by the District of Columbia's three Mobile Community Outreach Treatment Teams (MCOTT) assist individuals in getting and keeping their own housing in mainstream, non-specialized housing. Thus the two programs differ in the way in which mental health and housing supports are organized, but still provide a range of community support services roughly equivalent in intensity to one another. For MCOTT clients, supports are adjusted as the individual's needs change. Consistent with the ACT model and a supported housing approach, an MCOTT client generally would not be expected to move to an alternative housing setting as might happen in the continuum housing approach. Thus, the MCOTT program seemed to be an ideal comparison for addressing the relevant questions about linking housing and supports.

Second, the logic model was useful in identifying appropriate process measures. An ACT-fidelity measure already developed by Teague et al. (1998) was available for use in assessing how similarly the three separate MCOTT teams were delivering services. Because we planned to aggregate data from the three sites, it was important to us to evaluate how closely they adhered to a single, well defined model. That same fidelity scale will also be used to document the degree of overlap between the case management model at Community Connection and the MCOTTs.

In addition, we wanted to quantify the similarities and differences between Community Connection's and MCOTT's approaches to housing. We subsequently developed a simple Housing Fidelity Scale to capture the relevant dimensions. Dimensions assessed by the housing fidelity scale include five which should differentiate the two programs, and three on which we expect no differences. Those which should differentiate the two programs are: *Housing Control* (MH agency vs. independent landlord); *Separation of Providers* (clinical vs. housing supports); *Integration vs. Separation* (based on disability status); *Tenancy Decisions*; and reliance on *Live-In Staff*. We expect no differences on: *Consumer Preference for Services* (participation in decision-making); *Community-Based Services* (vs. office-based); and availability of *24 hour Services*. The logic model helped to highlight the key dimensions to be assessed in our process evaluation.

The logic model was also helpful in identifying variables and instruments to be used in the outcome evaluation. Though we clearly planned to assess housing outcomes, we had not adequately planned to capture several short-term and intermediate changes related to risk factors which we believe must be addressed to assure long term housing stability. Progress toward recovery from substance abuse is one such variable.

Finally, the logic model proved to be very useful as a communication tool with outsiders. For example, intensive discussions with a site-visit team revealed that we had inadvertently perpetuated the misconception that the Community Connections housing continuum is a linear one. This was an important revelation as program staff are careful not to operate the continuum in a linear fashion and instead work to maintain a high degree of flexibility and individualized planning in making decisions with residents about housing moves.

THE AGENCY MANAGER'S PERSPECTIVE

In my experience as the director of a large alcohol, drug and other behavioral health treatment services organization which has participated in numerous evaluation projects, projects have had trouble achieving their goals for one principal reason: The project is not as well-managed as it needs to be in order to ensure success. In the face of complex projects in which there are multiple stakeholders, the failure usually is one of management.

My aim in this section is to describe the experience of one organization, Arapahoe House (see Kirby et al., 1999, for a detailed description) in the application of logic models to the evaluation of behavioral health services delivery programs. More specifically, I will be addressing the central role and value of logic models in the overall management of these kinds of projects, in which evaluation and services delivery are linked from the outset.

The Team Approach to Development of the Logic Model. We used a team approach to develop our logic model. I chaired the team, referred to here as the steering committee, which was comprised of the following representatives: (1) the administrative project coordinator; (2) the manager or managers of the clinical programs most directly involved in the project–in the Homelessness Prevention PROUD Project, the Manager of Case Management services and the Detoxification Programs Manager; (3) the housing coordinator; (4) the Manager of Research and Program Evaluation and key staff members from that department; (5) our evaluation consultants, for this project from the University of Denver; and (6) others invited to meetings with a specific agenda, including other consultants, case managers, and program care coordinators.

This approach, in which each of the major stakeholders for the project is included on the steering committee, has proven to be very effective for our organization. It is a perfect fit with our culture and has led to success in both the development of proposals to secure funding for new projects and the management of existing projects. The steering committee convenes to develop the concept and proposal for each project, then continues intact as the key coordinating entity throughout the course of implementation of the project.

The Logic Model as a Management Tool. The other authors discussed the value of the logic model in guiding the evaluation. However, the logic model is also beneficial in providing a basis for ongoing management of the project from inception to completion.

What is meant by "management of the project?" In this context, we define management as the oversight of the project in an efficient and effective manner to assure that it is designed, implemented, and completed in the manner envisioned. Where deviations from the original vision must occur, they do so as the product of deliberations in the steering committee. This oversight includes not only adherence to the logic model, but adherence to the project time line and delivery of proposed products. Management thus has responsibility for oversight of the process and the quality of the outcomes of the project.

For us, management occurs on several levels. In each of our steering committee meetings, which typically occur on average every two weeks throughout the intensive phases of a project and monthly in the less intensive phases, we review the status of the project. Fundamental to this status review is the logic model. In effect, the logic model serves as our road map in managing the project. If a discrepancy occurs between the logic model and practice, we surface the relevant issues in a timely manner; usually we reaffirm the model and modify our practice, but it is also possible to modify the logic model. In either case, adherence to the logic model provides for us assurance that the intervention is being implemented to maintain fidelity to the model. Therefore, at the level of the steering committee, the advantages of the logic model as a management tool can be summarized as follows:

- Management has responsibility to provide staff with "the big picture." The logic model fosters this process by visually graphing the interrelationships between clinical services, administration, and evaluation; staff can identify in the logic model their respective roles in the larger enterprise.
- Team development of the logic model produces a richer and more comprehensive final product.
- Team development of the logic model substantially increases "buy-in" for all stakeholders.
- Team development of the logic model provides multiple perspectives reflecting the agency administration, clinical services providers, and evaluators.
- The logic model serves to facilitate more effective and efficient decision-making.
- The logic model is vital to ensure that program implementation and evaluation adhere to the model.
- Team monitoring of the logic model enhances accountability across all major stakeholders.
- The logic model is a schematic that can improve communication between steering committee members, managers, and their respective staffs.

At the level of individual managers, the logic model also serves as a management tool for each of them with their respective areas of responsibility, to ensure that their decisions and actions are consistent with the model. In our agency, with this particular project, for example, the Manager of Case Management Services and the Detoxification Programs Manager meet with their respective staffs on a regular basis to review the status of the project, utilizing the logic model as the key document in this ongoing process. If problems arise in the programs, these program managers either surface the issues in the next steering committee meeting or, in some cases, bring to the meeting the staff who are raising the issues. Again, we are convinced, based on our own experience, that this kind of inclusive process, which occurs at multiple levels within the organization and across our consultants as well, results in a more tightly managed project and one in which fidelity to the logic model is enhanced.

The following summarizes the advantages of the logic model as a management tool for individual managers with their respective staffs:

- Managers can manage to the logic model to assure that day-to-day activities encompassed by the model are carried out as designed.
- Communication across departments within the organization, with referral sources, and with funding sources can center on the logic model. We have found that communication in this manner is significantly improved and is achieved more efficiently than is the case with other forms of communication.
- Training of staff is enhanced through use of the logic model. Clinical staff can readily grasp the nature of the intervention, the target population(s) and the outcomes expected. Evaluators and administrative staff comprehend these same features in a manner that is devoid of clinical jargon.
- The administrative and clinical staff learn, through the regular application of logic models, the vital role of program evaluation in the activities of the organization. The interrelationships between clinical services, administration, and evaluation are clarified. It becomes clear that the purpose of evaluation is to improve the efficacy of services, and does not simply reflect more paperwork and burden for the staff.

We have experienced numerous occasions in which the logic model has served to avoid inadvertent deviation from our desired course of action. For example, in one evaluation project, when we were beginning interviews, we discovered that we had no measures in the interview to adequately assess some of the critical short-term outcomes specified in the logic model. In other cases, through developing iterations of the logic model, we have refined the linkages between the intervention(s) and the short-term, intermediate, and long-term outcomes. In the present Homelessness Prevention PROUD project, for example, there was a total of eight iterations of the logic model, spanning more than a year, before the model attained "final" status.

CONCLUSION

In conclusion, the kinds of projects in which we are engaged are complex, often with mixed funding sources; typically we must rely not only on program staff and a team of evaluators, but also on other programs in the agency and on other human services agencies who provide referrals and vital services for clients. In many cases all must work closely in order to collect data for the evaluation. These kinds of complex projects, entailing as they do multiple stakeholders, can founder at many points, and it has been our experience that the team model such as that embodied in the steering committee at Arapahoe House affords the most efficacious management strategy for management of them. The logic model is at the center of every project; it is generated by the team of stakeholders and monitored by the steering committee at regularly established intervals. It becomes an essential management tool, providing assurance that all are "speaking a common language" regardless of their respective roles in the project and that, throughout each stage in the course of the project, the interventions maintain fidelity to the model.

For the evaluators, the logic model ensures them that the program is evaluable and provides the formula which enables the scientific need for replicability. For the funding agency, the logic model serves a similar purpose: it provides the blueprint on which decisions are made as to the fidelity of the project to its original design. In all cases, it serves as an excellent tool to promote communication among a wide variety of stakeholders.

REFERENCES

Bickman, L. (1987). *Using Program Theory in Evaluation, New Directions for Program Evaluation*, no. 33, San Francisco: Jossey-Bass, 19-42.

Conrad, K.J., Matters, M.D., Hanrahan, P., Luchins, D.J., Savage, C. Daugherty, B. & Shinderman, M. (1999). Representative Payee for Individuals with Severe Mental Illness at Community Counseling Centers of Chicago. *Alcoholism Treatment Quarterly*, 17(1/2, 169-186.

Conrad, K.J., Matters, M.D., Hanrahan, P., Luchins, D., Savage, C. Daugherty, B. (1998). Describing patients with mental illness in representative payeeship. *Psychiatric Services*, 9, 1223-1225.

Conrad, K.J. and Hughes, S.L. (1989). *Adult Day Care Assessment Procedure: Research Manual.* Evanston, IL: Northwestern University, Center for Health Services and Policy Research. Working Paper # 188.

Kirby, M.W., Braucht, G.N., Brown, E., Krane, S., McCann, M., & Van DeMark, N. (1999). Dyadic Case Management as a Strategy for Prevention of Homelessness Among Chronically Debilitated Men and Women with Alcohol and Drug Dependence. *Alcoholism Treatment Quarterly*, 17(1/2), 53-71.

Krueger, R.A. (1988). *Focus groups: A practical guide for applied research.* Newbury Park, Calif.: Sage Publications, Inc.

Teague, G.B., Bond, G.R., Drake, R.E. (1998). Program fidelity in assertive community treatment: Development and use of a measure. *American Journal of Orthopsychiatry*, 68, 216-232.

Trochim, W. (1989). An Introduction to Concept Mapping for Planning and Evaluation. *Evaluation and Program Planning 12*, (1), 1-16.

Trochim, W. (1993). *The Concept System* (Manual). Concept Systems: Ithaca, N.Y.

Weiss, C.H. (1997). Theory-Based Evaluation: Past, Present, and Future. In Rog, D.J. & Fournier, D. *Progress and Future Directions in Evaluation: Perspectives on Theory, Practice, and Methods. New Directions for Evaluation, no. 76*, San Francisco: Jossey-Bass.

Wholey, J.S. (1994). Assessing the feasibility and Likely Usefulness of Evaluation. In Wholey, J.S., Hatry, H.P., & Newcomer, K.E. *Handbook of practical evaluation.* San Francisco: Jossey-Bass.

Wholey J.S. (1987). Evaluability assessment: Developing theory. In: Bickman, L. (ed.) *Using program theory in evaluation: New directions for program evaluation, no. 33.* San Francisco: Jossey-Bass.

Wholey J.S. (1979). Evaluation: promise and performance. Washington, D.C.: Urban Institute.

Homelessness Prevention Therapeutic Community (TC) for Addicted Mothers

JoAnn Y. Sacks, PhD
Stanley Sacks, PhD
Michael Harle, MHS
George De Leon, PhD

JoAnn Y. Sacks is Project Director; Stanley Sacks is Deputy Director; George De Leon is Director; all are affiliated with the Center for Therapeutic Community Research (CTCR) at National Development and Research Institutes, Inc. (NDRI), 2 World Trade Center, 16th Floor, New York, NY 10048. Michael Harle is Executive Director, Gaudenzia, Inc., 106 West Main Street, Norristown, PA 19401.

Address correspondence to Dr. JoAnn Sacks.

The authors acknowledge the leadership shown by the Gaudenzia staff in developing this innovative homelessness prevention program for addicted mothers and in contributing to this paper, including: Michael Harle, the Executive Director; Jim Leake, the Regional Director; Sandra Murphy-Grover and Avis Sawyer, the Program Directors of New Image and Kindred House, respectively; Leslie Ziegler and Joan Groves, the Clinical Supervisors at New Image and Kindred House, respectively; and the staff and clients of the program.

The authors also express their appreciation to Dr. Dwayne Simpson and Dr. Barry Brown for their assistance and special consultative advice in conceptualizing the homelessness prevention program and in outlining the evaluation approach; further appreciation to Dr. Barry Brown for his thoughtful critique of this paper.

This paper was supported by funding from the Center for Mental Health Services and the Center for Substance Abuse Treatment, Grant # 1 UD9 SM51969-01/02, Modified TC to Prevent Homelessness in Addicted Mothers.

[Haworth co-indexing entry note]: "Homelessness Prevention Therapeutic Community (TC) for Addicted Mothers." Sacks, JoAnn Y. et al. Co-published simultaneously in *Alcoholism Treatment Quarterly* (The Haworth Press, Inc.) Vol. 17, No. 1/2, 1999, pp. 33-51; and: *Homelessness Prevention in Treatment of Substance Abuse and Mental Illness: Logic Models and Implementation of Eight American Projects* (ed: Kendon J. Conrad et al.) The Haworth Press, Inc., 1999, pp. 33-51. Single or multiple copies of this article are available for a fee from The Haworth Document Delivery Service [1-800-342-9678, 9:00 a.m. - 5:00 p.m. (EST). E-mail address: getinfo@haworthpressinc.com].

© 1999 by The Haworth Press, Inc. All rights reserved.

SUMMARY. This chapter describes a homelessness prevention therapeutic community (TC) for addicted mothers and their children developed by Gaudenzia in response to increasing numbers of homeless addicted mothers and families entering the Philadelphia shelter system. The program uses TC principles and methods as the foundation for recovery and the structure within which the homelessness prevention interventions unfold. The mothers progress through program stages and typically move from residential to permanent housing. The chapter describes the program's conceptual framework and logic model, setting, client profiles, goals and interventions. The specific homelessness prevention activities include 14 distinctive interventions that address family preservation, employment; housing stabilization; societal reintegration and building a supportive community. The study design includes two groups and 185 subjects: a homelessness prevention TC (n = 104); and a standard TC (n = 81). The process evaluation assesses the fidelity of implementation of the homelessness prevention interventions. The outcome evaluation compares the effectiveness of the homelessness prevention TC with a standard TC on both traditional outcomes (e.g., substance abuse) and homelessness prevention outcomes (e.g., housing stabilization). This program has considerable significance for policy and planning, especially for the development of integrated mother-child programs and for the application of TC principles and methods to homelessness prevention. *[Article copies available for a fee from The Haworth Document Delivery Service: 1-800-342-9678. E-mail address: getinfo@haworthpressinc.com]*

KEYWORDS. Therapeutic community (tc), addicted/single mothers, family preservation, "housing as treatment," housing stages perspective, program evaluation

THE PROBLEM OF HOMELESS SUBSTANCE ABUSING WOMEN WITH CHILDREN

Homelessness represents one of our most pressing and complex social problems. Homeless people suffer from a variety of associated difficulties, including those related to health and medical problems (Institute on Medicine, 1990), HIV disease (Schutt & Garett, 1992), criminality (both as victims and participants; Rahav & Link, 1995), alcohol and drug use (Fischer & Breakey, 1991), and mental illness (Rossi, 1990).

A rapidly increasing number of women are joining the ranks of the homeless (Merves, 1992). For the past decade, the fastest growing subgroup of the homeless population in the US has been women with children; families comprised 33% of the total homeless population in 1987, rising to 38%

by 1996 (US Conference of Mayors, 1987; 1996). Homeless women face more discrimination than men in seeking shelter, food, and employment; homeless mothers are substantially more likely to be on welfare (Merves, 1992; Calsyn & Morse, 1990). The generally poorer economic state of women, combined with the demands of single parenthood are seen to imperil a woman's ability to maintain her home (Bassuk, 1993).

Diminished social supports have been cited as a significant factor in placing the family at risk for homelessness (McChesney, 1992; Wood, Valdez, Hayashi, & Shen, 1990); the loss of social supports are often a component of the process of becoming homeless. Homeless mothers report perceiving the members of their social support system as unavailable to assist them with housing, finances or child care, suggesting that even those with an identified support network of family and friends may have "worn out their welcome" by the time they became homeless. Other homeless women are members of social networks whose constituents are only marginally better off than themselves (Shinn, Knickman & Weitzman, 1991; Letiecq, Anderson & Koblinsky, 1996). Increased time homeless, transient homelessness, and maternal substance abuse are each associated with reduced assistance from the social network (Letiecq et al., 1996).

Homeless women with children, interviewed in the Maryland shelter system, differed from other homeless women in citing needs for child care, parenting skills training, help with their children, job training, finding work, education, and service coordination (DiBlasio & Belcher, 1995). Not surprisingly, a growing body of studies of homeless families provides evidence that homelessness profoundly and disproportionately affects the youngest family members. Homeless children are at increased risk for: severe and chronic health problems; poor and inadequate nutrition; developmental and emotional problems; educational problems; and child abuse (Bassuk & Cohen, 1991; Bassuk, Rubin & Lauriat, 1986).

Evidence of increased drug use among homeless women has emerged throughout this decade; many of these women have children and/or are pregnant (Hausman & Hammen, 1993). Homeless women with dependent children report rates of drug abuse ranging from two to eight times higher than those for housed women with children (McChesney, 1995; Robertson, 1991). Substance abuse poses a threat to housing, not only by causing disrupted functioning, but also by virtue of evictions as a consequence of national policy for public housing (Cranston-Gonzalez Affordable Housing Act, 1990). Homelessness and substance abuse also present serious threats to family preservation by virtue of being major factors in the decision to separate children from their mothers for placement in foster care (Allen, 1991; Steinbock, 1995).

The therapeutic community (TC) is a program model capable of addressing the extensive needs of homeless women with dependent children. A comprehensive, psychosocial intervention, the TC approaches substance abuse as a "whole person disorder." TC programs are designed to treat substance abuse and foster change in psychological functioning and social behavior. As modified for women and children, the TC incorporates the educational, developmental and social needs of the children.

THERAPEUTIC COMMUNITIES (TCs)

Several articles (De Leon, 1995; De Leon & Ziegenfuss, 1986) describe the perspective and approach of the traditional TC for recovery from drug abuse. Briefly, drug abuse is a disorder of the whole person reflecting problems in conduct, attitudes, moods, emotional management and values. The goals of the TC approach are to promote freedom from alcohol and illicit drug use, to eliminate antisocial behavior, and to affect a global change in lifestyle, including personal attitudes and values.

A number of NIDA-funded, multi-site, and program-based evaluations document the effectiveness of TCs. Short- and long-term follow-up studies show significant decreases in alcohol and other drug use, reduced criminality, improved psychological functioning, and increased employment (De Leon, 1984; Simpson & Sells, 1982; Hubbard, Craddock, Flynn, Anderson, & Etheridge, 1997; Condelli & Hubbard, 1994). The demonstrated effectiveness of the TC, in terms of drug use, prosocial behavior, and psychological outcome, provided the rationale for the development of TCs for special populations such as homeless mentally ill chemical abusers (MICAs) and homeless addicted mothers.

The past decade has seen the development of modified TC programs relevant to the current article. Modified TCs for homeless individuals, often developed within the shelter systems, are generally of shorter duration than traditional TC programs and focus on engaging clients in the peer community and initiating treatment. Homeless, addicted clients have multiple needs and modified TC treatment programs for these populations incorporate educational, vocational, legal and housing placement services (Liberty et al., in press; Leaf et al., 1993). Specialized, modified TCs for homeless MICAs are more flexible and less intense than standard TCs and provide a comprehensive multi-dimensional program of integrated mental health, substance abuse, and rehabilitative services designed to meet the complex needs of the population (Sacks et al., 1996; 1997). Modified TCs for women and children provide family style housing, day care and after-school programs, a gender-specific curriculum focusing on parenting issues for the mothers and modifications of the daily program routine to accommodate the mother's parenting responsibilities (Stevens & Glider, 1994; Wexler, Cuadrado & Stevens, in press; Coletti et al., 1997).

The findings from this work indicate: (i) homeless substance abusing men participating in shelter based short-term TCs showed significant declines in alcohol and drug abuse, criminal activity (drug possession and property offences), and depression (Liberty et al., in press); (ii) homeless MICA men and women show significantly greater improvement for the modified TC group on measures of illegal drug use, crime and depression as compared to a treatment-as-usual group receiving standard services (Sacks et al., 1997; De Leon, Sacks, Staines & McKendrick, submitted); and (iii) women in TCs modified to accommodate mothers with their children show decreases in alcohol and drug use, increases in employment, decreased depression, and improvement in other measures of mental health (Wexler et al., in press).

The TC approach, based on several core principles and methods now widely accepted in the drug treatment field, may be ideally suitable to address the needs of homeless, substance abusing women with children. These core principles and methods include: providing a highly structured daily regimen; coping with life difficulties through personal responsibility and self-help; using peers as role models and guides; recognizing the peer community as the healing agent and employing community-as-method (the community as both the context of and mechanism for change); understanding change as a gradual, developmental process, reflected by movement through treatment stages; stressing work, self-reliance, and acquiring skills to support vocational development and independent living; and promoting prosocial values accompanied by healthy social networks to sustain recovery.

The current project, evaluating a homelessness prevention TC, advances research in several ways. First, it documents specific homelessness prevention program elements, greatly increasing the ease of future applications. Second, although treatment effectiveness has been documented for homeless substance abusers, evaluations of homelessness prevention programs, especially those that provide services for addicted mothers and their children, are virtually nonexistent. The proposed study will provide a rigorous evaluation of an innovative homelessness prevention TC program and data on outcomes for both the mothers and their children. Third, the study will provide data on the relationship between process measures (i.e., specific homelessness prevention elements) and outcome measures, thereby identifying the "active ingredients" of the homelessness prevention program. Finally, and perhaps most significantly, the project evaluates TC methods found effective in reducing substance abuse, extending both the range and potential of these methods by adding components specific to homelessness prevention.

PROGRAM DESCRIPTION

This paper describes a modified TC program that focuses on the prevention of homelessness in substance abusing women with dependent children. This program is similar to other TC programs for women and children, but differs in its focus on preventing homelessness and in the richness of services designed to achieve this goal.

The goal of the present program is to prevent homelessness among homeless, substance abusing women and their children. The program addresses homelessness by focusing on several broad and interrelated goals: (1) using recovery from substance abuse as a foundation for homelessness prevention; (2) improving parenting and the mother-child relationship; (3) reuniting the family; (4) sustaining gainful employment; (5) stabilizing housing; (6) building a healing and supportive community; and (7) achieving reintegration with mainstream society. During the course of the program, mothers progress through program stages and move from residential to transitional and/or permanent housing. The specific homelessness prevention interventions begin early in the residential phase, increase in frequency and intensity (especially in the latter part of the residential program), and continue at somewhat reduced frequency upon entry into transitional and permanent housing (see Figure 1).

Setting

Agency and Facilities. Gaudenzia is a private, not-for-profit TC-oriented agency, incorporated in Pennsylvania in 1968, to provide treatment, prevention and other services to people with substance abuse and related problems. Two of Gaudenzia's 34 programs, New Image in Philadelphia and Kindred House in Westchester, were developed in 1989 (in cooperation with the City of Philadelphia Health Department and the US Public Health Service) as programs to prevent homelessness among those homeless, substance abusing women who were pregnant and/or who were parenting one or more children. Each mother entering the program is allowed to bring up to two of her dependent children with her.

Both program sites share similar physical design elements, including: bedroom space occupied by two or three mothers and their young children; gender-specific dormitory bedrooms shared by up to four older children; communal dining and recreational space; infant and pre-school nursery/day care space; group meeting rooms and office space for administrative work and individual counseling.

Staffing

The residential program is staffed 24 hours a day, seven days a week, with a combination of supervisors, counselors, and house managers. Three staff

FIGURE 1. Illustration of the Homelessness Prevention TC

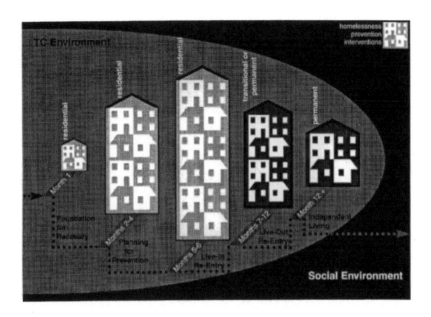

members, including at least one supervisor, are present during peak programming hours (9 a.m. to 9 p.m.); two staff members are present overnight. The Director and Clinical Supervisor are available for consultation on an emergency pager system when they are not present on-site. The Prevention Specialist provides special parenting skills training groups on weekdays and substance abuse prevention groups for children during the family education activities on Sunday, enriching the staffing at those times. The Transitional program is staffed with one counselor/case manager for approximately 20 individuals. The Child Care program is staffed by a Prevention Specialist and Child Care Worker. In addition, between two and three mothers are assigned to participate in the Child Care program each day as part of their parenting training.

Almost all staff members employed in the program are graduates of programs (including the Gaudenzia programs) for substance abuse treatment, and have subsequently acquired credentials in that area. The supervisors of the child care and children's prevention programs have training and experience in the field of education. Direct care and supervisory staff are female; their ages, ethnic and racial backgrounds reflect those of the residents within the program. The child care program operates five days/week with an adult:child ratio that varies between 1:4 and 1:6, depending on the age of the child. In total, 14 staff members are assigned to each program site.

The section that follows describes the conceptual framework of the homelessness prevention program in terms of a perspective, approach and interventions.

Perspective

The Individual. The nature of the problem of homelessness is viewed from the perspective of the individual, and encompasses the aspects of: the disorder, the person, recovery, and "right living." The disorder is perceived as one affecting the whole person; the person is viewed as having multiple deficits accompanied by multidimensional needs and problems. Recovery is viewed as a developmental process in which change continues to take place over time. The view of "right living" (prosocial change) highlights the need to focus on attitudes and values as well as behavior. The disaffiliation of the individual from society is most evident. Thus, TC programs are multi-faceted, focusing on changing attitudes, behavior and values and facilitating reintegration with mainstream society through the use of community-as-method (i.e., the community as the healing agent).

The Mother-Child Dyad. In the present project on homelessness prevention, the perspective also includes the mother-child dyad. Homeless, substance abusing mothers must learn to manage their own lives while providing proper care, guidance, and a secure environment for their child(ren). The educational, developmental and social needs of the children must be addressed. The mother-child relationship requires special attention in order to strengthen, and in some cases develop, the bonds between mothers and children, many of whom have lived apart. In addition, consideration needs to be given to the poverty, economic dependence, family deterioration and alienation that have formed the social context for these families. Successful homelessness prevention interventions must provide tools and supports to help the mother break the cycle of poverty and family disintegration for herself and for her children. The homelessness prevention TC program for women and children provides a unique opportunity for the correlated work of facilitating personal change in the mother, nourishing growth and development in the child and forging strong parent-child bonds for the future.

Approach

Structure. The structure of the program is defined in terms of the daily regimen, the role of staff, the peer hierarchy, and the role of the peer community. The daily regimen provides a predictable pattern to the day, and a predictable environment within which mother and child(ren) learn and practice consistency, responsibility, "right living" and community living skills. The daily schedule is structured and group-oriented, but flexible enough to accommodate mothering tasks and the special needs of the child, determined on an individual basis. The staff serve as role models and guides for the mothers, using their own experiences and current behavior to set examples for clients, providing supportive guidance and skills training to facilitate achievement of program goals. The peer hierarchy, which operates the facility, promotes personal responsibility and self-reliance. The role of the peer community is to provide support, leadership and mentoring for other members, building mutual self-help supports, and a peer "safety net" for mothers who have moved with their children into individual apartments in the community.

Process. The treatment process is defined in terms of program stages that reflect a developmental perspective of change (for the mother and for the mother-child dyad). Program stages provide opportunity for a gradual, incremental transformative process and the assumption of increased responsibility. Table 1 provides a brief description of the five program stages.

Successful progression through the program stages is dependent on demonstrating attainment of short-term goals and development of the next level of goals that are designed to bring the mother closer to self-management and independent functioning. As she completes each stage in the program, the mother conducts a self-assessment of goal achievement, then presents this assessment to her peers and receives their response. This procedure provides a peer feedback loop that supports the mother's successes as well as her

TABLE 1. Program Stages

Stage	Description	Goals
Stage 1	**Foundation for Recovery**–establishing a foundation for homelessness prevention	• affiliation with the peer community • stabilization of the family • assumption of personal responsibility and commitment to recovery from substance abuse
Stage 2	**Planning for Prevention**–introducing activities focused on obtaining housing and work	• abstinence from substance abuse • intensification of parent-child interventions
Stage 3	**Live-In Re-Entry**–intensifying all homelessness prevention activities	• preparation of the mother and family to move into the community
Stage 4	**Live-Out Re-Entry**–reintegration with the community	• stabilization of the family in the community • support for and consolidation of the self-management of all activities to prevent homelessness
Stage 5	**Independent Living**	• sustaining independent living in the community

struggles, and further strengthens her affiliation with the peer support network.

Homelessness Prevention Activities

Foundation for Recovery. Many of the core elements and activities of therapeutic community programs are present, as described in other writings (De Leon, 1996; Sacks et al., 1996). The basic elements of the TC are broadly grouped into four classifications of elements: (1) Community Enhancement; (2) Therapeutic/Educative; (3) Community and Clinical Management; (4) Vocational. These interventions include, for example: (i) morning meetings–to establish community affiliation for the future construction of a supportive community; (ii) encounter groups–to resolve personal and interpersonal conflicts and to facilitate personal growth; (iii) peer-work hierarchy–to increase personal responsibility and begin the process of vocational training; and (iv) educational seminars–to transmit basic information regarding substance abuse, social responsibility and daily living skills. These core TC elements are present in the current program, in adapted form, to address the problem of substance abuse, to provide a framework for a full personal recovery or change, and to furnish an environment within which homelessness prevention interventions occur.

Homelessness Prevention Specific Interventions. Table 2 describes the homelessness prevention interventions distinctive to the homelessness prevention TC in four categories: family preservation; world of work; housing stabilization; and building a supportive community. Along with core TC elements, the program employs a total of 22 homelessness prevention interventions; 14 are distinctive to the homelessness prevention TC (described in Table 2). The other interventions, although important in combination with the 14 distinctive interventions of the present program, may also be present in standard TCs.

The interventions specific to homelessness begin on entry to the residential setting and intensify over time, becoming predominant in the re-entry phase. The interrelationship between program stages and the homelessness prevention interventions is illustrated in Table 3.

Eligibility Criteria

Referrals to the residential programs come from homeless shelters, outpatient treatment programs, and the correctional system throughout Philadelphia and surrounding communities; because of the agency's high community visibility, some clients are self-referred. Program eligibility criteria are inclusionary in four areas: (i) clients are women; (ii) who have children and/or are

TABLE 2. Homelessness Prevention Interventions

Intervention	Goals and Description
Family Preservation	**Goals** • addresses the specific needs of mother, child(ren) and family
Child Focus	**Description**
*Structured child care/school	• daily child care program for infants and toddlers • provides a nurturing environment • addresses social, emotional and developmental needs
*Assessment and early intervention	• history of homelessness and substance abuse places children at risk • facilitates comprehensive assessment within 30 days of program entry • provides entree into early intervention and/or special needs programming
*Children's prevention group	• engages children in age-appropriate substance abuse prevention activities • provides a forum for the child to discuss concerns about his/her mother's past substance abuse and effects on his/her life
*Prevention group for visiting children	• provides prevention activities for children not living with their mothers • uses abbreviated materials from standard prevention resources
Mother and Family Focus	**Description**
*Parents' Group	• improves parenting and strengthens the mother-child relationship • provides a forum for mothers to discuss the problems, difficulties and pleasures of parenting and daily child care • focuses on self-expression, self-awareness, and problem solving
*Child care participation	• improves parenting skills and reinforces the mother-child relationship • mothers participate on a rotating assignment • staff guide interactions and discuss childcare principles
*Family Education Day	• fosters relationships between mother and her extended family • improves relationships between mother and children not living with her • children not in residence can visit weekly and participate in the Family Education Day • promotes family reunification
*Mother-child group	• improves communication between mother and child • increases the expression of personal feelings between mother and child • reduces acting-out or behavioral problems of children
*Individual/Family counseling	• improves mother-child relationship and strengthens the family unit • helps the mother to change the family dynamic through increased understanding of herself, her child(ren), and the family unit
World of Work	**Goals** • prepares the mother for work • focuses on obtaining and sustaining employment • fosters development of positive work attitudes and skills integral to TC programs
*Recovery and the World of Work	**Description** • focuses on self-monitoring of work performance, plans for improved performance and career development • sustains awareness of relationship between work-related issues and recovery.

TABLE 2 (continued)

Intervention	Goals and Description
Housing Stabilization	**Goals** • moving into stable, interim housing during the residential phase • moving to agency-operated transitional housing apartments (located at a common site) or other subsidized apartments during the transitional, live-out re-entry stage
*Case assistance	**Description** • provides critical case-specific support for the family's reintegration with community, either in a transitional housing apartment or in an independent apartment • provides regular counselor visits: to assess the status of the apartment; to monitor home management (maintaining sufficient food, cleanliness of apartment, etc.); to provide assistance with immediate problems; to assess emotional stability of the mother and the family unit; to monitor evidence of substance abuse; and to monitor compliance with aftercare plan (including linkage to outpatient services)
*Transitional housing group	• improves ability to sustain housing using a discussion format • focuses on issues of housing, homemaking and community living • includes Section 8 applications, leases, household budgeting and management
*Re-entry group	• facilitates re-entry into the community at large • assists with self-management of all the factors related to homelessness prevention, with special emphasis on peer support • focuses on daily review of a 17-point Self-Management Checklist maintained by the mother as a tool to help her track the relevant issues related to family preservation, work, housing stabilization, and extension of the support network
Building a Supportive Community	**Goals** • facilitates the assimilation into the community of peers • strengthens the individual's perception of community as a nurturing entity, enhancing the capacity of the community to teach and to heal • promotes affiliation with the extended, community-based "family" of mothers, and single individuals, within a recovery fellowship
*Re-entry board	**Description** • provides peer review of Live-Out Re-Entry candidates • refines the policies and procedures that govern re-entry • provides input for program development and planning

pregnant; (iii) who exhibit a substance abuse disorder, based on referral information, intake interview, and administration of the Addiction Severity Index (ASI; McLellan et al., 1985); and (iv) who are homeless or at-risk for homelessness. To be considered homeless, or at-risk for homelessness, clients must currently meet one of the following criteria:

1. reside in a group shelter, domestic violence safe home, hotel or motel paid for with public or charitable funds, or a mental health, drug or alcohol facility including prison programs
2. have received verification that their children are to be placed in foster care placement solely because of lack of adequate housing, or children currently in foster care could return to parental care if housing were adequate

3. reside in a doubled-up arrangement on a temporary basis that is in violation of the lessee's rental agreement
4. reside in a condemned building
5. reside in housing in which the physical plant presents life-threatening conditions; e.g., dangerous structural defects, or lacking heat, plumbing or utilities
6. reside on the streets, in cars, doorways, face eviction, etc.

Who Is Being Served?

Demographic Profile. The vast majority of women (75%) at New Image and Kindred House are African-American; 10% are Caucasian, and 15% are Hispanic. Their average age is 30, with a range from 17 to 47. The 32 women currently in the two programs have 98 children (an average of 3), 41 of whom are also in the program and 57 of whom are not. The ages of the children in the program range from newborn to 12, with an average age of four; the children outside the program average nine years of age. The inclusion of some, but not all, children creates an opportunity for the mother to develop parenting skills. The program promotes family reunification with the remaining children during the move to independent living.

Of the 32 women in the program, about half (47%) have obtained a high school diploma or GED; over two thirds (68%) have never been married. Prior to admission, over the same proportion (68%) were unemployed; virtually all (91%) were on welfare. This demographic data provide a portrait of under-educated single mothers, raising their children in conditions of homelessness and poverty, with limited opportunity for change in lifestyle.

Substance Abuse. All of the women admitted to the two programs have a substantial history of substance abuse. The profile of substance use is as follows: roughly 72% abuse crack cocaine; 19% abuse heroin (sniffing and snorting are more common than injecting); and 3% abuse cocaine in forms other than crack. Agency records reveal a significant history of poly-substance abuse including combinations of cocaine, marijuana and alcohol. The majority of women report a prior history of alcohol/drug treatment.

Psychopathology. A significant number of women in the programs (approximately 60%) suffer from a variety of psychological problems and psychopathology, including anxiety, depression, phobia, antisocial personality and other characteristics that are often part of a dual disorder profile. In general, the program screens out those with serious mental illness and addresses the psychological problems of those remaining within the context of TC programming, an approach with demonstrated success in other TC research (De Leon & Jainchill, 1982).

TABLE 3. Interventions by Stages

Intervention	Stage 1 Foundation for Recovery	Stage 2 Planning for Prevention	Stage 3 Live-In Re-Entry	Stage 4 Live-Out Re-Entry	Stage 5 Independent Living
Core TC Elements					
(e.g. morning/evening meetings, seminars, encounter groups, peer work hierarchy)	√	√	√		
Homelessness Prevention Interventions					
Family Preservation					
Child Focus					
*Structured child care/school	√	√	√		
*Assessment and early intervention	√	√	√	√	√
*Children's prevention group	√	√	√	√	
*Prevention group for visiting children	√	√	√		
Mother and Family Focus					
Family focus/Parenting seminar	√	√	√		
*Parents' Group	√	√	√		
*Child care participation	√	√	√		
*Family Education	√	√	√		
*Mother-child group	√	√	√		
*Individual/Family counseling		√	√	√	√
World of Work					
Education preparation	√	√	√	√	
Work readiness seminar		√	√		
Job search/location			√		
*Recovery and the World of Work			√	√	√
Housing Stabilization					
Independent living skills class	√	√	√		
*Case assistance			√	√	√
Individual and group counseling (outpatient)	√	√	√	√	√
*Transitional housing group				√	
*Re-entry group			√	√	
Building a Supportive Community					
Seminar leader/mentor				√	√
12-Step meetings		√	√	√	√
*Re-entry board				√	√

*Distinctive homelessness prevention interventions–Presented in idealized form for clarity; somewhat greater overlap occurs between specifc homelessness prevention interventions and program phases for each individual.

Implementation

Table 4 summarizes the principles of successful program development, and attempts to illuminate the practitioner's basic question concerning innovative programming: "How is it done?"

TABLE 4. Principles of Implementation

Area of Action	Means of Achieving
How to Organize	• develop project team that is skilled, representative, with decision-making responsibility • use a field demonstration framework in which cross-fertilization exists between program design and evaluation
How to Integrate with the Health Care System	• follow system guidelines, policies and constraints • respond to system changes • form partnerships with system stakeholders • use imprimatur of federal grant to facilitate system accommodation and change
How to Integrate with the Service Agency	• select an agency committed to research-based programming • form collaborative relationships, based on mutual commitment, at all levels of the organization
How to Refine and Implement Program Elements	• develop a planning group involving all key staff that meets regularly • provide training and technical assistance in the context of implementation • ensure staff and client orientation to all new program elements • codify program in manual form and use manual to guide program QA

LOGIC MODEL

The program as described above can be summarized schematically by the logic model (see Figure 2). The logic model depicts the relationship between the population/environment, conceptual framework, interventions, and expected outcomes in this project, focusing on the homelessness prevention specific interventions of the program.

EVALUATION PLAN

The study design includes two groups and projects a total of 185 subjects: a homelessness prevention TC (n = 104); and a standard TC (n = 81). The subjects, as previously described, are homeless, substance abusing women and their dependent children. The standardized battery includes cross-site and project specific measures to assess both traditional outcomes (e.g., substance abuse, crime) and homelessness prevention outcomes (e.g., family preservation, work, housing stability, and building a supportive community). The subjects are compared at baseline, six and twelve months follow-up. The main outcome goal is to determine the differential efficacy of the homelessness prevention TC in comparison with a standard residential TC. Significantly greater improvements are predicted for the homelessness prevention TC in comparison with the standard TC.

FIGURE 2. Homelessness Prevention TC for Addicted Mothers

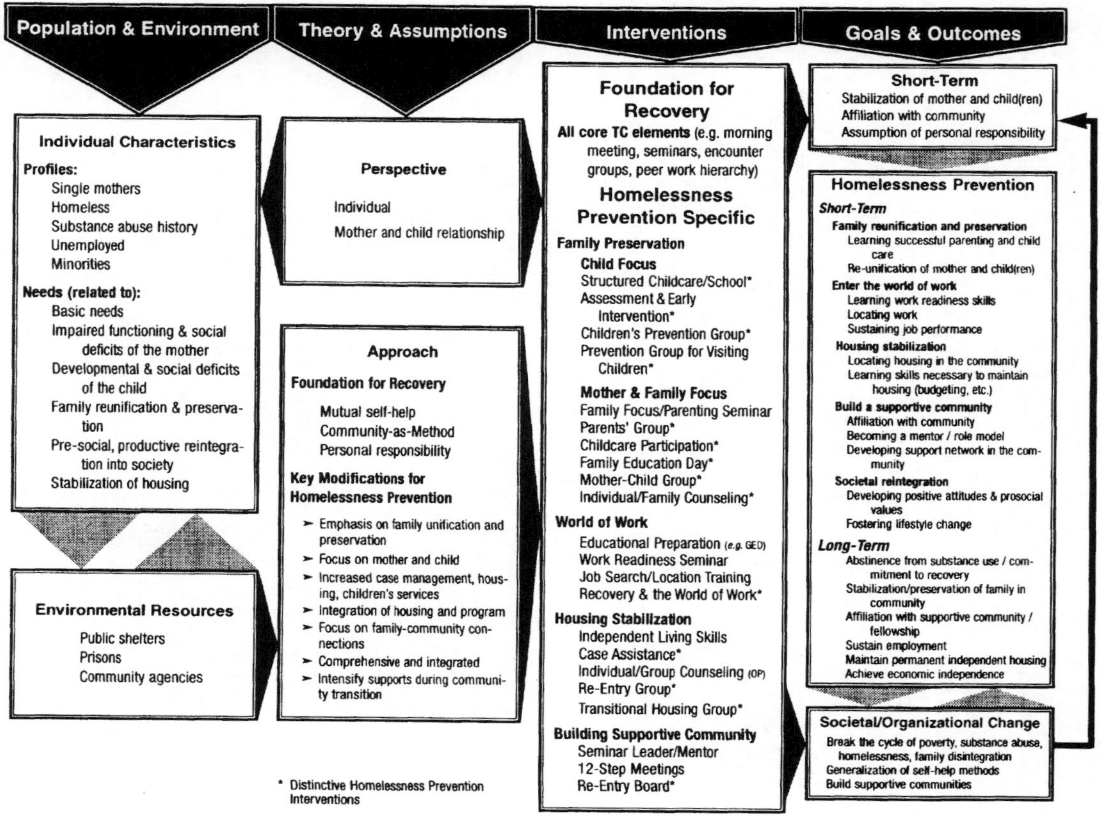

Population & Environment

Individual Characteristics

Profiles:
- Single mothers
- Homeless
- Substance abuse history
- Unemployed
- Minorities

Needs (related to):
- Basic needs
- Impaired functioning & social deficits of the mother
- Developmental & social deficits of the child
- Family reunification & preservation
- Pre-social, productive reintegration into society
- Stabilization of housing

Environmental Resources
- Public shelters
- Prisons
- Community agencies

Theory & Assumptions

Perspective
- Individual
- Mother and child relationship

Approach

Foundation for Recovery
- Mutual self-help
- Community-as-Method
- Personal responsibility

Key Modifications for Homelessness Prevention
- Emphasis on family unification and preservation
- Focus on mother and child
- Increased case management, housing, children's services
- Integration of housing and program
- Focus on family-community connections
- Comprehensive and integrated
- Intensify supports during community transition

Interventions

Foundation for Recovery
All core TC elements (e.g. morning meeting, seminars, encounter groups, peer work, hierarchy)

Homelessness Prevention Specific

Family Preservation

Child Focus
- Structured Childcare/School*
- Assessment & Early Intervention*
- Children's Prevention Group*
- Prevention Group for Visiting Children*

Mother & Family Focus
- Family Focus/Parenting Seminar
- Parents' Group*
- Childcare Participation*
- Family Education Day*
- Mother-Child Group*
- Individual/Family Counseling*

World of Work
- Educational Preparation (e.g. GED)
- Work Readiness Seminar
- Job Search/Location Training
- Recovery & the World of Work*

Housing Stabilization
- Independent Living Skills
- Case Assistance*
- Individual/Group Counseling (OP)
- Re-Entry Group*
- Transitional Housing Group*

Building Supportive Community
- Seminar Leader/Mentor
- 12-Step Meetings
- Re-Entry Board*

Goals & Outcomes

Short-Term
- Stabilization of mother and child(ren)
- Affiliation with community
- Assumption of personal responsibility

Homelessness Prevention

Short-Term

Family reunification and preservation
- Learning successful parenting and child care
- Re-unification of mother and child(ren)

Enter the world of work
- Learning work readiness skills
- Locating work
- Sustaining job performance

Housing stabilization
- Locating housing in the community
- Learning skills necessary to maintain housing (budgeting, etc.)

Build a supportive community
- Affiliation with community
- Becoming a mentor / role model
- Developing support network in the community

Societal reintegration
- Developing positive attitudes & prosocial values
- Fostering lifestyle change

Long-Term
- Abstinence from substance use / commitment to recovery
- Stabilization/preservation of family in community
- Affiliation with supportive community / fellowship
- Sustain employment
- Maintain permanent independent housing
- Achieve economic independence

Societal/Organizational Change
- Break the cycle of poverty, substance abuse, homelessness, family disintegration
- Generalization of self-help methods
- Build supportive communities

* Distinctive Homelessness Prevention Interventions

SIGNIFICANCE

The project has the potential to have a positive impact on policy and planning. The study will expand the knowledge base regarding homelessness, substance abuse, and families. Specific homelessness prevention interventions are delineated and "best practices" of general applicability will be identified. Further, empirical support for other applications of the program principles and methods will be provided, and the importance of integrated mother-child programs will be reinforced. Perhaps most significantly, the project uses TC principles and methods found effective in reducing substance abuse, extending both the range and potential of these principles and methods by adding components specific to homelessness prevention.

REFERENCES

Allen, M. (1991). Creating a federal legislative framework for child welfare reform. *American Journal of Orthopsychiatry, 61*, 610-623.

Bassuk, E. L., & Cohen, D. (1991). *Homeless families with children: Research perspectives.* Final Report, NIMH and NIAAA Conference. Rockville, MD: DHHS.

Bassuk, E. L. (1993). Social and economic hardships of homeless and other poor women. *American Journal of Orthopsychiatry, 63*(3), 340-347.

Bassuk, E. L., Rubin, L., & Lauriat, A. (1986). Characteristics of sheltered homeless families. *American Journal of Public Health, 78*, 783-788.

Calsyn, R. J., & Morse, G. (1990). Homeless men and women: Commonalities and a service gender gap. *American Journal of Community Psychology, 18*(4), 597-608.

Coletti, S. D., Schinka, J. A., Hughes, P. H., Hamilton, N. L., Renard, C. G., Sicilian, D. M., & Neri, R. L. (1997). Specialized therapeutic community treatment for chemically dependent women and their children. In G. De Leon (Ed.), *Community As Method: Therapeutic Communities for Special Populations and Special Settings.* Westport, CT: Greenwood Publishing Group, Inc.

Condelli, W. S., & Hubbard, R. L. (1994). Client outcomes from therapeutic communities. In F. M. Tims, G. De Leon, & N. Jainchill (Eds.), *Therapeutic community: Advances in research and application*, Research Monograph 144, pp. 80-98. Rockville, MD: National Institute on Drug Abuse (NIDA).

Cranston-Gonzalez Affordable Housing Act of 1990. United States Congress, 42 USC 12701.

De Leon, G. (1984). *The therapeutic community: Study of effectiveness.* National Institute on Drug Abuse (NIDA) Research Monograph, DHHS Pub. No. ADM 84-1286. Superintendent of Documents, US Government Printing Office, Washington, DC 20402.

De Leon, G. (1995). Therapeutic communities for addictions: A theoretical framework. *International Journal on the Addictions, 30*(12), 1603-1645.

De Leon, G. (1996). Integrative recovery: A stage paradigm. *Substance Abuse, 17*(1), 51-63.

De Leon, G., & Jainchill, N. (1982). Male and female drug abusers: Social and psychological status 2 years after treatment in a therapeutic community. *American Journal of Drug Alcohol Abuse, 8*(4), 465-496.

De Leon, G., Sacks, S., Staines, G., & McKendrick, K. (submitted). Modified therapeutic community for homeless MICAs: Treatment Outcomes. *Archives of General Psychiatry.*

De Leon, G., & Ziegenfuss, L. J. (Eds). (1986). *Therapeutic Communities for Addictions: Readings in Theory, Research, and Practice.* Springfield, IL: Charles C. Thomas Publishing.

DiBlasio, F. A., & Belcher, J. R. (1995). Gender differences among homeless persona: Special services for women. *Journal of Orthopsychiatry, 65*(1), 131-137.

Fischer, P. J., & Breakey, W. R. (1991). The epidemiology of alcohol, drug, and mental disorders among homeless persons. *American Psychologist, 46*(11), 1115-1128.

Hausman, B., & Hammen, C. (1993). Parenting in homeless families: The double crisis. *Journal of Orthopsychiatry, 63*(3), 358-369.

Hubbard, R. L., Craddock, S. G., Flynn, P. M., Anderson, J., & Etheridge, R. M. (1997). Overview of 1-year follow-up outcomes in the drug abuse treatment outcome study (DATOS). *Psychology of Addictive Behaviors, 11*(4), 261-278.

Institute on Medicine (1990). *Treating drug problems: A study of the evolution, effectiveness, and financing of public and private drug treatment systems.* Report by the Institute of Medicine Committee for the Substance Abuse Coverage Study, Division of Health Care Services, Washington, DC: National Academy Press.

Leaf, P. J., Thompson, K. S., Lam, J. A., Jekel, J. F. Armand, E. T. Evans, A. E. Martinez, J. S., Rodriquez, C., Westman, W. C. Johnston, P., Roew, M. & Hartwell, S. (1993). Partnerships in recovery: Shelter-based services for homeless cocaine abusers. In Conrad, K. J., Hultman, C. I. & Lyons, J. S. (Eds.) Treatment of the chemically dependent homeless: Theory and implementation in fourteen American projects, pp. 77-90. New York, NY: The Haworth Press, Inc.

Letiecq, B. L., Anderson, E. A., & Koblinsky, S. A. (1996). Social support of homeless and permanently housed low-income mothers with young children. *Family Relations, 45*(3), 265-272.

Liberty, H. J., Johnson, B. D., Jainchill, N., Ryder, J., Messina, M., Reynolds, S., & Hossain, M. (In press). Dynamic recovery: Comparative study of therapeutic communities in homeless shelters for men. *Journal of Substance Abuse Treatment.*

McChesney, K. Y. (1992). Absence of a family safety net for homeless families. *Journal of Sociology and Social Welfare, 19*(4), 55-72.

McChesney, K. Y. (1995). *A review of the empirical literature on contemporary urban homeless families.* Social Service Review, Chicago, IL: University of Chicago.

McLellan, A. T., Luborsky, L., Cacciloa, J., Griffith, J., Evans, F., Barr, H. & O'Brien, C. (1985). New data from the addiction severity index. Reliability and validity in three centers. *Journal of Nervous and Mental Disease, 173*(7), 412-423.

Merves, E. S. (1992). Homeless women: Beyond the bag lady myth. In M. Robertson & M. Greenblatt (Eds.)., *Homelessness: A National Perspective* (pp. 229-243). New York, NY: Plenum Press.

Rahav, M., & Link, B. G. (1995). When social problems converge: Homeless, mentally ill, chemical abusing men in New York City. *International Journal on the Addictions, 30,* 1019-1042

Robertson, M. J. (1991). Homeless women with children: The role of alcohol and other drug abuse. *American Psychologist, 46*(11), 1198-1204.

Rossi, P. H. (1990). The old homeless and the new homeless in historical perspective. *American Psychologist, 45,* 954-959.

Sacks, S., De Leon, G., Bernhardt, A. I., & Sacks, J. (1996). *Modified therapeutic community for homeless MICA individuals: A treatment manual.* New York, NY: NDRI/CTCR.

Sacks, S., De Leon, G., Bernhardt, A. I., & Sacks, J. (1997). A modified therapeutic community for homeless MICA clients. In G. De Leon (Ed.), *Community As Method: Therapeutic Communities for Special Populations and Special Settings.* Westport, CT: Greenwood Publishing Group, Inc.

Sacks, S., Sacks, J., De Leon, G., Bernhardt, A. I., & Staines, G. L. (1997). Modified therapeutic community for mentally ill chemical abusers: Background; influences; program description; preliminary findings. *Substance Use and Misuse, 32*(9), 1217-1259.

Schutt, R. K., & Garett, G. R. (1992). *Responding to the homeless: Policy and practice.* New York, NY: Plenum Press.

Shinn, M., Knickman, J. R., & Weitzman, B. C. (1991). Social relationships and vulnerability to becoming homeless among poor families. *American Psychologist, 46,* 1180-1187.

Simpson, D. D., & Sells, S. B. (1982). Effectiveness of treatment of drug abuse: An overview of the DARP research program. *Advances in Alcohol and Substance Abuse, 2*(1), 7-29.

Steinbock, M. R. (1995). Homeless female-headed families: Relationships at risk. *Marriage & Family Review* (The Haworth Press, Inc.), *20*(1/2) 143-159.

Stevens, S. J., & Glider, P. J. (1994). Therapeutic communities: Substance abuse treatment for women. In F. M. Tims, G. De Leon, & N. Jainchill (Eds.), *Therapeutic community: Advances in research and application,* Research Monograph 144, pp. 162-180. Rockville, MD: National Institute on Drug Abuse (NIDA).

US Conference of Mayors. (1987). *A status report on homeless families in America's cities: A 29-city survey.* Washington, DC.

US Conference of Mayors. (1993). *A status report on hunger and homelessness in America's cities: A 26-city survey.* Washington, DC.

Wexler, H. K., Cuadrado, C., & Stevens, S. (In press). Residential treatment for women: Behavioral and psychological outcomes. In S. J. Stevens, & H. K. Wexler (Eds.), *Women and substance abuse.* New York, NY: The Haworth Press, Inc.

Wood, D., Valdez, R. B., Hayashi, T., & Shen, A. (1990). Homeless and housed families in Los Angeles: A study comparing demographic, economic and family function characteristics. *American Journal of Public Health, 80,* 1049-1052.

Dyadic Case Management as a Strategy for Prevention of Homelessness Among Chronically Debilitated Men and Women with Alcohol and Drug Dependence

Michael W. Kirby, Jr., PhD
G. Nicholas Braucht, PhD
Ellen Brown, PhD
Sigmund Krane, PhD
Mary McCann, MSW
Nancy VanDeMark, MSW

SUMMARY. *Background:* The PROUD Homelessness Prevention Project of Arapahoe House, Inc. in Denver, Colorado uses a pair or dyad of case managers to address the individualized client needs of a target population characterized chiefly by chronic utilization of public detoxification services. The local political and economic contexts affecting this population include a recent increase in poverty and decreased housing available to seriously debilitated individuals. Created in 1992, PROUD has expanded its housing services to address homelessness more fully.

Target Population and Theory of Treatment: PROUD clients exhibit substance dependence, co-occurring mental health disorders, and tend to be homeless or at serious risk of homelessness. Clients are primarily

---

Michael W. Kirby, Jr., G. Nicholas Braucht, Ellen Brown, Sigmund Krane, Mary McCann, and Nancy VanDeMark are affiliated with Arapahoe House, Inc., 8801 Lipan Street, Thornton, CO 80221.

[Haworth co-indexing entry note]: "Dyadic Case Management as a Strategy for Prevention of Homelessness Among Chronically Debilitated Men and Women with Alcohol and Drug Dependence." Kirby, Michael W., Jr. et al. Co-published simultaneously in *Alcoholism Treatment Quarterly* (The Haworth Press, Inc.) Vol. 17, No. 1/2, 1999, pp. 53-71; and: *Homelessness Prevention in Treatment of Substance Abuse and Mental Illness: Logic Models and Implementation of Eight American Projects* (ed: Kendon J. Conrad et al.) The Haworth Press, Inc., 1999, pp. 53-71. Single or multiple copies of this article are available for a fee from The Haworth Document Delivery Service [1-800-342-9678, 9:00 a.m. - 5:00 p.m. (EST). E-mail address: getinfo@haworthpressinc.com].

© 1999 by The Haworth Press, Inc. All rights reserved.

white males with a high-school education and an average age of 39. Based on a Stages of Change model and intensive case management theories, the PROUD dyadic case management model was innovated by Arapahoe House. This model is hypothesized to offer a cost-effective managed-care strategy for reducing overutilization while simultaneously coordinating a more optimal mix of substance-abuse and housing services.

Description of the Intervention and Development of the Program: The primary long-term objectives for PROUD clients are stabilized housing and ability to maintain treatment goals. The intervention model focuses on intensive contact with clients. Contact includes recruitment, engagement, relationship- and skills-building, housing stabilization, and advocacy. Individualized treatment and follow-up plans are designed to motivate clients, reduce individual risk factors, and strengthen protective factors. Careful recruitment of case managers and the use of a multidisciplinary team to design, revise, and implement the logic model are essential.

Evaluation Design: The research design for evaluating the effectiveness of this strategy in preventing homelessness with the target population calls for random assignment of clients into the PROUD program or into a course of customary services. Data were collected from clients in both groups by trained research interviewers at the point of enrollment and at six and twelve months after enrollment.

Preliminary Findings on Program Implementation: Informal evaluations have shown PROUD to be effective in reducing the number of days and the number of episodes of detoxification. The current more rigorous evaluation should provide information about the efficacy of the dyadic case management model to reduce homelessness and increase sobriety.

Lessons Learned and Implications: Listening to client feedback and learning to present clear, complete information to them is crucial for the client/case manager relationship. Development of internal housing expertise and options and careful supervision of the dyads also helps to provide sound housing alternatives for clients. *[Article copies available for a fee from The Haworth Document Delivery Service: 1-800-342-9678. E-mail address: getinfo@haworthpressinc.com]*

KEYWORDS. Dyadic intensive case management, detoxification services (overutilization), stages of change model, "housing as treatment", individualized treatment, client-centered services

"It's amazing how drugs can change your life," reported Richard. Ever since he left his wife and family in California two years ago and came to Denver, Richard, a 30-year-old African American male, has been

struggling to get by. Alcohol dependence had made it impossible for him to hold down a steady job. Evicted from his apartment for using and selling drugs, and with a history of incarceration, Richard tried to stay with family members. His grandmother, fearing his ways, refused to let him stay with her. Alone in his anger and frustration, Richard developed clinical depression and a severe addiction to crack cocaine. Because he had no permanent place to stay, detoxification facilities became comforting to him, especially during the cold and snowy Colorado winter months. During a period of one year, he admitted himself to detoxification facilities 71 times.

Domestic violence, alcoholism, physical and mental health issues have taken their toll on Sarah, a 33-year-old white female with good job skills, but diagnosed with bi-polar disorder. At one time Sarah lived with her two children and her mother, enjoyed solid employment, and never had to worry about being homeless. Then in a few quick months, everything changed. Sarah began using heroin, became addicted, and began neglecting her children. "I got myself in a huge amount of debt. I just basically charged myself up past what my house was worth and had to sell it just to get myself out of debt. I lost my car and my job and so I don't really have any options, and my family is not real tolerant of the situation I got myself into with drugs and such." She was at her lowest point ever, and she was very scared.

* * *

These stories illustrate experiences all too common among people who are homeless or at risk of homelessness in the metropolitan Denver area. Extreme levels of despair and substance dependence are experienced by people who are chronic users of the area's detoxification facilities. These people are the target population for the Arapahoe House homelessness prevention project entitled PROUD (*P*roject to *R*educe *O*ver-*U*tilization of *D*etoxification). This project invites the direct participation of clients in designing individualized plans to meet their needs. Using an innovative, potentially cost-effective intervention model of dyadic intensive case management, PROUD facilitates substance abuse treatment and assists clients in accessing the most self-sufficient housing appropriate to their level of functioning. Dyadic intensive case management assigns to each client a pair of case managers to provide direct services (outreach, substance abuse treatment plans, assessment, motivational interviewing, clinical intervention); advocacy (with landlords, legal systems, employers); and linkage to other services (housing, medical resources, vocational programs).

BACKGROUND

History of Arapahoe House and the PROUD Program. Established in 1976 as a community-based nonprofit organization, Arapahoe House, Inc. started as a social model detoxification program, following the passage of legislation that de-criminalized public intoxication. In the intervening 23 years, Arapahoe House has become the largest provider of substance abuse treatment services in Colorado, serving more than 17, 000 individuals annually. The Arapahoe House continuum of care encompasses the following services: detoxification; a transitional residential program for up to two years; adult and adolescent intensive residential treatment; case management services for consumers with serious and persistent mental illness as well as other case management services (including PROUD); a comprehensive residential program for women with dependent children; vocational services; short-term treatment for offenders on probation or parole; housing services; adult and adolescent outpatient services; school-based services; specialized women's services; and education and therapy for multiple DUI offenders. The extensiveness of these services provides PROUD staff with a continuum of care options to which they may link clients. In addition linkages are made to an array of other community agencies.

PROUD was designed in response to a call by the Colorado General Assembly in 1990 to reduce the inappropriate and repeated use of detoxification facilities by chronically debilitated persons, approximately half of whom are dually diagnosed. After a statewide competitive process, Arapahoe House was selected to establish PROUD, which began serving clients in 1992. In 1996, Arapahoe House became part of the Collaborative Project to Prevent Homelessness sponsored by the Center for Mental Health Services (CMHS) and the Center for Substance Abuse Treatment (CSAT). This paper discusses both the intervention documented in the manual produced during the first year and the subsequent, current evaluation study.

Local Political and Economic Contexts Affecting the Program. In a 1994 report on poverty in Denver, the Piton Foundation found that poverty had increased in three out of four Denver neighborhoods during the decade of the 1980s and that the disparity between the "haves" and the "have nots" in the city was increasing. Although the 1990 census counted approximately 3,000 people living on the street or in shelters in Colorado, homeless service providers estimate the total homeless population is between 7,000 and 10,000 persons. The majority of the state's homeless population live in the core city areas near downtown Denver.

Several trends currently affect this population. Federal legislative changes in income and benefits have devastated some PROUD clients who have lost their SSI (Supplementary Security Income for the disabled) benefits and, thus, their only source of income. Changes in federal subsidized housing policies create greater competition nationally, resulting in fewer units locally. A demeaning attitude among some community service providers towards substance abusers affects their ability to access services and housing. Moreover, soaring housing prices in the metropolitan area have diminished low-cost housing alternatives. Furthermore, a lawsuit against the state has resulted in several board and care homes being shut down, thus decreasing housing available to seriously debilitated individuals. Additionally, homeless units developed on a vacated air force base are virtually inaccessible to poor people without cars.

TARGET POPULATION AND THEORY OF TREATMENT

Description of the PROUD Target Population. "Before I was admitted to PROUD, I went to the liquor store, 2, 3 times a day. Usually drank a pint of gin and 3 to 4 quarts of beer every day," reported Josie, a typical PROUD client. PROUD has served over 1,200 clients as of 1997. Approximately two-thirds of clients have been Caucasian and one-third people of color. The predominant minority group served has been African Americans, with Latinos and Native Americans composing a very small percentage. The gender composition of PROUD clients has changed dramatically in the last few years. In 1992, 12% of clients served were female; more recently, about 40% of PROUD clients are female. The average age of clients is 39; average educational level is twelfth grade.

Characteristics that place PROUD clients at risk of homelessness include problems with maintaining stable income and employment; shattered relationships with families, friends, and other social support networks; chronic substance abuse; and mental illness. PROUD clients typically meet the DSM-IV criteria for substance dependence. Three-quarters have experienced prior episodes of homelessness. And for *all years* of the program's history, approximately 95% report *not* having had full-time employment during the year before entering PROUD. Approximately half are divorced or separated; under 10% are currently married. Typically, alcohol is the drug of choice for 85% and cocaine for 15%.

Eligibility Requirements for PROUD Homelessness Prevention Project. For the CMHS/CSAT collaborative project, the Arapahoe House management team developed specific eligibility criteria based on past experience with PROUD clients. To be eligible, an individual must:

- be at least age 18 and be formerly or currently homeless or at-risk for homelessness;
- have a diagnosable substance abuse disorder, or be dually diagnosed;
- heavily use detoxification services. *For men,* this means four or more admissions to detoxification in the previous twelve months. *For*

women, this means either four or more admissions to detoxification in the last year, or two admissions to detoxification within the past twelve months, along with involvement with either the criminal justice system or the social services system. The criteria for men and women differ based on evidence that women with chronically debilitating substance dependence often divert to other systems, resulting in fewer admissions to detoxification than men.

Once clients are enrolled in PROUD, they are supported to attain and maintain sobriety, but they do not have to be in treatment or stay straight/sober to obtain and maintain housing. Currently, about 10-15% of clients are provided housing through Arapahoe House in-house programs while the majority is connected to housing programs outside the agency.

Description of Client Needs. Clients with the kinds of substance disorders and histories depicted above evidence multiple problems and multiple (usually unsuccessful) attempts to seek treatment for substance abuse and mental illness. The clients interviewed during the documentation period of the CMHS/CSAT grant specifically aimed at homelessness prevention (*clients from spring of 1997 only*) reported the following experiences and needs, which are typical of PROUD clients:

- *Substance Abuse.* These clients had a *long history of prior treatment* (mean 7.9 prior treatment episodes). At the time of enrollment into PROUD, 75% had experienced problems with alcohol within that last month, while half reported problems with drug use. The mean number of years of alcohol use was almost 16.
- *Mental and Physical Health.* Seventy percent had experienced depression during their lives, and 40% during the last month. Thirty-five percent had been prescribed psychotropic medications and a quarter had attempted suicide during their lifetimes. While none had health insurance, 55% reported medical problems, some serious, in the last 30 days.
- *Social Relations.* A majority reported conflict with family within the last month as well as a lifetime history of emotional, physical, and/or sexual abuse.
- *Economics.* Most were unemployed (average household income of $304 in the last month).

The above needs and experiences exacerbate at-risk factors for homelessness. When asked at the intake interview to describe their living situations during the two months preceding enrollment to PROUD, clients from the spring of 1997 reported spending time in cars, on the street, in shelters or motels, and in someone else's house or apartment.

Description of the Dyadic Intensive Case Management Model. Case management has been used with the chronic mentally ill (Bond, Miller, Krumwied, & Ward, 1988), the homeless mentally ill (Ridgway, 1986), homeless substance abusers (Kirby & Braucht, 1993), and in the substance abuse treatment field (Ridgely & Willenbring, 1992). Studies are starting to show successes of case management approaches with homeless populations in meeting the diverse needs of a heterogeneous homeless population (Stephens, Dennis, Toomer & Holloway, 1991). Recently, a study by Cox et al. (1997) found favorable outcomes in income, number of days drinking, and number of days spent in "own place" using case management with chronic alcoholics.

An important distinction in the literature emphasizes differences between "broker" case management, which focuses on service linking and monitoring, and more intensive and clinical forms of case management, such as assertive community teams (Morse et al., 1997; Wolff et al., 1997; Drake, Antosca, Noordsy, Bartels, & Osher, 1991). Similar to these assertive community treatment teams that have been found effective for homeless mentally ill clients (Morse et al., 1997), PROUD is an intensive clinical model providing services whose frequency and duration depend on client need, not a predetermined program formula.

An important element of the PROUD program and other programs at Arapahoe House is the "transtheoretical" model known as the Stages of Change (SOC) model (Prochaska, Di Clemente, & Norcross, 1992; Miller & Rollnick, 1991). This model holds that a person changes behaviors by progressing through stages of change: *precontemplation*-not open to/thinking about changing a particular behavior; *contemplation*-thinking about changing a behavior, but hasn't made up mind; *preparation*-seriously planning to change/has taken steps to change behavior; *action*-actively doing things to change or modify behavior; *maintenance*-maintaining behavioral change until it becomes permanent; *relapse*-returning to pattern of behavior that he or she has begun to change.

More than just a "brokerage model," PROUD functions as a clinical case management model in several ways. Case managers are required to have or be working toward clinical Certification for Addictions Counselors (three levels in Colorado). They use their clinical training during comprehensive assessment of clients as well as during motivational interviewing, which helps them to adjust the approach and content of their intervention according to where the client falls on the SOC scale. PROUD staff take every opportunity possible to interact clinically with clients. While transporting clients to appointments or waiting with them for a court appearance, case managers are provided with many opportunities for substance-abuse counseling. Thus, the PROUD staff provide many direct clinical services to clients in addition to connecting them to other community resources.

The key difference between PROUD and other programs using clinical intensive case management, however, is its use of case manager dyads, an innovation developed by Arapahoe House. The program matches pairs of case managers who jointly work with assigned caseloads to develop a helping relationship and serve as a catalyst for change. This dyadic model offers some of the principal advantages of the multidisciplinary team model (Drake et al., 1991) without the disadvantage of cumbersome coordination among numerous team members (Reinke & Greenley, 1986); fewer staff can also cost less. The dyadic model has several other putative benefits, including:

- clients are assured continuity of services, even in the face of case manager turnover or illness;
- the strengths and expertise of two case managers are blended to the benefit of clients;
- pairs provide greater personal safety when conducting street outreach;
- case managers can conduct clinical interventions requiring a combination of confrontation and empathetic support, with each case manager taking on a different role; and
- partners brainstorm and problem-solve together from different but informed perspectives.

Dyadic Partner Interactions. In the dyadic model it is important for the program manager to define clear expectations, roles and accountability, so that levels of responsibility are definite and understood by all case managers. Among themselves, dyads must agree who will document joint contacts with the client and how the services plan will be modified. The supervisor must work with all case managers to prevent the creation of individual caseloads. To ensure fruition of the benefits of the dyadic model, PROUD has developed expectations for dyad interactions. Dyad partners share the same office and receive supervision together once a week. Partners meet together at least once per week to update one another about mutual clients. Partners also cover for each other during absences.

Because the clients in PROUD are frequently difficult to recruit, engage, and motivate, case managers must be willing to provide aggressive outreach, follow-up, and support for clients. This may include transporting them to dental appointments, serving in an advocacy role with a potential landlord or employer, or rotating with other case managers to provide 24-hour, on-call crisis case management. In situations that can often be bewildering, explosive, or even physically dangerous as case managers track clients in crime-ridden neighborhoods or unsafe tenements, an essential element of dyadic case management is the partners' support not only of clients but also of each other.

DESCRIPTION OF THE INTERVENTION/DEVELOPMENT OF THE PROGRAM

The matrix of theory and praxis encompassed within the logic model has guided the development of the PROUD program and analysis of its outcomes (see Figure 1 for logic model). Arapahoe House relies on a multidisciplinary team to design, revise, and implement the logic model, allowing for its use as a management tool on several levels. (Using the logic model as a management tool is discussed in more depth in a separate article of this volume.) The current multidisciplinary management team includes specialists with years of experience in administrative supervision, program services management, and evaluation. For the PROUD program, the team meets formally at least once a month, with informal interactions, updates, and meetings conducted as needed to carry out plans. The logic model is the touchstone for program ownership, policy development and adherence, and evaluation of the program.

Objectives of the Program. The long-term objectives of the program, which are delineated in the logic model, are that each PROUD client will maintain treatment goals and will be able to live in the most self-sufficient setting possible for him or her. Other objectives include the ability to access helping and human services resources when needed rather than resort to acute care, to rebuild social networks, and to develop a stable, adequate income from work or benefits. Increased sobriety and stabilized housing are always crucial yet extremely difficult goals to achieve with these recalcitrant clients who have learned through repeated admissions that a detoxification facility is a safe, quick, free, and easy way to access temporary housing. Being able to establish and measure the gradual steps along the way to these long-term goals is an important task for the management team designing the logic model. Outcomes need to reflect, then, clients' *movement toward* sobriety and stable housing as well as their *arrival*. Thus, the essential difference between the short- and long-term outcomes is not arrival at separate goals but a question of the degree to which one is able to maintain and commit to them. Outcomes, whether short- or long-term, depend on educating clients (community resources), helping them access resources (advocacy, transportation), and motivating them (getting a new set of dentures) to maintain gains.

Homelessness Prevention Intervention Process. <u>Homelessness Prevention Activities</u>. For the homelessness prevention project, key components of the dyadic intensive case management model include the following:

- *Case Managers as Catalysts for Change.* Case managers apply motivational interviewing and other techniques to help clients progress through the stages of change. Case managers identify small, manageable steps toward change, involve clients in treatment planning, discuss

the potential obstacles clients may face, and strategize tactics for handling difficulties and building relapse prevention skills.
- *Client-Centered Services.* The client determines the order in which his or her needs should be met. For example, the dyad may help a client to obtain photo identification or have an eye exam weeks before the client agrees to seek substance abuse treatment. This strategy meets the client's needs, overcomes distrust, and eventually leads to client engagement in treatment.
- *Intense Service.* The case management dyads have low caseloads, usually no more than 24 per dyad. This allows the dyad to work closely with clients and to bond with them.
- *Community Location.* Services are field-based, not office-based. Dyads spend much time in the community conducting outreach, networking with agencies and clients, and advocating for clients.
- *Flexible Program Length.* Length of enrollment is not pre-set, but depends on clients' needs.
- *Comprehensive Activities.* Case manager dyads take on comprehensive roles that include: client identification; outreach and engagement of the client; assessment; service and treatment planning; securing linkages both within the Arapahoe House continuum of care and with outside agencies; monitoring the quality and quantity of services received; crisis intervention; and systems advocacy and intervention.

By acting as an advocate for the client, and providing a consistent presence, case managers begin to remove barriers and overcome client distrust.

Identification and Recruitment of Clients. A key feature of PROUD is that, historically, case managers become involved with the client from the point of identification. In many case management models, case managers step in when service linkages are needed. In PROUD, the case managers usually provide the initial and ongoing contact with the client, thus establishing relationships that engage clients and overcome their natural fear and distrust of the system. Thus, "homeless prevention activities" begin by building trust between the client and the dyad.

During the current evaluation phase of this grant, Program Evaluation (PE) staff are the primary recruiters of clients into PROUD. Using information from Arapahoe House client charts entered into our UNI/CARE database system, PE staff generate daily a list of admissions to each of our three agency detox sites. The list identifies clients who have multiple detox admissions in the past year. PE staff can thus identify clients who are eligible before they are discharged from detox. PE interviewers then approach clients about their interest in being in the homelessness prevention study.

Clients who are randomly assigned by the study evaluation design to PROUD are matched to a dyad where the skills and expertise of the dyad

FIGURE 1. Final PROUD Homelessness Prevention Logic Model

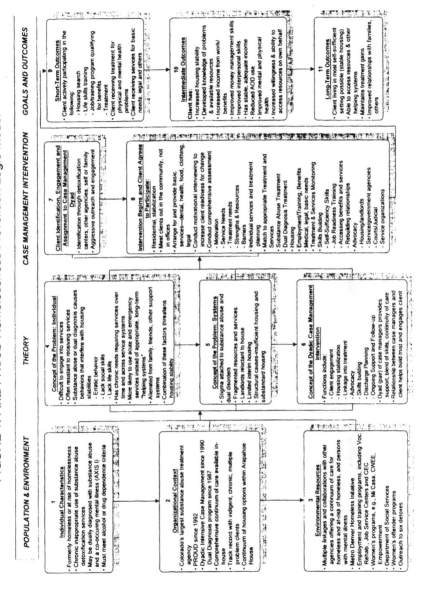

members complement the unique strengths and needs of the client. If clients are HIV positive, for example, they will be assigned to a dyad containing the case manager who has received in-depth training on HIV/AIDS issues. Similarly, because many of the female clients have histories of physical or sexual abuse, they are usually assigned to female case managers who have expertise in domestic violence counseling and who are more readily trusted by these clients.

Assessment. Assessment includes a full review of prior medical, substance abuse, and psychiatric histories. To assess motivation, PE staff administer the Addiction Severity Index to determine issues related to substance abuse; the SOCRATES instrument (Miller, 1991; Miller & Tonigan, 1995), designed to assess the level or stage of personal motivation and readiness for change in alcohol abusers; and the agency's own Checklist for Change. This assessment is shared with the case managers. Assessment of medical needs may include a complete physical exam of the client, as well as testing the client for TB, Hepatitis B, STDs, hepatitis, bacterial pneumonia, and other infectious diseases. HIV counseling and testing is available on a voluntary basis.

An extensive Case Management Client Assessment is conducted to identify needs in the following areas: threats to housing stability; other housing needs; immediate needs for clothing or other necessities; educational or academic remediation needs; employment/vocational needs; legal and other support needs. The case managers also assess the client's eligibility for Medicaid, Medicare, Supplemental Security Income, food stamps, and other public assistance.

Finally, through structured interviews and observation, the case managers assess the client's strengths and motivation. This assessment will form the basis of helping the client set his or her own goals and progress through the stages of change. These interviews help the dyads identify various "carrots" that may motivate the client.

Engaging and Motivating Clients. Case managers understand that many of the individuals referred to PROUD may be at least initially uninterested in case management or not know what it has to offer. The case managers must be very skilled at identifying needs they can fill that are likely to have immediate value to the client. During this phase of engagement, dyads work with clients to convince them to participate in some minimal way, encountering clients with varying levels of motivation, from those who are consistently motivated to those who refuse to participate.

Case managers will make numerous attempts to locate difficult-to-engage clients, including contacts with friends and relatives, jails, shelters and public hospitals, and visits to locations the individual is known to frequent. For clients who refuse to participate, case managers will continue to make periodic contact using various motivational strategies, until either the client's motivation changes, or the supervisor determines that the case managers have exhausted all motivational strategies. Still, the individual is given the case manager's card and an open invitation to contact the case management team for assistance any time.

Prior to transferring an individual to an inactive status (and eventual discharge), the case manager and/or supervisor complete and document three steps. A minimum of three face-to-face contacts with the individual have been made. An assessment of motivation using the SOCRATES instrument has been completed, if possible, and the client has been engaged in motivational strategies. The PROUD supervisor has reviewed the client and case manager records and has determined that a genuine and rigorous attempt has been made to contact and engage the individual in services.

Stabilizing Client Housing Through Advocacy, Education, and Resources. The chronic substance dependence and frequent symptomatic behavior associated with mental illness that PROUD clients exhibit may jeopardize their housing stability. Thus, integrating housing assistance into the case management program is a critical component of the intervention. Housing services offered by PROUD case managers include *evaluating current housing; offering emergency rental assistance; helping the client locate housing; providing skills training; linking the client with permanent housing resources; and advocating with landlords or housing agencies.*

Case managers work with landlords and housing authorities to *negotiate agreements about behavior and rental payments,* so that clients can maintain their current housing. Advocacy includes explaining the PROUD program, including its goals and how it operates, e.g., informing landlords that case managers will be working with the clients on strengthening social skills and financial management. When needed, case managers *link clients with representative payee programs* to ensure that the client's housing will be paid. Case managers also *link clients to resources for emergency relief,* such as rental payment assistance, foreclosure assistance, utility payment plans, and other emergency resources.

Additionally, case managers work with the housing resources available in-house at Arapahoe House (see below) and at other community agencies and shelters to *help identify temporary housing for the client, then develop a plan for longer term housing.* The case management department has conducted an extensive networking effort so that they can personally contact providers of every type of housing in the metropolitan area. This includes Arapahoe House services as well as other community shelters, board and care homes, halfway houses, structured group living programs, transitional living programs, and various public housing options, including apartments that accept Section 8 vouchers.

Arapahoe House Role in Housing. Recognizing the importance of housing in recovery, Arapahoe House has strengthened its ability to house clients in the last few years by developing *staff positions* and *programs* related to housing needs. Arapahoe House currently has two staff positions devoted to coordinating housing options for clients. We have also applied for a grant to fund a future housing specialist to coordinate information and develop materials for our agency on emergency, transitional, and permanent housing alternatives in the metro Denver area.

In addition to the residential treatment program and a transitional housing programs (the latter with a maximum stay of two years), Arapahoe House has expanded its housing resources to include:

- Sixty-three (63) *Section 8 housing vouchers* that clients can redeem in the private housing market, paying only 30% of their income for rental housing.
- *"Shelter Plus Care."* This Department of Housing and Urban Development (HUD) program provides tenant-based rental assistance plus supportive services throughout the Denver metropolitan area for families who have chronic problems with substance abuse, and/or who are serious mentally ill, and who would otherwise have difficulty maintaining housing even with Section 8 vouchers.
- *Transitional Housing For Families.* This HUD program provides tenant-based rental assistance for 18 families, who can be housed for two years while receiving intensive support services from agency staff.
- A *"practice apartment"* for lower-functioning chronically mentally ill individuals who can learn how to live independently.
- *Emergency rental assistance* funded through Denver Social Services and foundations providing short-term rental assistance for individuals and families close to eviction.
- A new *transitional housing program* being established at one of our detoxes to provide a dry, sober environment with a length-of-stay of 30 days for clients awaiting intensive substance-abuse treatment.

Beyond its own walls, Arapahoe House has partnered with other agencies to increase the availability of housing stock for those vulnerable to homelessness. In collaboration with the Colorado Coalition for the Homeless, Arapahoe House helped secure funding to develop The Forum, a new single-room-occupancy building for 100 individuals. Arapahoe House is currently partnering with a mental health agency and an agency serving individuals with developmental disabilities to construct 80 units of housing, 16 of which will be set aside for special needs populations. Arapahoe House is also an active participant and board member of the Metro Denver Homeless Initiative, a nationally recognized consortium of thirty agencies organized to provide housing and comprehensive wrap-around services for homeless people.

Strengthening in-house programs and networking with other community agencies dramatically increase the agency's ability to conduct homelessness prevention interventions for individuals whose chronic substance abuse and serious mental illness jeopardize their housing stability in the private market.

EVALUATION DESIGN

How well do the homelessness prevention activities of the dyadic case management model work? Earlier non-experimental evaluations of the PROUD program have shown it to reduce both the number of episodes and the number of days of detoxification for clients participating in the program. The current two-year research design for evaluating the effectiveness of this strategy in preventing homelessness within this chronically debilitated population is a much more rigorous design. Eligible clients are randomly assigned to either the PROUD case management program or to a course of customary services. The customary services typically consist of detoxification, followed by referral to substance abuse treatment, or self-help groups such as Alcoholics Anonymous, or to other appropriate health or human services agencies. Data are collected from clients in both groups by trained research interviewers at the point of enrollment, six months after enrollment, and again twelve months after enrollment. In addition, substantial services utilization data will be available for all study clients.

The outcome evaluation will address three major issues. First, the main effects of the PROUD program as compared to usual-care treatment will be estimated. Second, the degree to which the PROUD program has different effects for different types of clients will be assessed. We will examine differences in effects on the outcome measures both across clients with different scores on the baseline measures and across *a priori* and empirically derived categorizations of clients based on background characteristics, such as gender and ethnicity. We will be particularly attentive to differential effects across categories of gender and ethnicity. Third, the impact of individual service components will be estimated. This will include an assessment of how later effects (i.e., at 12 months) are dependent on earlier outcomes (i.e., at 6 months), which in turn are dependent on different types and amounts of services received. This evaluation will guide Arapahoe House in assessing the ways to improve its homelessness prevention intervention and services.

PRELIMINARY FINDINGS ON PROGRAM IMPLEMENTATION

The Arapahoe House PROUD program has been in existence for six years, with a special focus on homelessness prevention activities as a part of the CMHS/CSAT Collaborative Project. During each of the pre-collaborative years, a non-experimental evaluation was conducted, comparing days and episodes of detox for PROUD clients prior to, during, and following the program. Those informal evaluations showed a significant reduction in the utilization of detoxification services. In 1995, the University of Denver's Department of Psychology conducted a series of statistical analyses on the data collected on PROUD. Regression and correlation analyses were conducted to determine whether seasonal and/or relapse effects might have confounded the standardized variables. An outcome analysis was also conducted to differentially determine outcomes among clients with varying degrees of motivation. This study confirmed that PROUD produces statistically significant reductions in both number of episodes of detoxification and days in detoxification for the total target group of clients who participate in the program.

The current evaluation is needed, however, because it will provide new information on several levels. First, as opposed to the earlier, less formal evaluations, it is a true experimental design, randomly assigning an equal number of participants into the experimental PROUD group or a control group. In addition, this evaluation will focus more fully on the efficacy of the homelessness prevention activities for this chronically debilitated population. Finally, our dissemination of the findings will increase the knowledge base of homelessness prevention interventions as the evaluation will focus on the unique aspect of dyadic case management.

LESSONS LEARNED AND IMPLICATIONS

PROUD continues to evolve, providing opportunities for staff to learn how to refine services delivery, re-conceptualize the dyadic model of case management, and explore new housing options.

Listen to Client Feedback, and Present the Client with Clear and Complete Information. A key lesson gleaned from client interviews is that case managers need to provide detailed accounts of activities they are engaged in on behalf of the client for clients who want this information. For example, some clients did not fully understand the range of services available through the case management component because case managers were presenting information and options to address immediate needs (e.g., housing) first. Thus, the client did not necessarily understand that case management could help them with long-term goals like vocational training and employment. This problem can be compounded with clients whose thinking is not clear due to years of substance abuse or mental illness. As a result of this insight, case managers now provide an overview during the initial client meeting of all services and activities available through PROUD, and explain that they will be available when the client is ready to pursue these goals.

Work to Develop Internal Housing Expertise and Options. The documentation period of the CMHS/CSAT collaborative agreement allowed Arapahoe House to examine PROUD specifically in terms of homelessness prevention. We interviewed clients, case managers, and others during this period to identify gaps in the current services systems. In Denver, the primary gap we identified was short-term transitional housing for people at risk of homelessness who are substance dependent. Scarce housing exists for clients who are leaving residential treatment and who need placement in a stable setting while they are transitioning back to the community. Arapahoe House has been working on developing some housing options with a highly flexible length of stay to meet this client need.

Another lesson related to homelessness prevention is that the control the case management department has over the agency's housing resources, such as its ability to provide clients with Section 8 vouchers, is a vital piece in stabilizing client housing. Case managers believe it significant to directly link clients with housing resources provided by Arapahoe House rather than having to clear other agencies' eligibility requirements (which often screen out substance abusers).

We also learned the importance of specialized training in housing issues and resources to help case managers effectively engage in homelessness prevention. During the first year of the project, Arapahoe House provided specialized training in tenant advocacy, housing terminology and housing resources in the metropolitan area. Uniformly, case managers stated that this was very important training to help them do their jobs.

Provide Experienced, Ongoing Supervision for Case Managers. For the PROUD program, the best supervisor of dyads is one with extensive case management expertise and experience working with the chronically debilitated population PROUD serves, and one who is adept at managing and supporting case managers. Ongoing supervision of individual case managers as well as dyads keeps staff motivated and supports them in work that can often be frustrating and discouraging. The case managers receive close supervision through weekly staff meetings, dyad supervision meetings, and individual clinical supervision, all of which reinforce the spirit needed to build strong relations with clients and to persevere in outreach.

Arapahoe House mandates that all staff providing Clinical Supervision have Level II state certification for substance-abuse counseling–which requires numerous additional hours of training, courses in Clinical Supervision, a minimum of two years experience in providing substance abuse treatment services, and two years experience in providing supervision of substance abuse treatment staff.

As we continue to evaluate PROUD through formal and informal systems of assessment, Arapahoe House will energetically pursue resources and knowledge to adapt the program in light of changing trends in client care, homelessness prevention theories, and substance abuse treatment issues. Seeking to improve services delivery and to re-design the program in light of the lessons learned ensures that Arapahoe House will continue to reach out to clients like Stan who conclude, "It's reassuring to know that there's somebody I can call that can help me out."

REFERENCES

Bond, G.R., Miller, L.D., Krumwied, R.D., & Ward, R.S. (1988). Assertive case management in three CMHC's: A controlled study. *Hospital and Community Psychiatry, 49,* 411-418.

Cox, G.B., Walker, R.D., Freng, S.A., Short, B.A., Meijer, L., & Gilchrist, L. (1997). Outcome of a controlled trial of the effectiveness of intensive case management for chronic public inebriates. Unpublished Manuscript.

Drake, R.E., Antosca, L.M., Noordsy, D.L., Bartels, S.J. & Osher, F.C. (1991). New Hampshire's specialized services for the dually diagnosed. In K. Minkoff & R.E. Drake (Eds.), *Dual diagnosis of major mental illness and substance disorders: Vol. 50. New directions for mental health services* (pp. 57-67). San Francisco, CA: Jossey-Bass.

Kirby, M.W. & Braucht, G.N. (1993). Intensive case management for homeless people with alcohol and other drug problems. *Alcoholism Treatment Quarterly, 10* (3/4), 187-200.

Miller, W.R. & Rollnick, S. (1991). *Motivational interviewing: Preparing people to change addictive behavior.* New York: The Guilford Press.

Miller, W.R. (1991). The stages of change and treatment eagerness scale. Unpublished manuscript, University of New Mexico at Albuquerque.

Miller, W. R. & Tonigan, J. S. (1995). Assessing drinkers' motivation for change: the stages of change readiness and treatment eagerness scale (SOCRATES). *Psychology of Addictive Behaviors, 10* (2), 81-89.

Morse, G., Calsyn, R., Klinkenberg, W., Trusty, M., Gerber, F., Smith, R., Tempelhoff, B. & Ahmad, L. (1997). An experimental comparison of three types of case management for homeless mentally ill persons. *Psychiatric Services, 48* (4), 497-503.

The Piton Foundation. (1994). *Poverty in Denver: Facing the facts.* Denver, CO: Author.

Prochaska, J.O., DiClemente, C.C., & Norcross, J.C. (1992). In search of how people change: applications to addictive behaviors. *American Psychologist, 47,* 1102-1114.

Reinke, B. & Greenley, J. (1986). Organizational analysis of three community support models. *Hospital and Community Psychiatry, 37*, 624-629.

Ridgely, M.S., & Willenbring, M.L. (1992). *Application of case management to drug abuse treatment: Overview of models and research issues.* Bethesda, MD: National Institute on Drug Abuse.

Ridgway, P. (1986). Case management services for people who are homeless and mentally ill. Report from an NIMH workshop.

Stephens, D., Dennis, E., Toomer, M. & Holloway, J. (1991). The diversity of case management needs for the care of homeless persons. *Public Health Reports 106*, 15.

Wolff, N., Helminiak, T., Morse, G., Calsyn, R., Klinkenberg, W., & Trusty, M. (1997). Cost-effective evaluation of three approaches to case management for homeless mentally ill clients. *American Journal of Psychiatry, 154* (3), 341-348.

Preventing Homelessness in Florida

Colleen Clark, PhD
Gregory B. Teague, PhD
Robert M. Henry, BS

SUMMARY. Essential elements of a housing intervention designed to serve people who are homeless or risk becoming homeless, have severe mental illness, and may have a substance use disorder are described and summarized in a logic model. Characteristics of the target population, the community and the service system are examined, and how this program serves to address the issues. The effectiveness of this intervention appears to be the result of the organizational characteristics. The organizational structure and climate provide: (a) integrated services under one "umbrella"; (b) flexible, responsive service delivery; and (c) a treat-

---

Colleen Clark is Associate in Research in the Department of Community Mental Health, Louis de la Parte Florida Mental Health Institute, University of South Florida, Tampa, FL. She serves as Project Director for the contract with Boley Centers for Behavioral Healthcare, Inc. to document and evaluate their Homelessness Prevention Project. Gregory B. Teague is Chair and Associate Professor in the Department of Community Mental Health, Louis de la Parte Florida Mental Health Institute, University of South Florida, Tampa, FL. Robert M. Henry is Senior Behavioral Program Specialist on the Clinical Research and Education Unit, Louis de la Parte Florida Mental Health Institute, University of South Florida, Tampa, FL.

Address correspondence to: Colleen Clark, Department of Community Mental Health, Louis de la Parte Florida Mental Health Institute, University of South Florida, MHC 1345, 13301 Bruce B. Downs Blvd., Tampa, FL 33612-3807 (Email: cclark@hal.fmhi.usf.edu).

This work was funded in part by a contract with Boley Centers for Behavioral Healthcare, Inc. in accordance with grant number 1 UD9 SM51965-01 from the Center for Mental Health Services and the Center for Substance Abuse Treatment, Substance Abuse and Mental Health Services Administration.

[Haworth co-indexing entry note]: "Preventing Homelessness in Florida." Clark, Colleen, Gregory B. Teague, and Robert M. Henry. Co-published simultaneously in *Alcoholism Treatment Quarterly* (The Haworth Press, Inc.) Vol. 17, No. 1/2, 1999, pp. 73-91; and: *Homelessness Prevention in Treatment of Substance Abuse and Mental Illness: Logic Models and Implementation of Eight American Projects* (ed: Kendon J. Conrad et al.) The Haworth Press, Inc., 1999, pp. 73-91. Single or multiple copies of this article are available for a fee from The Haworth Document Delivery Service [1-800-342-9678, 9:00 a.m. - 5:00 p.m. (EST). E-mail address: getinfo@haworthpressinc.com].

© 1999 by The Haworth Press, Inc. All rights reserved.

ment philosophy which builds on the strengths of residents through effective staff-resident relationships. *[Article copies available for a fee from The Haworth Document Delivery Service: 1-800-342-9678. E-mail address: getinfo@haworthpressinc.com]*

KEYWORDS. Psychosocial rehabilitation, strength-based treatment, integrated services, "housing as treatment"

Set in an urban county in West Central Florida, the Boley Homelessness Prevention Project was developed in response to the community's need for stable and supportive housing for individuals who have experienced homelessness or been at risk of homelessness, have severe mental illness and may also have substance abuse disorders. Boley Centers for Behavioral Healthcare, Inc. is a comprehensive psychosocial services agency with a long history of developing housing choices for individuals with severe mental illness, creatively matching individuals' needs with community resources. The Homelessness Prevention Project is this agency's response to the special needs and strengths of this population, including their lack of material resources, resistance to traditional mental health treatment approaches, lack of history in maintaining a stable home and lifestyle and simultaneous desires for independence and community.

The intervention provides three types of service to the target population:

1. Consumers are assisted in finding their own apartment and negotiating a lease. Based on need, choice, eligibility and availability, the housing may be transitional or long-term, and may be either owned and managed by Boley Centers, or independent free-market housing.
2. Support services are offered to help residents become established in their home such as assistance with locating household supplies and in budgeting.
3. Staff link residents to services either within Boley Centers or with other agencies to meet the social, medical, clinical and vocational needs and goals of the resident.

Essential elements of this intervention are summarized in a logic model in Figure 1. The theory and nature of the intervention are described in terms of an organizational structure that provides an umbrella of services, an organizational climate that supports a flexible and responsive delivery of services, and a treatment philosophy of building on the strengths of residents through effective staff-resident relationships.

FIGURE 1. Logic Model for the Boley Homelessness Prevention Project

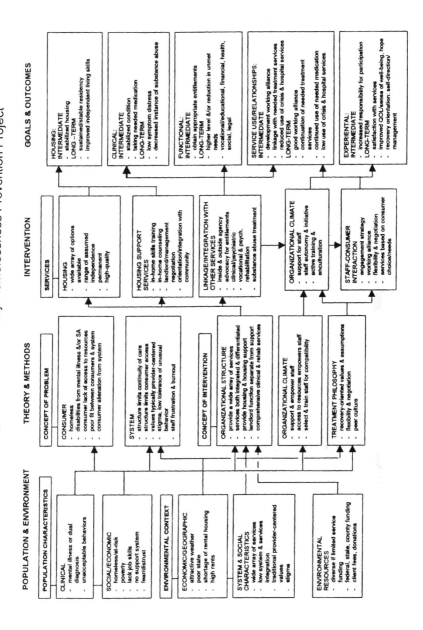

POPULATION AND ENVIRONMENT

Population Characteristics

Demographic and Clinical Characteristics. The Homelessness Prevention Project at Boley served ninety-two (92) persons in 1996. These persons had all been homeless or at-risk of homelessness when they entered the program or when they entered the hospital or crisis stabilization unit from which they entered the program. The most typical person served in 1996 was male, white, never married, and in his forties. Overall, (a) gender was 30% female and 70% male; (b) ethnic/racial mix was 79% white, 18% black, and 2% other; (c) 42% were never married and 51% divorce or separated. None were married at intake into the program. Ages fell in ranges as follows: 19-29 years old (18%); 30-39 (34%); 40-49 (36%); and 50-63 (12%). Racially and ethnically these individuals are fairly representative of Pinellas County in general. Data on the homeless population in Pinellas is more difficult to come by. One survey does suggest that African-Americans are a significantly larger portion of the homeless population than of the general population. A "snapshot" survey was taken by the Pinellas County Coalition for the Homeless on one night in January of 1995: the survey looked at 297 people using cold night shelters, soup kitchens, and transitional shelters and found that 37% were black, 61% were white, and 2% "other."

Clinically, the majority of residents entering the Homelessness Prevention Project have been assessed as having a primary diagnosis of a psychotic disorder. A review of medical charts revealed primary diagnoses: schizophrenia or other psychotic disorder (48%); mood disorder (45%); and anxiety disorder (1%). Secondary diagnoses are substance abuse problems (43%) and personality disorder (40%). Twenty-two per cent (22%) have both substance abuse disorders and personality disorders. Of those with substance abuse disorders, the most frequent problem is polysubstance dependence–usually alcohol and cocaine dependence. The majority of residents enter the program with serious symptoms and/or serious impairment of daily functioning; the average Global Assessment of Functioning (GAF) is 47.

Social and Economic. At the time of entering the project, most of the residents had "slipped through the cracks" of the existing mental health system or chosen not to use traditional services. For those with mental illness in Florida, the primary vehicle for publicly funded services is the Continuity of Care Case Management System, and 62% of the Boley Homelessness Prevention Project residents do not receive services in this system. This lack of involvement in formal systems of care is seen by some as a strength. Some staff members describe the residents in the homelessness program as less "passive" and less "institutionalized" than the traditional consumer of mental health services.

Most people enter the Homelessness Prevention Project with few entitlements or regular sources of income. Residents also report very little financial support from (or contact with) their families. Again, this lack of reliance on entitlements is seen by some as a strong point. The director of Boley Centers' Supported Employment Program sees residents from the homelessness programs as less dependent on entitlement income and more committed to employment.

Finally, most of the residents (74%) enter the Boley Homelessness Prevention Project having lived on the streets or in shelters for the homeless. The other 26% are considered at high risk for homelessness because of histories of multiple hospitalizations and difficulty with living in the community. Many have lived in various group settings and been evicted due to illegal, disruptive, or erratic behaviors. However, this history of unstable housing appears to some to contribute to the value the residents place on their home once obtained. As one consumer mentioned, "Having a nice place makes you want to care for it; you feel like your in it for the long run." For many consumers, the sense of being a part of a community is a valued and appreciated experience after years of transience or feeling like an outcast.

Environmental Context

Demographic. In 1994 the unemployment rate in the local district was 5.95%. Seven per cent of the district's families had incomes below the poverty level. St. Petersburg is less ethnically diverse than many major metropolitan areas in Florida. Racial/ethnic minorities comprise 23.9% of the population: 19.4% are African-American, 2.6% are Hispanic. The ethnic diversity of the area is increasing. However, the trend toward income disparity between minorities and the white majority is also increasing. Minority households accounted for less than 15% of all home owners, but over 26% of all renters.

Service System Characteristics. State funded services for those with serious mental illness are primarily for case management services, state hospitals, psychiatric emergency units, and funds for Adult Living Facilities. The state of Florida assigns priority to those who have been in the state hospital or had multiple visits to psychiatric emergency units. Often individuals who are homeless, or recently homeless, are not eligible for case management services as they frequently have not had long-term involvement with the mental health system. They are also often ineligible to live in Adult Living Facilities as admission requires entitlements to already be in place. Many mental health services, especially outpatient, are only available to those with Medicaid or other third-party payers.

Services and funding for substance abuse services are generally in separate systems. Providers from each system are reluctant to handle issues related to the other, in part due to a lack of cross-training, but also because they are not reimbursed for services in the other. This bifurcation affects all level of services. Until recently many mental health providers refused to serve those with substance abuse problems, and substance abuse providers resisted serving those with serious mental illness.

Environmental Resources. It is estimated that, on any given night, there are approximately 1,637 homeless persons in Pinellas County (Pinellas County Coalition for the Homeless, 1995); 75% are single individuals, 25% are members of homeless families. Approximately 3% of homeless persons are under 18 years of age. There are approximately 1,400 beds available to homeless persons in Pinellas County, fewer than 500 are in emergency shelters. Also, there is a great need for additional services for those persons considered to be chronically homeless. Nearly 50% of all Pinellas County homeless persons suffer from drug or alcohol dependency, and 32% have a serious mental illness.

A Comprehensive Housing Affordability Strategy was prepared for Pinellas County on a five-year planning period (1994-1998). This study found that very few affordable rental units have been constructed since the mid-1980s. Of the 762 homeless persons surveyed about their situation, 446 or 59% said they could not afford rents and the high cost of deposits. At the time of this report, approximately 5,400 Pinellas County residents with a serious mental illness had supportive housing needs, with system capacity to serve only about 200.

THEORY OF THE INTERVENTION

Concept of the Problem

Consumer Issues. People who have a diagnosis of severe mental illness and are also homeless (or at-risk of homelessness) present numerous issues to address in order to achieve and maintain housing stability. This population is heterogeneous (Rossi, 1990). Approximately half have a co-existing alcohol or other drug use disorder (Fischer & Breakey, 1991). Symptoms of mental illness such as paranoia or hallucinations may result in unpredictable and unacceptable behaviors or apathy and withdrawal. These in turn may lead to poor hygiene and housekeeping, failure to pay rent, hospitalization and loss of Supplemental Social Security Income, and, thus, eviction (Lezak & Edgar, 1996).

Conversely, being homeless appears to exacerbate mental illness (Winkleby & White, 1992), or could result in conditions that might lead to a psychiatric diagnosis (Lovell & Shern, 1990). The 10% to 20% of the homeless population who are dually diagnosed with severe mental illness and alcohol or other drug problem (Tessler & Dennis, 1989) are likely to experience greater poverty, more behavior problems and exacerbation of mental illness. Desjarlais (1994) observed long-term homeless people in a Boston shelter as tending to "struggle along" rather than experience and integrate daily living. Those at risk of homelessness coming from jails, long term psychiatric facilities, and boarding homes may be out of touch with their strengths and abilities.

The most prevalent risk factor for homelessness is poverty, and individuals with psychiatric disabilities existing on Supplemental Security Income (SSI) are indeed poor. The increase in the number of poor combined with the decrease in low-income housing has driven up housing costs (Reamer, 1989). Tanzman (1993) states "Nowhere in the United States can people living on SSI afford to rent, much less obtain goods and services (transportation, telephone, food and clothing) identified in consumer surveys as necessary to succeed in preferred housing." They may also lack adequate social and support networks, and face stigmatization and discrimination in seeking housing (Lezak & Edgar, 1996). All of these economic and social stresses contribute to the day-to-day difficulty of managing a serious mental illness.

System Issues. Other external risk factors for the homeless individuals with mental illness include the unavailability of safe, decent housing and lack of integrated support systems (Carling, 1993; Weir, 1995). Some may have found being homeless preferable to living in available housing that may have restrictive rules, unsanitary facilities or dangerous high-crime neighborhoods. Some may need to be homeless to access other necessities, such as free health care. Others may not be willing to accept the "package deal" of treatment with housing (Carling, 1990; Drake, Osher & Wallach, 1991). What the consumer prefers and what the clinician recommends are often at odds (Susser, Goldfinger & White, 1990).

The 1994 CMHS Interim Status Report of the McKinney Demonstration Program for Homeless Adults with Serious Mental Illness reported that homeless people with severe mental illness use accessible, relevant community mental health services. Further appropriate services decrease homelessness and advocacy helps increase access to entitlement income. Substance abuse was found to be a major factor in homelessness among persons with severe mental illnesses and formerly homeless persons with severe mental illnesses are an important resource. Finally the findings of this report demonstrate that housing stability, appropriate treatment, and increased income lead to an improved quality of life.

Concept of Intervention

The Boley Homelessness Prevention Project can best be understood in terms of the importance of three hypothesized organizational and interactive factors: (a) consumer-provider relationships, (b) organizational climate, and (c) organizational structure. These three aspects of service structure and delivery are linked and integrated throughout the program. At the level of service delivery, the Boley model emphasizes the importance of the relationship between service providers and consumers, i.e., on the ability of staff to form effective "working alliances" with consumers. More than just a basis for carrying out the practical and instrumental transactions of services, these relationships provide an interpersonal grounding for the adaptive development of recovery. At the second level, the Boley model assumes that in order to establish and negotiate productive connections with clients, staff must work in an organizational context that explicitly values those relationships and actively allows them the flexibility and autonomy to invest in them.

At the third level, the Boley model provides both integration and differentiation of organizational functions. By providing a comprehensive array of clinical, rehabilitative, and housing services, the agency can ensure their availability to meet the individual needs of a wide variety of consumers and can provide staff with ready access to the resources. A wide organizational umbrella enhances the dissemination of the values of client recovery and staff support. At the same time, the agency's structure separates the functions of residential management and consumer service. This differentiation offers the opportunity for effective consumer advocacy and greater consumer independence.

Treatment Philosophy. The Homelessness Prevention Project has its theoretical origins in the psychosocial rehabilitation principles on which Boley Centers, the parent organization is based. These principles have been adapted to address the specific needs of those individuals who are homeless or at immediate risk of homelessness.

Primary in the psychosocial rehabilitation approach is the consumer-staff relationship. Dincin (1975) states that the rehabilitative relationship is characterized by an ability to develop a feeling of "dynamic hopefulness" in the member; creativity that enables the worker to use the center for the member's involvement; great frequency of interpersonal contact; and a deep-seated investment in all areas of the member's current life situation. Boley Centers encourages staff to make decisions based on what works with each consumer. Boley Centers promotes empowerment of staff by helping staff realize the decision-making that is invested in them and encouraging staff to speak up for the needs of consumers. This trust in staff judgment is passed on to trusting the strengths of consumers.

Anthony (1996) has used the term "recovery" to describe using skills and techniques to fulfill a chosen role in a chosen environment, not merely controlling symptoms or heading off crises. Psychosocial rehabilitation, assertive community treatment, and treatment of people who carry dual diagnoses share certain principles. These include: building on a person's strengths rather than focusing on deficits; an initial engagement stage of the helping relationship during which trust and rapport are developed; integrated services provided in vivo; and "tailoring" services to fit the needs and desires of the consumer. The research suggests approaches guided by these principles may be well-suited to assisting people whose background of falling between the "cracks" has left them cynical, skeptical, wary, and untrusting of the mental health "system" and its practitioners.

Organizational Climate. One possibility for increasing the involvement in treatment of this heterogeneous population may be the establishment of a significant relationship between the consumer and the service provider (Solomon et al., 1995; Blankertz & Cnaan, 1993; McGrew, Wilson & Bond, 1996). The development of such a relationship may greatly depend upon the organizational climate in which the consumer and provider find themselves (Friedman, Jeger & Slotnik, 1982). The social climate within the organization should allow consideration of consumer choices, tapping their experiences by having consumers on boards and advisory committees, and as providers of services. Formerly homeless people frequently have an advantage in relating to their peers effectively and providing support services (Mowbray et al., 1996). The practice of hiring consumers as providers also creates an employment option for which this hard-to-employ group are uniquely qualified (Warner & Polak, 1995; Besio & Mahler, 1993).

As the staff are called upon to act as "generalist" in the psychosocial model of service, the organization must also be flexible in its role expectations and allow for a high level of autonomy of staff decision-making (Dougherty, 1994).

Organizational Structure. The availability of a range of housing options offering a variety of services may be essential in the long term process of preventing homelessness and promoting stabilization (Shern, Surles & Waizer, 1989). Two types of housing alternatives for people who have severe mental illness are described in the literature: (a) supportive (or transitional) housing which usually involves a continuum of housing options progressing toward community living (Pyke & Lowe, 1996; Drake, Bartels, Teague, Noordsy & Clark, 1993), and (b) supported (or independent) housing which is community-based housing with a comprehensive support system (Hogan & Carling, 1992). Consumers are much more likely to maintain permanent housing if they take an active role in choosing their own housing (Carling, 1990; Shern et al., 1989). Recommended is a range of housing options, the choice being made by the consumer (Carling, 1993) and emphasizing the importance of supportive services only as needed and desired (Cnaan, Blankertz, Messinger & Gardner, 1988).

Integrated services have been recommended for successfully treating mentally ill homeless people (Bachrach, 1993; McGrew & Bond, 1995) and people who are dually diagnosed (Drake et al., 1993). Continuity of care, when contrasted to compartmentalized service provision, more readily fosters engagement, which may result in a working alliance in a therapeutic relationship (Solomon, Draine, & Delaney, 1995; Blankertz & Cnaan, 1993). Beginning the process of assisting people who have an alcohol and/or drug use problem (Pinsker, 1983) closely parallels descriptions of the process of the psychosocial rehabilitation model. Specifically, an initial "low demand" relationship is an effective engagement strategy, as the person moves to a stage of "readiness" for change. Once this point is reached goals may be gradually increased step-by-step (Anthony, 1996).

The service provider should be prepared to mediate landlord-tenant negotiations, in addition to communicating with neighbors, local businesses, and law enforcement agencies to develop the optimum means of relating to the consumer (Bond, Witheridge, Dincin, Wasmer, Webb & DeGraff-Kaser, 1990). Likewise family mediation is a service which helps many of the target population maintain housing stability (Knisely & Fleming, 1993).

The Homelessness Prevention Project operates within a larger agency–Boley Centers for Behavioral Healthcare, Inc. Boley Centers is a private, not-for-profit, psychosocial rehabilitation agency. Since 1970, Boley has been providing residential and supportive services for residents of Pinellas County, Florida, who have severe and persistent mental illness including those who also have alcohol and other drug related disorders. Boley currently has 17 residential facilities including enhanced group homes, group homes, supervised apartments and permanent independent housing. Boley provides day treatment services, case management, job evaluation, job placement, sheltered and supported employment, psychiatric services, partial hospitalization, outpatient counseling and a consumer-run drop-in center. Currently, Boley has the capacity to serve 600 persons at any given time and served over 900 persons in 1996.

In addition to the influential Boley Centers psychosocial rehabilitation philosophy, the fact that the Project is within Boley Centers is significant for a number of reasons. A comprehensive array of services is available within the same "bureaucratic" structure. This facilitates flexibility and choice of services, minimizes roadblocks to services, and provides for enhanced continuity of care. A wide variety of housing options are available within Boley Centers, varying on continuums of structure, permanency, and privately versus Boley owned and managed. A sense of community is provided which facilitates a sense of belonging and normalcy for residents, staff and administrators.

DESCRIPTION OF THE INTERVENTION

Services

Individuals are referred to the Project from a wide variety of sources. Except for a few self referrals, most residents do not come directly from the streets, but rather from shelters, hospitals, or emergency stabilization units where they have been identified as being homeless upon admission and are then referred to screeners from Boley Centers. Outreach for recruitment to the Supported Living Program (open-market housing) portion of the program consists primarily of meeting with discharge workers at the state mental health facility, psychiatric emergency units, and local hospitals to divert individuals from being committed to the state hospital. As with the rest of the project, as the community becomes aware of the program, little outreach and recruitment is needed. The first step of the intervention is assisting the consumer in finding their own apartment and negotiating a lease agreement.

The second part of the intervention is the provision of support services aimed at helping the client become established in their home and may include anything from locating household supplies to assistance in budgeting. Discussions are begun regarding the social, medical, clinical and vocational goals of the client for the third step which is establishing linkages to services either within Boley Centers or with outside agencies. These direct support services and linkages to other services continue throughout the resident's tenure, varying as needed and requested.

Housing. Each individual coming into the Boley Homelessness Prevention Project is given assistance in locating high quality, affordable housing. Based on assessed functioning level and degree of substance abuse, the individual may be offered transitional or permanent housing situations. Individuals without funds are usually placed in apartments owned and managed by Boley Centers. The apartments at the Oaks (the transitional housing complex) are generally shared with a roommate; otherwise all apartments are for single occupancy.

For those choosing to live in the community in independent, open-market housing, landlords are approached first by the supported living worker. They look for accommodating landlords, and talk to them about the specific client they want to place. They try to match the client to an apartment complex and take them to look at many places before they move. A major problem is credit and background checks: many clients have a criminal background and have poor or no credit. Established complexes with property managers are less likely to work with staff, but the smaller places where they can deal directly with the owner do. They try to place only one person in a complex to not overload the landlord, and to maximize privacy and normalcy for the client. Most live in one bedroom efficiency apartments. For Boley owned and managed apartments, deposits are not required. In the privately owned apartments, the program assists with deposits as needed. Staff also orients consumers to the neighborhood, transportation, and other Boley facilities.

While some apartments in the Boley Homelessness Prevention Project are owned and managed by Boley Centers, the leasing management staff is a completely separate division of the organization. It is the role of the leasing management staff to set up lease and fee agreements with residents in Boley housing. The supported housing specialists in these settings then work with the consumers on landlord and leasing issues.

The Oaks is the transitional housing facility and is designed for stays from 18 to 24 months; the average is 11 months. About half the residents move from the Oaks into the Permanent Housing facilities. The second most frequent move is into other Boley housing, usually because they need more structure and support than the independence of the Permanent Housing program provides.

Residents of Permanent Housing may live there indefinitely. While they are eligible for the housing support services as long as they live there, services and support tend to be much more intensive initially. Over time residents appear to require fewer services and to get support more from peers and the community. Residents in the open-market housing of the Supported Living Program are eligible for services as long they are needed and desired. Once a resident has been stabilized for a significant amount of time, services will be faded and eventually the resident may be graduated from the Supported Living Program.

Housing-Related Support Services. This group of services could be called "eviction prevention," and comprises an amazing medley. Staff work the hours necessary to help residents, including evening hours and weekends. As one supervisor states, "basically we do whatever is needed to keep people in the community, out of the hospital, and off the streets." They see the residents as often as needed, guided by the resident. They will also make frequent phone contacts.

Supported housing staff working with residents in privately owned apartments also find that major problems are often associated with leases and paying bills. This program has $1,200 per year per resident available for assistance with deposits, rent, furniture, linens, cooking utensils, or whatever is needed by the resident to help him or her get established in an apartment. Staff work with landlords on becoming more accepting of the resident's behaviors, and may negotiate arrangements with the landlord such as splitting the cost of installing window air conditioners. Staff may also negotiate with landlords on issues such as possibly decreasing the rent slightly, or if the resident has done something that would normally be a "lease breaker." For example, one person got a cat, contrary to the lease, and didn't tell anyone. Staff worked with the landlord so she could keep the cat. If someone consistently doesn't pay bills, staff may try to get them payees.

In the Boley owned housing, supported housing specialists serve as resident advocates and assist in negotiating with leasing management staff. At times staff may use the property management arm of Boley to enforce rules.

Evictions are rare. Again staff provide many types of direct service, including hands on cleaning, if needed, of an apartment when a person moves in their new home. Other staff arrange "cleaning days" about once a month to assist residents in maintaining their homes. Initially, most residents have few of the household items needed to start a home. The program may provide, for example, personal hygiene items, detergent, toilet paper, food from a pantry at Oaks, bus tokens, or clothes from Boley's thrift store.

Staff describe much of what they do as education. They teach residents budgeting, cleaning, daily living skills, how to use transportation, how to take their medications, how to grocery shop and time management skills. Staff also monitors progress: how residents are doing in the apartment, do they have enough food, are they taking medications, is the apartment clean, and are they stable both mentally and physically. A great deal of the supported housing staff time is engaged in transporting residents to buy resources, for appointments, or to take care of personal business.

The results of a focus group with residents suggested that the role of the staff as friend and advocate is the one most valued by residents. "Staff make you feel like you are part of their families. They take you into their hearts." In these roles staff may feed resident's pets, keep in touch with family members, or hold family problem-solving sessions.

Staff assist with getting a resident hospitalized if needed or if there is an ex parte order. They will then visit them in the hospital, take things to them in the hospital, keep in touch with hospital staff or participate in hospital staffings. Staff may also assist with any legal problems, go to court with residents, and keep in touch with probation officers. If a consumer is incarcerated they may get things to them, accompany them to court, or visit them in jail.

Linkage/Integration with Other Services. As soon as the resident has had an opportunity to settle into their apartment, the initial assessment is developed. Discussions with their supported housing specialist will include what the resident's service needs and goals are and how these can best be met. Many of the services can be obtained within the Boley Centers organization. The staff member will begin to arrange for meetings that will include the residents, their primary staff member and a representative from the other program such as the day treatment program or vocational program. Initially the supported housing specialist arranges the first appointments with the psychiatrist or psychiatric nurse. If any problems arise for a consumer in these other Boley programs, the staff member will participate in Boley staffings.

Boley seeks to meet the needs of consumers by offering an array of services that foster community integration and independence. By offering comprehensive services consumers do not have to negotiate a separate set of service providers. However, linkages are also made outside of Boley Centers as wanted or desired, especially, for example, for entitlements and medical services.

Organizational Climate. Rather than formalized policies and procedures, program decisions are primarily negotiated among administrators, staff and residents. For example, drug or alcohol use is not allowed in the transitional housing program. If a resident is found using or dealing on the property they will be discharged immediately, but this has happened only once. Alcohol is not allowed in the common areas of any of the Permanent Housing settings, but there and in the Supported Living Program people have the freedom to do as they wish in their own homes.

The overriding goal of each of the programs is to support the residents' community tenure. Substance abuse is assessed in terms of the problems it causes for the resident and addressed accordingly. Although there is an official policy that relapse may be cause for eviction, all of the staff agreed, "you just can't kick someone out and tell them to go to a 28-day program. It just won't happen." Encouragement to attend substance abuse groups is intensified, as is one to one counseling and AA. Brief stays in a detoxification unit or a hospital program may be arranged so as to allow the resident to keep their apartment. A Boley group home for those with co-occurring disorders may be used for detoxification.

Staff-Consumer Interaction. The Boley Homelessness Prevention Project seeks to build on a resident's independence and individuality primarily through respecting their choices as to what level of services, supports and interventions they need and desire. As a residential supervisor phrased it, "we try to balance what they need, with what they accept." This appears to be primarily a negotiation approach rather than a prescriptive one. As one resident describes this process, "staff don't push me to go too fast, they let me go at my own pace." These negotiations may be difficult when the client is less stable, or still actively abusing substances. This appears to be the one situation where staff may push for the relatively structured environment of The Oaks (Transitional Housing) which may not be the client's preference in housing. One resident later observed: "I had to learn to live in a structured environment that I resisted, but really needed." On the other hand, the supported living staff relate the case of one resident who had a heart condition but chose to live in an apartment without air conditioning. Despite their efforts to relocate him to a nicer apartment with air conditioning, he was firm about staying where he was.

This same flexibility and responsiveness can be seen in the housing-related support services. One resident stated, "I get a foundation of support that I can choose to use or not." Material needs are provided in a practical manner, focusing on what it takes to build and maintain a household, while responding to the creativity and individuality of each resident by supplying or helping them obtain things such as posters and decorative pillows. The long-term support again is very individualized. Staff describe two residents living in the permanent housing apartments who exhibit paranoia but do not accept the label of "mentally ill," and thus refuse to apply for services or benefits. They continue to live there for free. One man has had an apartment for four years with enough income to pay rent but wants no other services.

GOALS AND OUTCOMES

The Boley Homelessness Prevention Project is designed to arrange housing and provide housing-related services to individuals who have experienced homelessness or been at risk of homelessness, and have severe mental illness and may have alcohol or other drug problems. The provision of housing and/or housing-related services endeavors to increase the housing stability of these individuals; to improve their quality of life; and to promote rehabilitation and recovery from the debilitating effects of homelessness, mental illness, and substance abuse.

The goal of the linkage to services is to reduce the level of unmet need for each consumer. In other words there are no generic service goals. Each person's service plan is carefully negotiated with their primary support team and other staff and providers as relevant. The goal is to work with the consumer to: (a) determine their individual desires and needs; (b) plan together the best means for addressing these; and (c) determine which resources are accessible, acceptable to and appropriate for each resident. It is also intended that the participants will have fewer unmet needs for clinical, psychosocial, medical, housing, and vocational services. Further, those participants with substance abuse problems will have decreased use of alcohol and other drugs and fewer associated problems.

It is anticipated that housing stability and increased availability of needed services will result in associated benefits for participants that include: (a) stable income from benefits or work; (b) improved physical health; (c) reduced level of mental, emotional and behavioral symptoms; (d) an increased level of functioning; (e) improved social support; (f) reduction in substance use or abstinence; and (g) an improved quality of life.

Outcomes. Of residents served in 1996, most had been in the program prior to 1996 (63%). Thirty-four individuals were admitted this year. Throughout the year only 3 residents stayed less than 6 months. Many of the new admissions were due to expansion of capacity. The program acquired 16 new apartments designated for Permanent Housing in September of 1996. Of the 92 individuals served in 1996, 59% were still in the Boley Homelessness Prevention Project at the end of the year. Twenty-six people (or 28%) were "closed" to the Project but still receiving services and/or housing from Boley Centers. Thirteen per cent were closed to the Project and to Boley Centers.

Focus groups with residents and staff confirmed that the Boley Homelessness Prevention Project is characterized by a flexible, creative and responsive style. This aspect appears to be very influential in the power of the intervention. It does involve balancing and negotiating with limits however and may create some problem areas. For example, in order to be responsive in outreach and recruitment, screening has historically been very individualized. Depending on the client situation, the screener may meet with the client promptly, bypass some procedural requirements and match them with an suitable apartment quickly. At other times more formal procedures were followed or appropriate matches were not available. A problematic result of this responsive style was that some referral agencies felt frustrated with the inconsistencies and not sure how to "get a client in the program." Another example is the handling of relapses. Staff are careful to evaluate the extent of problem caused by relapses for each resident. This allows them to respond in a manner effective for that individual. The balancing problem in this case is that some residents feel that the policy is inconsistent and perhaps "unfair."

In the history of the program, there have been only 2 evictions from the permanent housing setting. Both of these were for significant, long-term nonpayment of rent; severe destruction of the apartments; and after many attempted interventions. Substance abuse was involved in many of the cases closed or discharged in 1996, usually because the individual chose to leave the program or to go into another Boley residential program specifically for those with co-occurring disorders. Residents with co-occurring disorders comprise 43% of the people served in 1996 but 53% of those who left the program.

The research literature consistently confirms the importance of: (a) using individualized approaches; (b) addressing the real needs of the recipients of services; (c) flexibility and offering a variety of options; (d) considering individual preferences; (e) providing access and linkages in ways that cut across bureaucratic lines; (f) facilitating staff responses that engage the consumer; and working consistently *with* the consumer to achieve their own life goals.

Line staff, both from Boley Centers and from Florida Mental Health Institute confirm this. For example they describe one resident who needs all her possessions with her at all times to feel secure, so she carries the bags everywhere. There was no "treatment plan" stating what staff think she needs to feel secure (for example, more restrictive setting, increased medications), the bag-carrying is not described as a problem or symptom to be "cured."

IMPLICATIONS

The issues that are raised in working with this most disenfranchised group, apply to all aspects of mental health and substance abuse systems of care. If a program cannot be responsive to the needs and wishes of those people that are disabled, have no property and no income then it is an inadequate system. We heard descriptions of the independence of thought of these individuals, the ingenuity, and the individuality. By forcing the system to acknowledge and respond to the uniqueness of each person that is homeless, they have helped shatter concepts that the individual must conform to or comply with the system to succeed.

The split between substance abuse and mental health systems is seen by many as originating at the federal level and this serves as an administrative disincentive to address the problems of the homeless population with co-occurring disorders. As funds are specifically set for housing needs, these funds clearly need to have sufficient operating expenses to allow staff to assist residents in obtaining entitlements and other support services needed for residents to become stabilized in the community.

REFERENCES

Anthony, W.A. (1996). Integrating psychiatric rehabilitation into managed care. *Psychiatric Rehabilitation Journal, 20* (2), 39-44.

Bachrach, L. (1993). Continuity of care and approaches to case management for long-term mentally ill patients. *Hospital and Community Psychiatry, 44*, 465-468.

Besio, S.W. & Mahler, J. (1993). Benefits and challenges of using consumer staff in supported housing services. *Hospital and Community Psychiatry, 44*, 490-491.

Blankertz, L.E. & Cnaan, R.A. (1993). Serving the dually diagnosed homeless: program development and interventions. *The Journal of Mental Health Administration, 20*, 100-112.

Bond, G.R., Witheridge, T.F., Dincin, J., Wasmer, D, Webb, J., & De Graaf-Kaser, R. (1990). Assertive community treatment for frequent users of psychiatric hospitals in a large city: A controlled study. *American Journal of Community Psychology, 18*, 865-891.

Cnaan, R.A., Blankertz, L., Messinger, K.W., & Gardner, J.R. (1988). Psychosocial rehabilitation: Toward a definition. *Psychosocial Rehabilitation Journal, 11* (4), 61-77.

Carling, P.J. (1990). Major mental illness, housing, and supports: The promise of community integration. *American Psychologist, 45*, 969-975.

Carling, P.J. (1993). Housing and supports for persons with mental illness: emerging approaches to research and practice. *Hospital and Community Psychiatry, 44*, 439-449.

CMHS Center for Mental Health Services. *(1994).Making a difference: interim status report of the McKinney demonstration program for homeless adults with serious mental illness.* Rockville, MD. Center for Mental Health Services.

Desjarlais, R. (1994). Struggling along: The possibilities for experience among the homeless mentally ill. *The American Anthropologist, 96,* 886-901.
Dincin, J. (1975). Psychiatric rehabilitation. *Schizophrenia Bulletin, 13,* 131-147.
Dougherty, S. (1994). The generalist role in the clubhouse model. *Psychosocial Rehabilitation Journal, 18* (1), 95-108.
Drake, R.E., Osher, F.C. & Wallach, M.A. (1991). Homelessness and dual diagnosis. *American Psychologist, 46,* 1149-1158.
Drake, R.E., Bartels, S.J., Teague, G.B., Noordsy, D.L., & Clark, R.E. (1993). Treatment of substance abuse in severely mentally ill patients. *The Journal of Nervous and Mental Disease, 181,* 606-611.
Fischer, P.J. & Breakey, W. R. (1991). The epidemiology of alcohol, drug, and mental disorders among homeless persons. *American Psychologist, 46,* 1115-1128.
Friedman, S., Jeger, A.M., & Slotnick, R.S. (1982). Social ecological assessment of mental health treatment environments: Toward self-evaluation. *Psychological Reports, 50,* 631-638.
Hogan, M.F. & Carling, P.J. (1992). Normal housing: A key element of a supported housing approach for people with psychiatric disabilities. *Community Mental Health Journal, 28,* 215-226.
Knisely, M.B. & Fleming, M. (1993). Implementing supported housing in state and local mental health systems. *Hospital and Community Psychiatry, 44,* 456-461.
Lezak, A.D. & Edgar, E. (1996). *Preventing homelessness among people with serious mental illnesses: a guide for states.* The Center for Mental Health Services; Substance Abuse and Mental Health Services Administration; U.S. Department of Health and Human Services, Rockville, MD.
Lovell, A., & Shern, D. (1990). Assessing mental health status among adults who are homeless. In Morrissey, J.P., & Dennis, D.L. (Eds.), *Homelessness and Mental Illness: Toward the Next Generation of Researh Studies* (pp. 69-77), Rockville, MD: National Institute of Mental Health.
McGrew, J.H., & Bond, G.R. (1995). Critical ingredients of assertive community treatment: Judgements of the experts. *Journal of Mental Health Administration, 22,* 113-125.
McGrew, J.H., Wilson, R.G., & Bond, G.R. (1996). Client perspectives on helpful ingredients of assertive community treatment. *Psychiatric Rehabilitation Journal, 19,* (3), 13-21.
Mowbray, C.T., Moxley, D.P., Thrasher, S., Bybee, D., McCrohan, N., Harris, S., Clover, G. (1996). Consumers as community support providers: Issues created by role innovation. *Community Mental Health Journal, 32*(1), 47-67.
Pinsker, H. (1983). Addicted patients in hospital psychiatric units. *Psychiatric Annals, 13*(8), 620-623.
Pyke, J. & Lowe, J. (1996). Supporting people, not structures: Changes in the provision of housing support. *Psychiatric Rehabilitation Journal, 19*(3), 5-12.
Reamer, F.G. (1989). The affordable housing crisis and social work. *Social Work, 34,* 5-9.
Rossi, P.H. (1990). The old homeless and the new homelessness in historical perspective. *American Psychologist 45,* 954-959.
Shern, D.L., Surles, R.C. & Waizer, J. (1989). Designing community treatment

systems for the most seriously mentally ill: A state administrative perspective. *Journal of Social Issues, 45,* 105-117.

Solomon, P., Draine, J. & Delaney, M.A. (1995). The working alliance and consumer case management. *The Journal of Mental Health Administration, 22,* 126-134.

Susser, E., Goldfinger, S.M. and White, A. (1990). Some clinical approaches to the homeless mentally ill. *Community Mental Health Journal, 26,* 463-480.

Tessler, R.C. & Dennis, D.L. (1989). A synthesis of NIMH-funded research concerning persons who are homeless and mentally ill. Rockville, MD: National Institute of Mental Health, Division of Education and Service.

Tanzman, B. (1993). An overview of surveys of mental health consumers' preferences for housing and support services. *Hospital and Community Psychiatry, 44,* 450-455.

Warner, R., & Polak, P. (1995). The economic advancement of the mentally ill in the community: 1. economic opportunities. *Community Mental Health Journal, 31,* 381-396.

Weir, D.S. (1995). Why are Americans homeless?: A review of research findings. *Erie County Commission on Homelessness: Report on the Causes of Homelessnes,* 1-3.

Winkleby, M.A., White, R. (1992). Homeless adults without apparent medical and psychiatric impairment: Onset of morbidity over time. *Hospital and Community Psychiatry, 43,* 1017-1023.

Housing Solutions: The Community Connections Housing Program: Preventing Homelessness by Integrating Housing and Supports

Richard R. Bebout, PhD

SUMMARY. Key features of a comprehensive housing program serving formerly homeless and at-risk adults with serious and persistent mental illness are described. The program combines intensive case management, integrated dual-diagnosis treatment, and other clinical services with a range of housing options which are operated under the auspices of a single agency. For individuals with co-occurring substance use disorder, housing responses are guided by a four stage model of treatment and recovery. The authors offer a rationale for the continuum approach's relevance for high risk populations, especially those in poor, urban settings where safety and harm-reduction are a high priority. A controlled study comparing the continuum housing approach to another leading model is underway. Primary outcomes of interest are engagement in services, establishing and maintaining high quality housing, and avoiding returns to literal homelessness. *[Article copies*

Richard R. Bebout is Research Director, Community Connections, 801 Pennsylvania Avenue, S.E., Suite #400, Washington, DC 20003.

This publication was supported by a grant from the Substance Abuse and Mental Health Services Administration (SAMHSA) through a Cooperative Agreement with the Center for Mental Health Services (CMHS) and the Center for Substance Abuse Treatment (CSAT).

[Haworth co-indexing entry note]: "Housing Solutions: The Community Connections Housing Program: Preventing Homelessness by Integrating Housing and Supports." Bebout, Richard R.. Co-published simultaneously in *Alcoholism Treatment Quarterly* (The Haworth Press, Inc.) Vol. 17, No. 1/2, 1999, pp. 93-112; and: *Homelessness Prevention in Treatment of Substance Abuse and Mental Illness: Logic Models and Implementation of Eight American Projects* (ed: Kendon J. Conrad et al.) The Haworth Press, Inc., 1999, pp. 93-112. Single or multiple copies of this article are available for a fee from The Haworth Document Delivery Service [1-800-342-9678, 9:00 a.m. - 5:00 p.m. (EST). E-mail address: getinfo@haworthpressinc.com].

© 1999 by The Haworth Press, Inc. All rights reserved.

available for a fee from The Haworth Document Delivery Service: 1-800-342-9678. E-mail address: getinfo@haworthpressinc.com]

KEYWORDS. Harm reduction, four-stage model of housing and recovery, intensive case management, "housing as treatment," housing continuum model, dual diagnosis treatment

INTRODUCTION

Formerly homeless persons with serious mental illness (SMI) face an ongoing threat of housing loss due to their multiple interacting impairments. Those at-risk for homelessness are a heterogeneous subgroup with diverse needs that change over time. Compared to other mentally ill persons, those experiencing homelessness are more likely to have become ill earlier in their lives, to have multiple interacting impairments such as co-occurring personality disorders, and to have untreated physical illness (Federal Task Force, 1992). Other complicating factors, such as exposure to sexual abuse and other traumatic violence and the prevalence of co-occurring substance use disorders among persons with severe mental illness, act in combination to dramatically increase an individual's risk of housing loss. Those with co-occurring substance use disorders and mental illness, for example, are known to face harsher living conditions and to remain homeless longer once housing loss occurs compared to other subgroups of homeless persons (Fischer, 1990).

Studies of homeless adults with SMI show that intensive case management, improved access to housing, and housing support services are effective in increasing time in stable housing but that substance abuse improves only with specialized dual-diagnosis treatment (Caton et al., 1993; CMHS, 1994; Jerrel and Ridgely, 1995; Lipton et al., 1988; Morse et al., 1992; Wasylenki et al., 1993). Studies also show that housing stability is strongly mediated by substance abuse. For example, researchers from the San Diego McKinney study found that participants who reported no alcohol problems at study entry, and those reporting no problems with other drugs at study entry, were 2.04 and 2.66 times as likely to maintain consistent community housing as those with problematic alcohol and drug use patterns, respectively (Hurlburt et al., 1996). Similarly, data from the Boston McKinney Project, which evaluated two contrasting housing models, indicated that substance abusers used more inpatient hospital days and were much less likely to remain in stable housing compared to nonabusers (Dickey et al., 1996). These and other investigators consistently call for specialized dual-diagnosis treatment programs (Caton et al., 1993; CMHS, 1994; Desmond et al., 1991; Jerrell and Ridgely, 1995; Lipton et al., 1988; Wasylenki et al., 1993).

Recent experimental and quasi-experimental studies of integrated treatment approaches for homeless persons with dual-disorders examined highly specialized, heavily controlled residential treatment models in which housing and treatment were tightly bundled (Blankertz and Cnaan, 1994; Burnam et al. 1995; Rahav et al., 1995). These studies were hampered by recruitment and retention problems which the investigators attributed in large part to the level of structure and control featured in the study settings. To facilitate engagement and retention over longer service intervals, these researchers recommended a range of residential options flexibly tied to services.

One such approach to linking housing and supports is currently being evaluated in a randomized trial in Washington, DC, at Community Connections (CC), a large private non-profit mental health provider. The CC Housing Continuum represents a comprehensive housing response that includes a wide range of options that are linked to one another and to mental health services within a single organizational structure. The range includes several different levels of staffing and support intensities. Both permanent and transitional housing are available. Roughly 60% of the 360+ adults who receive community-based supports at CC live in housing units that are owned or leased by the agency. Housing supports, property management, clinical and rehabilitative services are all situated under one umbrella. Housing and clinical supports are integrated in an attempt to assure continuous access to decent, affordable housing with flexible supports. The study now underway in Washington, DC, seeks to build on the limited empirical research available on the two dominant models for linking housing and supports by comparing the continuum model against a supported housing approach using an experimental design.

CONTRASTING MODELS OF LINKING HOUSING AND SUPPORTS

Because of the complex interplay between the multiple risk factors observed among homeless and marginally housed persons with mental illness, how housing and mental health services are linked has important implications for housing stability, retention in services, and risk of homelessness. Two prevailing models have emerged: the HOUSING CONTINUUM approach and the SUPPORTED HOUSING approach. In the continuum model, housing functions as an extension of the mental health treatment system. The continuum model features a range of settings with different levels of on-site services. Continuum models often rely heavily on staffed, group living arrangements and assume that many persons with major mental illness cannot live successfully in ordinary, independent housing. Clinical considerations drive decisions about housing match, taking into account such factors as the need for structure and containment, instrumental skills and the need for tangible assistance, and the ability to tolerate interpersonal intensity (Bebout and Harris, 1992; Dickey et al., 1996; Lamb, 1980; Lamb and Lamb, 1990).

In contrast, the "supported housing" approach emphasizes "housing as housing" and is rapidly gaining popularity among consumers, consumer advocates, and system planners due both to its philosophical and fiscal appeal. Many state systems are moving to replace the continuum model with the supported housing model (Ridgway and Zipple, 1990; Carling, 1993). Supported housing emphasizes self-determination, consumer choice, individualized rehabilitation plans, and the creation of permanent homes in normal housing. Its proponents are critical of the residential continuum model for its reliance on staff-controlled, transitional preparatory settings and medical-model treatment philosophies (Ridgway and Zipple, 1990).

While the literature has perpetuated a dichotomous framing of these two approaches and the surrounding issues, it is possible to see these approaches as two, somewhat overlapping segments of a comprehensive housing response for persons with serious mental disorders (Fields, 1990; Bebout and Harris, 1992; Dixon and Osher, 1993). While many of the criticisms of the continuum model are deserved when the model is operationalized poorly, the concept of a continuum itself need not be abandoned. This seems especially true when the need for comprehensive responses to the problems of homelessness and residential instability among the mentally ill is so overwhelming. The continuum model may be particularly relevant for poor residents in dense, high crime urban areas and high-risk populations such as those with dual-disorders.

Studies of the Prevailing Housing Support Models. There have been several successful demonstrations of the supported housing model (Carling, 1993; Cohen and Somers, 1990). However, the supported housing approach has received mixed reviews for people with dual-disorders (Newman and Ridgely, 1994; Dixon et al., 1994; Dixon and Osher, 1993). In addition, investigators with the Boston McKinney project–the only direct test of the two prevailing model–found no differences based on housing type (Dickey et al., 1996). Service utilization in both groups in the Boston project was high and the vast majority of persons in both housing conditions remained in assigned housing and avoided returns to homelessness.

Further controlled evaluations of the continuum model are needed in order to compare housing outcomes and service utilization for consumers with access to an extensive range of housing settings, including more traditional staff-run group homes as well as supported apartment arrangements (single and shared). Claims that the continuum model meets a range of needs and facilitates the recovery process, that it can be operated in a fashion that is consistent with consumer choice and empowerment values, and that it promotes long-term stabilization require further study.

Previous Findings on the CC Housing Continuum. The Washington, D.C. Dual-Diagnosis Project compared an integrated treatment approach implemented at CC to a standard treatment control group, using a quasi-experimental design, for homeless, dually-diagnosed adults in inner-city Washington. Compared to controls, participants in the integrated treatment group experienced more days in stable housing, were judged to have advanced to a later stage of treatment on the SATS (McHugo et al., 1995), and demonstrated greater decreases in alcohol use (Drake et al., 1997). The Washington Project combined integrated mental health and substance abuse treatment with a housing continuum approach. One goal of the project was to help homeless persons with dual disorders attain permanent, high-quality housing over time rather than merely to keep them off the streets.

Detailed analyses of the housing records for the integrated treatment group in the Washington, D.C., project were reported separately (Bebout et al., 1997). Housing status was assessed along with residential history, substance use, treatment stage (SATS), psychiatric symptoms, and quality of life at baseline and at 6-, 12-, and 18-month follow-ups. Most participants were successfully absorbed into stable housing by study end, and progress toward substance abuse recovery at the 6- and 12-month assessment points–not pre-admission psychiatric or substance abuse status (duration or severity)–emerged as the only predictor of final housing status. Those with no detected use of illicit drugs during the 6-12 month period were almost three times as likely to achieve stable housing compared to those with known use. The findings suggest that the continuum model, together with integrated dual-diagnosis services, was helpful to formerly homeless persons with co-occurring substance use disorders.

HISTORY, SETTING, AND ENVIRONMENTAL CONTEXT

CC was incorporated as a private non-profit mental health agency in 1984. The Dixon Class Action Suit, filed in 1974, asserted the rights of civilly committed residents of St. Elizabeth's Hospital–the city's public psychiatric facility–to treatment in less restrictive settings. That action stimulated the creation and growth of a number of private non-profit and for-profit agencies that now provide a wide range of community services to many of the city's most seriously disturbed psychiatric outpatients. In addition to long-stay inpatients at St. Elizabeth's, homeless mentally ill persons have been identified as an additional priority group for referral to contracted services. Available data suggest that more than 2,500 severely mentally ill adults, including as many as 1,500 persons dually diagnosed with mental illness and substance abuse, are homeless on any given night in the District of Columbia. Due to this overwhelming need, several new outreach initiatives were undertaken to assure that mentally ill persons who were homeless were identified and linked to appropriate services.

When the city added crisis residential beds through contracts with CC and other providers, most observers envisioned only a very limited role for the mental health system in the provision of housing. However, this changed rapidly as the demographics of the public system shifted. Most people referred for contract services had only intermittent contact with the treatment system and had experienced only brief hospitalizations. This cohort of "never-institutionalized" young adults strained the system and demanded that new, innovative support strategies be developed. With this shift came a sharp rise in the rates of substance abuse, HIV risk behaviors and infection, and trauma histories among the mentally ill men and women we were serving. The scene had changed dramatically, and the existing network of housing resources was not equal to the task. The mental health system was forced to get into the housing business in a bigger way, like it or not.

The District of Columbia's mental health system and its contractors now provide a wide range of support services tied to a variety of different housing settings. Transitional housing units for the homeless and those at imminent risk for homelessness have since been developed along with several kinds of permanent housing with varying levels of support. The federal Department of Housing and Urban Development (HUD) and several sister agencies at the federal level took active leadership roles in stimulating innovative strategies for combining housing and supports to address the problems of homelessness among the most vulnerable of the nation's "outcasts." CC combines federal, local and private monies to renovate and purchase most of the buildings that now house the various staffed residences it operates, and the continuum is expanding all the time. CC now provides intensive case management services to more than 350 adults with severe mental disorders and has a capacity to house approximately 200 people in agency controlled housing units.

Clinical Services at CC. The housing program is nested in a comprehensive mental health agency that provides a full range of community supports. These include:

- outreach and intensive case management (1:15 ratio);
- 24 hour on-call back-up;
- representative payee services;
- psychiatric follow-up, including medication management, laboratory and pharmaceutical services (in the clinic, by arrangement);

- psychoeducational groups, such as trauma/recovery groups, HIV prevention and support, and cultural awareness groups; and
- linkage to medical care, vocational and other psychosocial services.

All clients at CC receive case management supports from a Master's level clinician who functions in a therapist/case manager role (Harris and Bachrach, 1988). A minimum of two weekly contacts is the expectation for clients served at this intensity level. However, it is not unusual for a case manager to have as many as 5 contacts or more per week with a client who is new to the agency, who is experiencing some acute psychiatric distress, or who is encountering other adjustment problems in the community.

Integrated Dual-Diagnosis Services at CC. The model of dual-diagnosis treatment employed at CC combines cognitive-behavioral and social network strategies with a model of integrated treatment originally developed by Drake and Osher in New Hampshire. The foundation of this approach is a stage-model of recovery advanced by Osher and Kofoed (1989). Each of the four stages is characterized by a set of related tasks and emerging clinical indicators: the emergence of a working alliance between the dually-diagnosed individual and treatment providers marked by growing trust and regular contact (ENGAGEMENT); heightened awareness in the client of negative consequences related to his substance abuse leading to increased motivation for recovery (PERSUASION); the emergence of an internalized commitment to reducing and then eliminating use (ACTIVE TREATMENT); and the acquisition of the life-skills necessary to maintain stable recovery (RELAPSE PREVENTION). This stage model also provides a useful framework for making housing decisions, as we discuss in a later section.

External Housing Resources. While nearly 60% of case management recipients at CC reside in housing units that are part of our continuum, 40% live in external housing resources. These include fully independent apartments, SRO settings, rooming houses, and community residences for mentally ill persons. An estimated 90% of consumers start in agency-managed housing.

DESCRIPTION OF THE CLIENT POPULATION

CC currently serves more than 350 adults with severe mental illness as certified by the D.C. Commission on Mental Health Services (DCCMHS). About three-quarters are African-Americans, one-fifth are Caucasian, and the remainder are from other ethnic minorities. At present, 55-60% of clients served here are female. Fewer than 5% of the clients are currently married, and nearly three-quarters have never married. Nearly one-third did not complete high school, and fewer than a quarter have any schooling beyond high school. More than 90% of individuals served at CC have a psychotic spectrum diagnosis. Specifically, 75% carry diagnoses of schizophrenia or schizoaffective disorder, and 20% have a diagnosis of mood disorder, most commonly with psychotic features. A small percentage (<5%) are seen as having a severe personality disorder and no other major mental illness. Lifetime incidence of substance use disorders is over 70%. Using case manager ratings, we estimate that 35-40% met the criteria for substance abuse or dependence during the past 12 months.

Risk Factors. Systematic attempts to document the incidence of various risk factors indicate that formerly homeless clients remain at risk of residential instability and homelessness even after being absorbed into services for an extended time. For example, clinical records indicate that nearly two-thirds of all clients at CC have some lifetime history of literal homelessness prior to enrollment in services. Nearly a third re-experience episodic homelessness after enrollment, though episodes tend to be quite brief because of aggressive efforts to re-house clients rapidly once housing loss occurs. Including stays in the Crisis Program, more than 40% have avoided a return to literal homelessness by staying in temporary/transitional housing following an eviction. As many as one-third have experienced a housing loss leading up to, or during, an institutional stay and returned to housing in the CC continuum. Still others reside with family members who have previously evicted them, or threatened to, after their behavior exceeded the limits of tolerance.

Substance abuse and histories of exposure to various forms of traumatic violence are prevalent. Both are linked to homelessness and residential instability and require specialized intervention. We estimate that half to three-quarters of the new clients referred to CC meet DSM criteria for a current substance use disorder. Also, our data show that the vast majority of women, and roughly half the men, have known histories of traumatic sexual or physical abuse in childhood, as adults, or both.

Singly, each of these factors is associated with greater risk of episodic homelessness. Most clients at CC present pictures in which the complex interplay of multiple risk factors renders them extremely vulnerable to housing loss. Network resources are limited and do not insulate these individuals the way people with more social support can expect.

THEORY OF THE HOUSING INTERVENTION

The CC housing approach is a non-linear continuum model. An individual can enter the housing continuum at any point and movement between components is fluid. Services are individualized and flexible, and both internal and external supports are adjusted over time as needs change. Housing changes are seen as clinical decisions. Consumers report that previous landlords have been intolerant of symptomatic behavior and/or essentially absent, neglecting to perform even minimal maintenance tasks in the housing units themselves. Rather than relegating these vital functions to an outside landlord, clinicians and consumers collaborate in matching individuals to housing settings where supports are tailored to the individual's needs.

In the description which follows, modifications for people with co-occurring substance use disorders are emphasized because drug and alcohol problems contribute so extensively to residential instability. There is growing evidence that suggests that progress toward recovery from substance abuse is the best predictor of housing stability among persons with severe mental disorders. Because substance abuse accounts for so much of housing loss, we devote more space and attention in this report (and the program manual on which this report is based) to this special needs group than any other.

The overarching goal of the program is to prevent housing loss and limit exposure to harm. Most people with prior homelessness and residential instability can be absorbed gradually into stable, high-quality housing if followed for sufficient periods of time. Intermediate goals include engagement and retention in mental health and related services, psychiatric stability, increased social support, and decreased substance abuse. Long-term goals include permanent housing and improved quality of life. Adoption of a longitudinal perspective is essential.

Clearly both housing and treatment are needed. However, organizing mental health and housing services under separate or parallel provider systems may not be enough as poor coordination of mental health and housing support services often undermines treatment gains, leads to clients dropping out of services, and perpetuates the cycle of instability and housing loss. Instead, integrated strategies are needed.

The Housing Continuum Approach: Principles and Practices. A few basic assumptions guide the operation of CC's Housing Continuum. First, mental health and housing supports should be *Integrated.* Because persons with mental illness and other interacting impairments have complex needs, mere coordination is not enough. Second, a *Broad Range* of housing options is needed. One-size-fits-all approaches cannot work. A comprehensive housing response should incorporate low demand environments, highly structured residences with varying degrees of staff supervision, as well as less intensively supported independent settings.

Third, stabilization in housing is a *Longitudinal Process.* Regaining housing stability, or achieving housing stability for the first time, is a longitudinal process. Providers should expect to see continued residential instability for months, sometimes years, during which people must be assured of continuous access to core services. Transitional settings with flexible time-limits have a role alongside permanent housing.

Fourth, the continuum is *Non-Linear*. In contrast to the traditional notion of a linear continuum, our residential model allows for multiple points of entry along the continuum. Participants need not move along the continuum in a pre-ordained fashion. Movement within the continuum is fluid; residents can move from any given setting to any other. Fifth, supports must be *Individualized and Flexible*. Diversity in this population means that supports must be individualized. Supports vary both across and within housing components. Matching the individual to the most appropriate housing resource requires a sophisticated understanding of the person's history and current needs. Flexibility in the operation of the residential continuum is essential if the goal is to accommodate the needs of the high-risk person with mental illness.

Sixth, the integrated continuum is designed to assure *Responsiveness*. We co-locate housing and clinical staff within a single organization to minimize barriers to effective communication, to assure early detection of problems, and to facilitate rapid responding. The integrated continuum responds rapidly to consumers' changing support needs by titrating both on- and off-site supports. An important aim of the program is to adjust supports without a residential change whenever possible.

Seventh, consumers and providers should make decisions *Collaboratively*. Clinicians, not landlords, have responsibility for tenancy decisions. We work hard to strike a balance between consumers' preferences and their legitimate need for self-determination on the one hand, and the necessity of factoring in sound clinical judgment on the other. For example, active substance abuse may mean that a provider will choose to override a client's stated preference for independent living arrangements in the short-run.

Logic Model. The logic model (see Figure 1) provides a schematic representation of the intervention, including our understanding of the problem, the underlying philosophy and assumptions which drive the intervention, our conceptualization of the homelessness prevention activities, the structure of the program and its distinctive features. The logic model also sets forth the intended outcomes, including short-term objectives and intermediate and long-term goals.

THE HOUSING COMPONENTS

The housing continuum at CC comprises a wide range of housing options supported through the collective efforts of clinical case managers, clinical housing coordinators, and property management staff. The housing opportunities range from intensively staffed crisis/respite beds and longer term supervised congregate residences to single and shared apartments with no on-site staffing. The continuum includes temporary, transitional residences as well as permanent housing. Although the component programs are function-

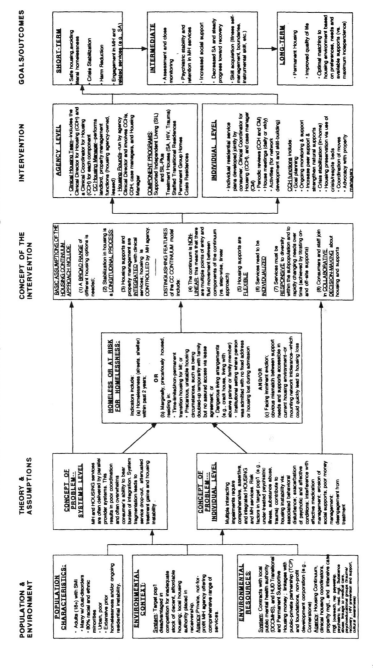

FIGURE 1. The Community Connections Housing Continuum

ally differentiated, they combine to form a whole which is more than the sum of its parts. Housing units are leased or owned by the agency. The components represent discrete but overlapping levels of care which are always evolving in response both to emerging client needs and to changing funding opportunities. Funds for the supportive housing program come from several sources: contracts with the District of Columbia Commission on Mental Health Services, HUD supportive housing grants, foundation money, and client rent payments. The component programs of the housing continuum identified here (see also Bebout and Harris, 1992) represent discrete but overlapping levels of care. Those components that might be conceptualized as "housing as treatment" are listed first, followed by the components which fall at the "housing as housing" end of the spectrum.

Crisis Residential Services. The Crisis Program operates two houses located in residential neighborhoods. The houses provide crisis care to six and eight residents respectively for up to 30 days (Desmond et al., 1991). Each house is staffed by three pairs of residential counselors that live-in for 48 hour shifts. The full-time clinical coordinator teams with a part-time psychiatrist and part-time psychiatric nurse to screen referrals, make assessments, plan and coordinate crisis services, and to support and supervise the residential counselors. The primary purposes of the crisis program are to resolve acute psychiatric crises and to facilitate rapid returns to, or new placements in, permanent housing. The availability of easily accessible crisis or respite beds is a key part of any community-based continuum.

Treatment Houses. Specialized residential treatment is offered to a small number of individuals from three sub-groups of adults with mental illness: persons infected with HIV, people with co-occurring substance use disorders, and women with extensive histories of sexual abuse or other forms of traumatic violence together with ongoing substance abuse problems. These houses feature round-the-clock staffing; 2 staff are on duty during peak evening hours (between 4 and 9 p.m.). Each house serves 6 residents concurrently. Currently, CC has two HIV houses, two dual-diagnosis houses, and one house providing trauma-recovery services for women. While there is not a set time-limit on a resident's stay in any of these houses, the treatment orientation assumes movement through a treatment sequence leading to some degree of resolution of the presenting problems. These are not intended to be permanent residences. This is "housing as treatment," not "housing as housing." These residences are an alternative to treatment in a more restrictive setting.

Transitional Housing Program. CC currently provides a total of 26 transitional beds in three separate residences. These residences are staffed round-the-clock; staff members work alone, living-in for 48 hour shifts. The transitional houses feature a 3-6 month stay and accommodate 8-10 residents. Emphasis is placed on careful assessment to identify and address specific behavior patterns which have interfered with successful community adjustment and which have contributed to residential instability. An important objective of this program is to improve matching to existing housing options upon discharge, based on the individual's need or tolerance for interpersonal contact and the level of structure and supervision required. Although the intended length of stay is 3-6 months, stays may extend as long as 24 months if indicated or if a suitable alternative cannot be located sooner. In order to be responsive to acute housing crises, however, we try to keep stays brief to assure that openings are available for those who might otherwise experience a return to literal homelessness.

Supported Independent Living (SIL & SIL-Plus). The supported independent living (SIL) program currently houses 120 individuals and has the capacity to expand flexibly as needed. SIL is the largest segment of the housing continuum, reflecting the desire most consumers express to live independently. While housing costs and the scarcity of rent subsidies mean that many people must share apartments with one peer, roughly one-third of those in the apartment program live alone in one-bedroom or efficiency apartments. Of those who share, most have their own bedrooms and live with roommates they have chosen themselves.

Within the supported independent living program, there are two distinct support levels. The majority (102) only receive brief weekly visits from one of the clinical coordinators (in addition to the supports they receive from their case managers). More support is available as needed during periods of difficulty or following a transition. A small minority of the residents in the independent living program receive more intensive support which is provided by staff who are on-site from 4 p.m. to midnight daily. Currently, 18 residents live in two separate rooming house settings which we refer to as the SIL-Plus program.

Within the continuum, the SIL units are closest to the "housing as housing" end of the spectrum. Supports are generally consumer-driven and are less frequent and intensive than elsewhere in the continuum. Here consumers enjoy a high degree of autonomy, and the rules are more or less the same as any other renter accepts. The rent has to be paid on time, neighbors' privacy rights have to be respected, and minimum standards for cleaning and upkeep of the units must be met.

Throughout the supported independent living program, clinical coordinators run weekly on-site meetings and conduct monitoring visits to individual apartments. On-site meetings focus on problem solving, household maintenance skills, and conflict resolution. Significant concerns are reported directly to the clinical case managers and supervisors involved as they arise. Additionally, emerging issues and persistent problems are identified and discussed in a weekly residential "rounds" meeting attended by all clinical staff. Support staff work in conjunction with case managers to obtain food stamps, housing subsidies (where available), and to coordinate the timely payment of rents and utilities. With the exception of six 2-person apartments funded with transitional housing dollars from HUD, all other apartments are permanent. The vast majority of units in the supported independent living program are clustered apartments in small buildings with 2-6 apartments located at scattered sites near the agency to maximize opportunities for staff and peer support while providing an independent living experience.

Permanent Staffed Group Homes. CC presently operates 3 permanent staffed residences each of which accommodates 6 residents. This level-of-care is for clients who need assistance with activities of daily living, medication management, and/or behavior management above the level ordinarily available to residents of privately operated community residence facilities. These residences are staffed 24 hours per day. One residential counselor is on duty at all times and is joined during peak hours by the second staff person. Both work under the supervision of the Clinical Coordinator. Behavior management issues are a focus of these residences. The goal of the program is primarily to accommodate the individual problems to a large extent while also seeking to maximize self-management of the behavioral and medical problems which led to referral in the permanent staffed residences.

CLINICAL HOUSING COORDINATORS

Each component within the housing continuum is supported by a clinical housing coordinator. The coordinators are master's level clinicians who provide specialized supports in housing and who work with primary case managers to prevent housing loss and to rapidly rehouse individuals who become displaced from housing. The clinical coordinators serve a number of key functions in housing, including: (a) initial assessment and recommendations about matching within the continuum; (b) individual service planning; (c) on-site assessment, monitoring and support; (d) supervision of residential support staff; (e) the development of social supports in housing; (f) crisis stabilization within an individual's current residence; (g) coordinating movement within the continuum, including the use of crisis/respite beds; and (h) advocacy with property management. The clinical housing coordinators are specialists in finding housing solutions, not merely gatekeepers who manage a discrete set of housing resources.

GOALS OF THE HOUSING CONTINUUM

The primary goal of the program is to prevent housing loss and to limit exposure to harm. Each component of the housing continuum has specific objectives and is intended to meet the unique needs of one or more subpopulations. However, the continuum-as-a-whole has a number of short-term and intermediate programmatic goals. Most people with prior homelessness and residential instability can be absorbed gradually into stable, high-quality housing if followed for sufficient periods of time. Intermediate goals include engagement and retention in mental health and related services, psychiatric stability, and decreased substance abuse. Long-term goals include achieving an optimal match to permanent housing with adequate, time-unlimited supports and improved quality of life.

PASSAGE THROUGH THE HOUSING CONTINUUM

A principal goal of the housing continuum is to promote stability through proactive planning, early identification of problems, an assertive system of supports, and integrated decision-making that involves all relevant parties. When problems arise, our goal is to obviate the need for any housing change. We first determine whether or not the crisis can be safely managed in the current housing situation through the addition of supports both on- and off-site. When it can, supports are added and then re-evaluated regularly, even daily, until the crisis resolves. When safety concerns require a change in the location, we first consider temporary moves either to hospital or to a Crisis Residence. Here the goal is to stabilize the situation sufficiently that the person is able to return to the prior residence, if they so desire. On return, additional supports are put in place and then gradually withdrawn, if appropriate. Sometimes a lateral move away from problematic network ties will work. At other times, a change in the level of residential care is indicated.

All housing changes are discussed in "housing rounds," a weekly forum co-led by the agency's clinical director and the clinical director for housing. All clinical housing coordinators and case management staff attend these meetings. Bringing all staff together facilitates early identification of emerging problems and allows us to formulate coordinated, strategic, individualized responses.

Stage of Treatment Considerations. Individualized planning is favored over uniform movement through the continuum. However, some broad generalizations and recommendations are possible. Particularly for persons with dual-disorders, housing support needs appear to change over time as a function of the stage of recovery. The recognition that substance abuse treatment and recovery occur in stages, an important, recent advance in dual diagnosis care, provides clinicians with a useful framework for selectively applying specific interventions at specific points in the recovery sequence (Drake et al., 1993). As noted earlier, we rely on the stage model outlined by Osher and Kofoed (1989) that describes treatment as proceeding along a dynamic yet predictable course involving the four stages of engagement, persuasion, active treatment and relapse prevention.

Housing responses are matched to the client's stage of treatment (Dixon and Osher, 1993). During the *engagement* stage, for example, the formation of an embryonic alliance often turns on the case manager's ability to address basic needs, securing access to decent, safe housing being chief among them. Clients are not yet engaged and have yet to experience abstinence for any length of time. Independent living in this phase, even with supports, is probably ill-advised. In our experience, clients generally failed in unsupervised apartments prior to reaching the active treatment phase. On the other hand, highly structured environments, though indicated, may not be accepted by clients in a pre-motivational stance. As a result, we sometimes need to locate transitional housing outside the mental health system or assist clients in finding other low demand environments. Rooming houses sometimes provide a modicum of safety and supervision, especially if a landlord or on-site manager is willing to provide some monitoring or at least to observe and report periodically on the client's activities.

As clients move into the *persuasion* stage, bonds between case managers and clients solidify and external structure may become more acceptable. Specialized transitional housing arrangements can serve an important role and seem to be accepted during the persuasion and active treatment phases at least in part because they are time-limited. Linking opportunities for more attractive independent housing to specified periods of abstinence can be powerfully persuasive (Dixon and Osher, 1993). Demonstrating to clients how their substance abuse restricts their housing options and has contributed to past residential instability helps to make substance use more ego-dystonic, a defining objective of the persuasion phase.

Somewhat surprisingly, many clients in the DC Dual-Diagnosis Project desired continued residential supervision even after achieving periods of abstinence of six months or longer, despite the fact that the active treatment and relapse prevention phases led to greater willingness by staff to explore independent options. A small cohort of individuals may require residential structure and supervision indefinitely because the internalization of controls seems not to occur as expected. Generally, though, clients in the *active treatment* and *relapse prevention* phases gradually lessen their dependence on external structure and controls. Opportunities for more flexible supports in ordinary housing are needed for clients in these latter stages as they become increasingly involved in other activities, such as work, while continuing to participate in office-based treatments designed to help them to cope with cravings, to refuse drugs, to recognize emotional and situational triggers, and to develop social ties that will reinforce abstinence.

Relapse Policy. To successfully meet the housing needs of the dually diagnosed, housing providers must bring admission and discharge policies in line with current knowledge about addictive disorders, chiefly, that they are chronic, remitting conditions of which relapse is a regular, expectable part. Exclusionary rules designed to keep mentally ill persons with addictive disorders out of housing are inappropriate, as are policies which impose uniform and automatic consequences for drug infractions.

Prescriptive policies, such as "three strikes, you're out!", are more likely to meet our needs as service providers–for order, predictability, simplicity–than those of the dual-disordered individuals we endeavor to serve. Clinical judgment must take precedence over administrative ease and individualized plans must be honored over the desire for absolute equity across all residents and situations. Rather than defining automatic "sentences," relapse policies can be most helpful when they establish "due process" rules to guide the decision-making process and identify a range of potential responses available to the unified housing/support team. Policies should also specify the kinds of assessment data needed for making sound decisions. Factors to be weighed in making housing decisions include: how well the individual is known to the system and the stage of treatment he has reached; the safety and security of the individual and other members of the immediate network; the length of abstinence prior to the current episode of use and whether it is judged to be a "slip" versus a downward spiraling pattern of relapse; the level of structure and support available within the existing residential setting; and, the presence or absence of problematic behavior frequently associated with substance abuse, such as stealing and fencing personal belongings and furnishings, threatening or violent behavior, prostitution, and other kinds of antisocial behavior.

It is important that we widen our focus and look beyond substance use *per se* to include use-related behavior and issues of manageability. Decisions are then both person- and situation-specific. For example, the policy we have adopted permits more flexibility within staffed residences than in independent apartments because light to moderate use often can be safely managed for individuals returning to controlled settings. By contrast, individualized plans for residents of supported apartments are often stricter, both because they are more difficult to enforce, and because use in an uncontrolled setting can escalate so rapidly to dangerous levels.

Stage considerations are given greatest weight when the individual's use is isolated and has little impact on others in the peer network. The case management team and the liaison retain a great deal of flexibility in determining the most appropriate response to episodic use. However, as the use escalates and is associated with more disruptive behavior or begins to involve others in the peer network, individual needs may be subordinated to system needs.

LESSONS LEARNED

We have a great deal more to learn and must continue to challenge our own, often unspoken, assumptions about what works and what doesn't. The program description provided here is drawn from a full length manual and reflects our current thinking about linking housing and supports to prevent homelessness. The process of developing the manual itself imposed a valuable discipline on us and required us to think about why we do what we do. It pushed us to articulate and make explicit our rationale for various practices. Frequently, we rediscovered sound reasons for certain conventions we had adopted. And sometimes we ended up abandoning practices that were out of sync with our own philosophy and mission. For example, current dangerousness or substance abuse are virtually the only factors that override client preference around housing. Part of this process is learning what we don't yet know how to do effectively and recognizing the limits of our current "technology." For example, we have learned that we cannot predict at the outset who will stabilize in housing quickly and who won't, which means we have to give everyone the best opportunity to succeed.

We have also learned something about the limits of flexibility and the importance of clear expectations. There is a fine line between flexibility and chaos. We place a very high premium on flexibility, but have found it increasingly necessary to structure the decision-making process. We have the freedom to depart from our own relapse policies in the housing network if we choose to, but we have to be able to justify departures from program guidelines. Developing a framework for thinking about difficult problems provides a common ground and serves to unify rather than divide staff whose goal is to provide a safety net that few will fall through. This work requires us to bring tremendous creativity to the business of finding housing solutions, whereas rigidity retards creative problem-solving, structure and clarity facilitate it.

We must also acknowledge that, for those at-risk for homelessness–due to recent homelessness or because of the presence of underlying factors such as co-occurring substance use disorder or traumatic violence that predispose people to housing loss–the threat persists for a very long time. Progress toward housing stability is in some ways analogous to progress toward substance abuse recovery: recovery occurs in dynamic stages which are marked by stage-specific needs and intervention strategies. The language of addictions encourages us to refer to someone as "recovering" rather than "recovered," suggesting that people may need services indefinitely to prevent a relapse, although their needs will obviously change over time. In the same way, people who are at-risk for homelessness will likely need supports indefinitely, although they will choose very different items from the menu as their requirements change.

REFERENCES

Baumohl J. (1989) Editor's introduction: Alcohol, homelessness, and public policy. *Contemporary Drug Problems, 16,* 281-300.

Bebout R.R., Drake R.E., Xie H., McHugo G.J., Harris M. (in press for July, 1997) Housing status among formerly homeless, dually-diagnosed adults in Washington, DC. *Psychiatric Services.*

Bebout R.R., Harris M. (1992) In search of 'pumpkin shells': Residential programming for the homeless mentally ill. In HR Lamb, LL Bachrach, FI Kass (Eds.), *Treating the Homeless Mentally Ill.* Washington, DC, American Psychiatric Association Press.

Blankertz L.E., Cnaan R.A. (1994) Assessing the impact of two residential programs for dually diagnosed homeless individuals. *Social Service Review, 68,* 536-560.

Burnam M.A., Morton S.C., McGlynn E.A., Petersen L.P., Stecher B.M., Hayes C., Vaccaro J.V. (1995) An experimental evaluation of residential and nonresidential treatment for dually diagnosed homeless adults. *Journal of Addictive Disorders, 14,* 111-134.

Carling P.J. (1993) Housing and supports for persons with mental illness: Emerging approaches to research and practice. *Hospital and Community Psychiatry, 44,* 439-449.

Caton C.L.M., Wyatt R.J., Felix A., Grunberg J., Dominguez B. (1993) Follow-up of chronically homeless mentally ill men. *American Journal of Psychiatry, 150,* 1639-1642.

Center for Mental Health Services (1994) Making a Difference: Interim Status Report of the McKinney Demonstration Program for Homeless Adults with Serious Mental Illness. Rockville, MD, Substance Abuse and Mental Health Services Administration.

Cohen M., Somers S. (1990) Supported housing: Insights from the Robert Wood Johnson Foundation Program on Chronic Mental Illness. *Psychosocial Rehabilitation Journal, 13,* 43-50.

Desmond M., Harris M., Bergman H.C. (1991) Crisis residential services. *T.I.E. Lines, 8,* 3-4.

Dickey B., Gonzalez O., Latimer E., Powers K., Schutt R., Goldfinter S. (1996) Use of mental health services by formerly homeless adults residing in group and independent housing. *Psychiatric Services, 47,* 152-158.

Dixon L.B., Krauss N., Meyers P., Lehman A. (1994) Clinical and treatment correlates of access to Section 8 certificates for homeless mentally ill persons. *Hospital and Community Psychiatry, 45,* 1196-1200.

Dixon L.B., Osher F.C. (1993) Housing people with severe mental illness and substance use disorders. *The Housing Center Bulletin, 2,* 3-10.

Drake R.E., Bartels S.J., Teague G.B., Noordsy D.L., Clark R.E. (1993) Treatment of substance abuse in severely mentally ill patients. *Journal of Nervous and Mental Disease, 181,* 606-611.

Drake R.E., Yovetich N.A., Bebout R.R., Harris M., McHugo G.J. (1997) Integrated treatment for homeless dually diagnosed adults. *Journal of Nervous and Mental Disease, 185,* 298-305.

Federal Task Force on Homelessness and Severe Mental Illness (1992) Outcasts on Main Street. Washington, DC, Interagency Council on the Homeless.

Fields S. (1990) The relationship between residential treatment and supported housing in a community system of services. *Psychosocial Rehabilitation Journal, 13*, 105-113.

Fischer P.J. (1990) *Alcohol and drug abuse and mental health problems among homeless persons: A review of the literature, 1980-1990*. Rockville, MD, National Institutes on Alcohol Abuse and Alcoholism.

Harris M., Bachrach L.L. (1988) *Clinical Case Management*. San Francisco: Jossey-Bass.

Hurlburt M.S., Hough R.L., Wood P.A. (1996) Effects of substance abuse on housing stability of homeless mentally ill persons in supported housing. *Psychiatric Services, 47*, 731-736.

Jerrel J.M., Ridgely M.S. (1995) Comparative effectiveness of three approaches to serving people with mental illness and substance abuse disorders. *Journal of Nervous and Mental Disease, 183*, 566-576.

Lamb H.R. (1980) Structure: the neglected ingredient of community treatment. *Archives of General Psychiatry, 37*, 1224-1228.

Lamb H.R., Lamb D.M. (1990) Factors contributing to homelessness among the chronically and severely mentally ill. *Hospital and Community Psychiatry, 41*, 301-305.

Lipton F.R., Nutt S., Sabatini A. (1988) Housing the homeless mentally ill: A longitudinal study of a treatment approach. *Hospital and Community Psychiatry, 39*, 40-45.

McHugo G.J., Drake R.E., Burton H.L. et al. (1995): A scale for assessing the stage of substance abuse treatment in persons with severe mental illness. *Journal of Nervous and Mental Disease, 183*, 762-767.

Morse G., Calsyn R., Allen G., Tempelhoff B., Smith R. (1992) Experimental comparison of the effects of three treatment programs for homeless mentally ill people. *Hospital and Community Psychiatry, 43*, 1005-1010.

Newman S.J., Ridgely M.S. (1994) Organization and delivery of independent housing for persons with chronic mental illness. *Administration and Policy in Mental Health, 21*, 199-216.

Osher F.C., Kofoed L.L. (1989) Treatment of patients with psychiatric and psychoactive substance abuse disorders. *Hospital and Community Psychiatry, 40*, 1025-1030.

Rahav M., Rivera J.J., Nutterbrock L., Ng-Mak D., Sturz E.L., Link B.G., Struening E.L., Pepper B., Gross B. (1995) Characteristics and treatment of homeless, mentally ill chemical-abusing men. *Journal of Psychoactive Drugs, 27*, 93-103.

Ridgway P., Zipple A.M. (1990) The paradigm shift in residential services: From the linear continuum to supported housing approaches. *Psychosocial Rehabilitation Journal, 13*, 11-31.

Wasylenki D.A., Goering P.N., Lemire D., Lindsey S., Lancee W. (1993) The hostel outreach program: Assertive case management for homeless mentally ill persons. *Hospital and Community Psychiatry, 44*, 848-853.

From Streets to Homes: The Pathways to Housing Consumer Preference Supported Housing Model

Sam Tsemberis, PhD
Sara Asmussen, PhD

SUMMARY. This paper describes essential elements of the Consumer Preference Supported Housing (CPSH) Model of homelessness prevention in use at Pathways to Housing, Inc. in New York City. This intervention prevents homelessness by engaging and housing homeless substance abusers with psychiatric disabilities whom other programs have rejected as "treatment resistant" or "not housing ready." The CPSH model is built on the belief that housing is a basic right for all people. As opposed to the housing continuum model, housing is based on consumer choice and is not connected to compliance or treatment. Housing is provided immediately, and there are separate criteria for housing and treatment needs. Support services are aimed at integration of mental health and substance abuse services.

In a randomized controlled study, individuals who are currently homeless and have psychiatric disabilities and/or substance abuse problems are randomly assigned to either the CSPH intervention or an intervention using the linear continuum model. Participants will be followed for a period of one year and the study will provide feedback

---

Sam Tsemberis is Executive Director and Sara Asmussen is Project Coordinator, both at Pathway to Housing, New York, NY.

Address correspondence to: Sam Tsemberis, Pathways to Housing, Inc., West 23rd Street, New York, NY 10011-2426.

Preparation of this chapter was funded in part by the Center for Substance Abuse and Mental Health Services Administration (SAMHSA) Grant # 1UD9SM51970.

[Haworth co-indexing entry note]: "From Streets to Homes: The Pathways to Housing Consumer Preference Supported Housing Model." Tsemberis, Sam and Sara Asmussen. Co-published simultaneously in *Alcoholism Treatment Quarterly* (The Haworth Press, Inc.) Vol. 17, No. 1/2, 1999, pp. 113-131; and: *Homelessness Prevention in Treatment of Substance Abuse and Mental Illness: Logic Models and Implementation of Eight American Projects* (ed: Kendon J. Conrad et al.) The Haworth Press, Inc., 1999, pp. 113-131. Single or multiple copies of this article are available for a fee from The Haworth Document Delivery Service [1-800-342-9678, 9:00 a.m. - 5:00 p.m. (EST). E-mail address: getinfo@haworthpressinc.com].

© 1999 by The Haworth Press, Inc. All rights reserved.

regarding the effectiveness of the CSPH model. *[Article copies available for a fee from The Haworth Document Delivery Service: 1-800-342-9678. E-mail address: getinfo@haworthpressinc.com]*

KEYWORDS. Consumer preference independent living (cpil), supported housing intervention, "housing as housing," assertive community treatment (act), harm reduction, representative payee

INTRODUCTION

The homelessness prevention program presented in this chapter, the Consumer Preference Supported Housing Model (CPSH), was developed by Pathways to Housing, Inc., a private non-profit social services organization in New York City. Pathways to Housing, Inc. was founded in 1992 to serve the most visible and underserved segment of New York's homeless population–persons with psychiatric disabilities and co-occurring substance use disorders who live on the streets, parks, subway tunnels, and other uninhabitable public places. The agency concentrates on individuals rejected by other housing programs due to refusal to participate in psychiatric treatment, active substance abuse, histories of violence or incarceration, and other behavioral personality disorders.

Pathways' CPSH program is the only one in the U.S. to offer homeless street dwelling individuals with dual diagnoses immediate access to independent apartments. The cornerstone of this intervention is the belief that housing is a basic right for all people. Unlike traditional housing programs, Pathways regards housing and treatment as two distinct domains with separate criteria for evaluation. Thus housing is not connected to compliance or treatment; however, every individual in the program receives support services or treatment from Pathways' Assertive Community Treatment (ACT) teams. The ACT teams are modeled after the original Stein and Test (1980) community based treatment teams and meet the majority of current program criteria for fidelity to ACT (Teague, Bond, & Drake, 1998), with some modifications to reflect the special needs of the agency's target population. This includes a significant number of peer counselors on the team and a nurse practitioner to tend to the numerous medical problems of this population. Consistent with many other aspects of the ACT model, the teams provide services to tenants in their new homes and communities, 24 hours a day, 7 days a week.

The CPSH program prevents homelessness by successfully engaging and housing a segment of the population that has resisted or been rejected by all other housing programs. This segment of the homeless population is often described as "treatment resistant" or not "housing ready" by other housing programs. In addition, the program prevents the cycle of recurring homelessness by achieving long-term housing stability through the provision of client centered, home/community based support services that are relevant to the tenants needs, such as rapid crisis intervention to avert unwanted hospitalizations, client-determined service plans, and a harm reduction approach to alcohol and substance use. The majority of clinical interventions are provided in the context of a radical acceptance of the point of view of the tenant.

This paper describes the essential ingredients of the CPSH model including the program's conceptual framework and logic model; a description of the concept mapping process that was used to obtain stakeholder perceptions; the logic model which resulted; a discussion of program effectiveness; and the lessons learned from the past five years of operation.

Foundation of the CPSH Model

To date, there have been no well-controlled randomized studies comparing different housing models to one another (Goldfinger et al., 1997); therefore, the CPSH program was developed based on findings from related studies, supported housing and psychiatric rehabilitation theoretical models, and years of clinical practice based on respect for individual's empowerment, and faith that tenants who had no previous experience can maintain independent apartments when provided with the right support. The model was developed by the first author after years of directing the Homeless Emergency Liaison Project (Project HELP), a large city-wide outreach psychiatric emergency team for street dwelling individuals with severe psychiatric disabilities (Katz, Sabatini, & Codd, 1993). In spite of Project HELP's best efforts to find housing for their clients, innumerable individuals continued to live on the streets (Tsemberis, Cohen, & Jones, 1993). A careful review of the mental health housing literature provides ample evidence that there are problems with the continuum of care housing model, the most widely used housing approach in the U.S.; problems with the fragmentation of mental health and substance abuse services; and very few programs where any attention is paid to consumer choice. The following is a brief synopsis of the existing literature in these areas.

HOMELESSNESS IN NEW YORK CITY

Homelessness in New York City has reached an all-time high. It is estimated that there are 100,000 to 120,000 homeless individuals in New York

City-approximately 50,000 to 80,000 homeless individuals are served by various social agencies during a one-year period with an additional 30,000 people on the street who receive no services (Barrow et al., 1989). Of the single adult homeless population, 25% to 37% exhibit serious mental disorders or have a history of psychiatric illness (Plapinger et al., 1988; Struening, 1987; Susser et al., 1988). These numbers clearly indicate that the existing system of care is simply ineffective for a large number of individuals who remain homeless and mentally ill.

HOUSING FOR INDIVIDUALS
WITH PSYCHIATRIC DISABILITIES

Most mental health systems have responded to the crisis of homelessness among individuals with mental illness by developing residential treatment programs. The prevailing treatment/housing model in the US is the linear continuum of care model. While the ultimate goal of this model is independent living, the environment fosters dependence. Residents have little choice or freedom concerning treatment or housing options and the move to independent housing may take years. Typically, a client is first placed in a residential treatment facility, such as a community residence, where he or she lives with others with similar levels of impairment or function, and by satisfying treatment goals set by staff may "graduate" to higher" levels in the continuum. Supervision and treatment is reduced along each step of this gradient, and programs are less structured and less restrictive (Bassuk & Lamb, 1986; Telson & Couco, 1993). It may take anywhere from one to five years to obtain independent housing through this model compared to days to several weeks in the CPSH model. Given that the continuum of care model has had a low success rate among the target population, CPSH was designed to resolve the barriers to housing for dually diagnosed individuals living on the streets.

Overall, consumers and researchers have attributed the model's low success rate to the following factors: (1) constant changes required by the continuum are very stressful for clients, demanding that clients abandon existing relationships formed in one setting only to start anew in another; (2) paradoxically, the changes along the continuum coincide with a decrease in staff support and treatment, in many cases it has proven unrealistic to expect people with psychiatric disabilities to fit into this highly structured linear progression; (3) skills learned for successful functioning for a structured congregate setting are not necessarily transferable to an independent living situation (Anthony & Blanch, 1989); (4) clients lack choices and freedoms, residential treatments offer standardized levels of care to which clients must adapt (Ridgway & Zipple, 1990); and (5) clients are placed into a level of supervised housing based on the decision of clinical staff and clients are afforded little privacy or control (Grunberg & Eagle, 1990).

Studies indicate that most consumers prefer to live independently (Owen et al., 1996; Shutt & Goldfinger, 1996). Many individuals prefer the relative independence of the streets to the structure of residential facilities (Howie the Harp, 1990). When consumers have a choice in housing options, this correlates with greater housing satisfaction, housing stability, and psychological well-being (Srebnik et al., 1995). In fact, numerous surveys indicate that consumers identify lack of income, not mental disability, as the main barrier to stable housing (Tanzman, 1993). In the CPSH model, the needs of the clients, from apartment and neighborhood selection to comprehensive service plans, are determined by the clients. There has been a national and state policy shift towards developing more of this type of supported housing (Carling, 1993); however, the CPSH program is one of the only operational models.

FRAGMENTATION OF SERVICES

There are systems variables which create an environment which may further foster homelessness. Fragmentation and lack of coordination between mental health, addiction, and housing services contribute to recurring homelessness (Oakley & Dennis, 1996). Mental health providers often assume that substance abuse providers are responsible for dually diagnosed individuals and vice versa. Housing programs are usually not even involved in this treatment process since the entire premise of the continuum of care model is that the person must first seek treatment to be "housing ready." Programs characterized by low demand and consumer driven approaches have not been widely used by traditional housing providers (Asmussen et al., 1994; Osher & Drake, 1996; Tsemberis, 1996; U.S. Dept. of HHS, 1994). Overall, research has shown that with adequate support services, even severely mentally ill persons can maintain stable housing (Brown et al., 1991; Livingston et al., 1992), even if they are substance abusers (Goldfinger, 1994). Other studies have shown that individuals are more willing to participate in and complete treatment for substance abuse if housed (Erickson et al., 1995).

Based on the barriers and weaknesses as described in the literature, the CPSH Model was developed on the following tenets: (1) homeless individuals with psychiatric disabilities can maintain independent housing of their choice with the right supports; (2) the consumer selects his/her own housing (apartment); (3) apartments are rented from landlords in the community and the landlord does not provide the support services; (4) clinical crises such as relapse to substance abuse or psychotic episodes, do not place the tenant at risk for losing his/her housing; (5) services are offered by an ACT team, in vivo, in the community, 24 hours a day; (6) type, frequency, and sequence of services is determined by the tenant; and (7) sobriety, medication compliance, or any other form of treatment is not a requirement, the staff use a harm reduction model for drug and alcohol abuse.

RELEVANT STUDIES

As stated earlier, there is a lack of controlled research in the field of housing which makes it difficult to assess the effectiveness of any model of housing. In an older analysis of the literature, continuum of care programs showed relatively little success in realizing the long-term goals of housing tenure and independent living. In a review of 109 studies on residential treatment facilities, no clear evidence for reducing symptoms, improving economic self-sufficiency, or community functioning were found (Cometa, Morrison & Ziskoven, 1979).

In a study conducted in Boston which assessed the effectiveness of the support systems used by two different supported housing programs, Goldfinger et al. (1997) randomly assigned and tracked 109 homeless individuals selected from the Department of Mental Health's shelter system to one of the two supported housing programs. At month 16, there was an 81% retention rate between the two groups, with 59% (n = 65) remaining in their original housing.

In another study of supported housing which examined the effectiveness of different case management models, Hough et al. (1997) randomly assigned 362 individuals from the San Diego area into one of four housing/case management groups. Across all four groups, at 18 months, 60% (n = 217) were still housed in independent living situations.

In an initial analysis of the existing data, over the past five years, the Pathways CPSH program has maintained 85% of all tenants who entered the program. In contrast, the continuum of care model in New York City that carefully selects out the very clients Pathways seeks to serve, reports the housing retention rate over the past 2 years at 60% (Tsemberis, 1996).

CONCEPT MAPPING

Representing the Views of the Program's Shareholders

In writing the manual that describes the CPSH program, it was essential to include the perspective of those who played an integral role in establishing and operating the program. This includes tenants, staff, and the board of directors. The concept mapping methodology developed by Trochin (1989) was adapted for the collection and analysis of data from these three groups. By examining the program descriptions offered by each of the groups, concept mapping allows for a representation of the key elements of agreement among the groups and the essential ingredients of the program can be identified and included in the manual and the logic model.

Different groups met individually to brainstorm assumptions, experiences, and approaches which operationally defined the topics as they related to the CPSH Model. Ideas were combined into lists resulting in 97 statements about the environment, 113 about supports, 30 about philosophy, and 72 conceptualizations about outcomes.

The groups then held an additional meeting where the ideas generated by all three groups were sorted and classified within each of the four domains. Each individual rated each statement as to its level of importance, accuracy or relativeness to the CPSH model. Data were entered into the Concept System8 computer software program. A total of 63 individuals consisting of staff, tenants, and board members participated in at least one of six meetings that served to drive the Concept Mapping process. By the end, 35 conceptual categories had been developed.

Logic Model

The Logic Model for the CPSH program was taken from the Concept Mapping exercise and is exhibited in Figure 1. The following is an explanation of the model.

Logic Model Inputs:
Population and Environment

The tenants currently in the program will be described in the Program Description section below. Resources available to tenants consist of benefit or entitlement systems from Federal, State, and City governments. Benefits/entitlements are often difficult to obtain and may be discontinued arbitrarily.

Logic Model Basis:
Theory and Assumptions

One of the basic assumptions of this model is that the tenants in this program consist of individuals who, although able to survive on the streets for long periods of time, are highly vulnerable to other stressors. Clients need access to housing and support services that do not make demands that compromise the individual's dignity or increase stigma. This group of individuals

FIGURE 1. Pathways to Housing, Inc.

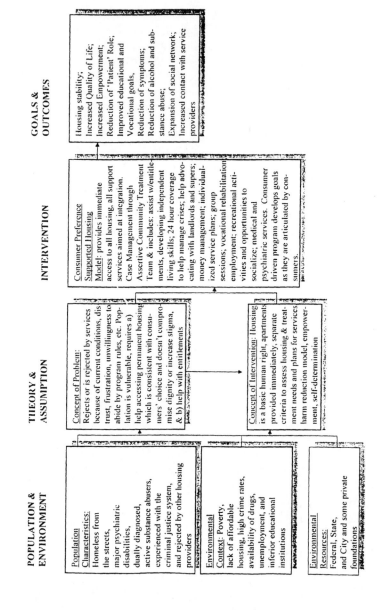

is somewhat distrustful and, as a whole, becomes easily frustrated by "rules and regulations." Many times, they simply leave situations in which they have housing, or they will lose their benefits, rather than deal with the frustration of dealing with a funding source.

Logic Model Thruput:
Intervention

More important than the specific interventions is the feeling and intention with which services are provided. The CPSH program interventions are comprised of numerous supported housing and ACT team services, comprising a conceptual framework that is an amalgamate of psychiatric rehabilitation, harm reduction, self-psychology, advocacy, and crisis intervention, among others, provided in an atmosphere that fosters the expression of love and respect and the creation of new possibilities. The specific services are listed in Figure 1.

Logic Model Output:
Goals and Outcomes

First and foremost is housing stability: to retain housing and prevent relapse into homelessness. Other outcomes can be sought such as increases in quality of life, empowerment, and obtaining needed services; reduction in the "patient" role, symptoms, alcohol and substance use; improvements in educational and vocational goals; and expansion of the social network. The outcomes for each tenant are individualized, based on the needs expressed by that person.

DESCRIPTION OF THE HOMELESSNESS PREVENTION INTERVENTION

Program Structure

A flexible program structure is central to the success of the CPSH program. The administration of the program, including the Board of Directors, fiscal operations, and clinical staff, are committed to the values of the program that emphasize consumer preference. Program staff have access to a flexible accounting system such that money is immediately available for emergencies without unnecessary paperwork. Program staff have flexibly scheduled hours and rotate the responsibility of on-call coverage. Funding sources must be informed about the program so that they are flexible regarding what expenses are reimbursable.

Eligibility Criteria for Admission to/Participation in the Program

Eligibility criteria for admission to Pathways' CPSH program are very simple. the individual must be homeless, must have a psychiatric disability that compromises their ability to function (active symptoms or history of hospitalization, primarily described by a DSM IV Axis I diagnosis), and during the first year of tenancy must be willing to meet with a service coordinator twice a month and participate in the money management program. There are no requirements for participation in psychiatric or substance use treatment, or in sobriety programs. A history of violence or prison time does not disqualify the applicant from entering the program.

CPSH Client Characteristics

In the CPSH program, all tenants are homeless and have psychiatric disabilities. Of the 218 current tenants, 79 are women (36%) and 139 are men (64%) with an age range of 18 to 51+ years. Of this group, 85 individuals (39%) have children, all of whom are in foster care or living elsewhere. Only 7% (n = 15) are married, 65% (n = 142) are single, 20% are divorced or widowed, and data are not available for 8% (n = 17) of the group. These numbers are suggestive of a disabled group and the 85% who are single or divorced closely matches the percentage found in other groups of people diagnosed with major mental illness. Thirty-six percent of the tenants (n = 79) were raised by someone other than their parents; 38 (17%) reported being sexually abused as children, and 55 (25%) reported being physically abused. Thirteen percent (n = 29) refused to answer these questions, so the numbers could be higher. Of those responding, 102 (47%) reported having been arrested and 82 (38%) reported being a victim of a crime.

The last place the person lived prior to entering the program was as follows: 65% living on the streets or using drop-in centers, 18% in shelters, 7% in treatment facilities, with the remainder in transitional hotels, the Y, or with friends. Levels of education and employment histories are consistent with other studies of psychiatrically disabled urban populations. Figures indicate a fairly disabled group with 77% receiving Medicaid and 67% receiving SSI.

Of the current tenants, 73% (n = 160) report past psychiatric hospitalizations. The diagnosis for this group are as follows: schizophrenia 52% (n = 113), mood disorders 27% (n = 59), other psychotic disorders 9% (n = 20), and other disorders including Axis II 13% (n = 28).

Finally, the most difficult numbers to obtain are those having to do with substance and alcohol abuse. Based on self-report, 36% (n = 78) of the tenants reported having actually received treatment for substance or alcohol abuse in the past, 9% (n = 33) reported that they currently abused substances, including alcohol. Staff, on the other hand, observed that 17% (n = 38) were currently actively using and overall, 60% of the tenants (n = 131) had been abusing drugs or alcohol within the past year. The high percentage of dually diagnosed tenants is consistent with estimates of dual diagnoses obtained from other samples of this population (U.S. Dept of HHS, 1994).

Staffing Selection and Staff Training

One of the most important aspects of staff recruitment is the establishment of cohesive teams of culturally diverse individuals who are creative, compassionate, and flexible and who have a willingness to put the needs of the tenants ahead of all other considerations. The most highly-rated staff characteristics in the Concept Mapping process was a "staff that is able to work inter-racially and inter-ethnically."

Gender composition of the 33 current staff at Pathways is 48% male and 52% female. Forty-two percent are African-American, 27% Caucasian, 24% Latino, 3% Asian-American, and 3% other. A total of five languages is spoken. Fifty percent of the staff are people in recovery, either from homelessness, substance abuse, or psychiatric disability.

Staff must be capable of understanding the need to attend to the spoken and unspoken needs of tenants. They must be able to separate societal and personal beliefs concerning mental illness and learn to listen to the needs of the individual with whom they are working. It is essential that the tenant be allowed to make his or her own mistakes. This was supported during Concept Mapping with the statement, "The program allows for every crisis to be an opportunity for growth," receiving a very high rating.

The harm reduction philosophy is one of the more controversial program practices and it is important for all staff to embrace this approach if it is to succeed. The CPSH harm reduction model offers an effective alternative to the prevailing 12-step program approach which may create problems for those individuals who are accustomed to enforcing strict behavior rules and sobriety. The statement, "The program does not require medication or sobriety compliance," was rating among the highest during Concept Mapping. The tenant who is actively using drugs or alcohol is offered a series of harm reduction objectives to reduce the harm that drug use causes in a manner that is supportive and empowering.

The staff characteristics which were rated quite high were, "a staff that can relate to people," "a staff that can work hands-on with people," and "a staff that is flexible." In part this is accomplished by careful selection of staff. Training is an ongoing process. Monthly in-service sessions encompass a variety of subjects including advocacy, managing benefits, domestic violence, preventing violence, legal issues, stress reduction, cultural sensitivity, and many others as well as presentations from Pathways' staff and tenants.

Training sessions range from traditional lecture presentations to on-site workshops offered by other agencies with compatible program approaches.

Other effective ways to increase staff effectiveness in the clinical application of the CPSH model are to provide staff support, ample and careful supervision, and staff retreats where work-related issues are discussed. Another support is the use of staff mutual support group session for staff to discuss work-related feelings and concerns. The support meeting is confidential and the team leader is not present.

Administrative Structure

Agency administration and leadership is always a challenge, especially when one is operating a service that challenges the prevailing views. The governance and decision-making process is a combination of hierarchical and collaborative. The Executive Director (ED), who reports to the Board of Directors, is also the agency's founder. He collaborates closely with the Board. The ED also meets with two management teams: the clinical management team comprised of the ACT Team Leaders and the Director of Programs and the Operations Team comprised of the Comptroller, Housing Director, Continuous Quality Improvement Director, and other relevant administrative staff.

Cost of Operating the Program

There has not been a formal cost analysis of the CPSH program. An estimate of program services during the 1997-1998 fiscal year was computed by dividing the total agency budget by the total number of funded apartments (including the current vacancies). The result is an estimated annual cost of $15,000 for the agency's share of the rent and support services for each apartment. To provide a context for this figure, the annual cost for a cot in a municipal shelter is $18,500 and the annual costs of congregate living supported housing ranges from $35,000 to $50,000. Though rudimentary, these figures strongly suggest that this supported housing program is a very reasonably priced intervention.

ACT Team Services

The Pathways ACT teams embody the philosophy and values of the organization's mission. Each tenant is assigned a case manager, but the entire team is involved in the planning and delivery of services. The primary case manager is responsible for charting and ensuring coordination of services, including referrals to other agencies. The team composition includes case managers who are often peer counselors or former consumers, a nurse, a psychiatrist, vocational rehabilitation counselor, social worker, drug counselor, and an administrative assistant. The team leader carries a small caseload, but the nurse, psychiatrist, and vocational rehabilitation counselor offer their services to all tenants referred by staff. When the team cannot provide the services directly, tenants are referred and escorted to the relevant programs including vocational training, psychosocial clubs, court appearances, job interviews, and medical and dental clinics. The type, frequency, and sequence of services is determined by the tenants. This flexibility is an essential ingredient to operate a program truly based on clients' preferences.

Housing

The goal is to obtain an apartment for the client as soon as possible. The three-person housing department keeps logs of all new acquisitions from brokers or landlords, lists new vacancies, and works closely with service coordinators to negotiate new tenant leases, complete Section 8 applications, and coordinate apartment repairs.

The agency leases two transitional apartments which can support two or three tenants at any one time and are always supervised by Pathways staff. The immediate access to these apartments is available for clients who have been accepted into the program, but have yet to find an apartment of their own. The other option for such temporary housing is using the local YMCA. In either case, tenants move out of transitional housing and into apartments of their own as an apartment is found. The average length of stay in a transitional apartment is 15 days for the small percentage of clients who cannot move directly into apartments of their own.

Money Management

Money management is part of the service coordinator's function. Money management is one of the two requirements for becoming a tenant of the Pathways CPSH program. This usually means that the tenant will make the agency a representative payee. This requirement is introduced at different points in time for individual tenants.

There are two major reasons for this requirement: (1) Pathways has the responsibility for paying the tenant's rent, including 30% of the tenant's income. Having a centralized banking system is much more efficient when such a large number of rents must be paid at the beginning of each month, and (2) money management ensures that tenants' utilities, food, and other essentials are provided for and, in instances of dually-diagnosed tenants, this service limits their expenditures for alcohol or drugs. The money management service is a central ingredient for effective homelessness prevention procedures with this tenant population.

After the rent is paid, a monthly budget is developed by the tenant and the service coordinator which meets the requirements set for Representative Payee responsibilities. Some tenants receive the entire balance of their funds while others may have weekly or biweekly budgets. Tenants receive monthly banking statements showing their deposits, credits, and balance for the month. The goal is for all tenants to eventually manage their own money after learning appropriate money management skills.

Comprehensive Service Plan (CSP)

The housing component is the first of ten domains addressed by the CSP. The remaining goal domains are education, vocation, mental health, physical health, alcoholism and substance abuse treatment, finances, self-care, social and family network/support, and other needs. The tenant selects the domains to be addressed, defines the objectives for each goal, and determines the rate of progress for each goal. After a period of time, not more than three months, the service coordinator and the tenant discuss the progress toward the goals and update the plan.

Exceptions to adhering to the plan occur in rare cases such as: (1) staff deems that the tenant is at risk to self or others; (2) legal constraints such as mandated services, including probation and conditional discharges are in place for the tenants; (3) rent or utility bills are not being paid by the tenant; (4) instances of violence; and (5) instances of child abuse.

Service Coordinators

The second program requirement is that the tenant agrees to meet with the service coordinator at least twice per month in the first year. The service coordinator is a member of the ACT team and shares the responsibility for the rotating on-call schedule. The purpose of the 24-hour, 7 days per week schedule is so that tenants will know they can obtain help whenever they need it. Another goal of the service coordinator is to provide and coordinate a comprehensive array of services determined by the tenant. These linkages are central to the success of the CPSH Model and there are many linkages already in place including individual providers and the numerous clinics and hospitals in the New York City area. The program places a strong emphasis on developing vocational opportunities and operates a tenant worker program. If a tenant enters long-term treatment, a psychiatric hospital, or jail, the service coordinator will continue to follow-up. The length of the intervention is as long as the tenant wishes it to be.

Evaluation

Finally, to assess the effectiveness of the Pathways CPSH Model as compared to other models of housing, a randomized, controlled study has been funded by SAMHSA and is currently underway. In this study, individuals who are currently homeless and have psychiatric disabilities and/or substance abuse addictions are randomly assigned to either the CPSH intervention or an intervention using the linear continuum model. The participants will be followed for a period of at least one year and the study will provide feedback regarding the effectiveness of the CPSH model, as well as for whom the model is most effective.

LESSONS LEARNED AND RECOMMENDATIONS

The lessons learned and recommendations made after operating the program for the past five years are presented separately for the areas of program/clinical issues, housing, and financial.

Program/Clinical Issues

1. The most important and exciting discovery of operating the Pathways CPSH program is that individuals who are homeless, living on the streets, in parks and other public places, who have severe psychiatric disabilities and/or substance abuse problems can be successfully housed in independent apartments with support services. However, it should not be assumed that because some people have successfully survived the hardships of life on the streets, those same people will not need assistance managing their new household.
2. The relationship between psychopathology, substance abuse, and level of functioning is not as strong as assumed by most clinicians and housing providers. People with a host of psychiatric symptomatology, as well as alcohol and drug addictions, can handily demonstrate the skills necessary for living in an apartment.
3. Treatment participation and housing tenure are achieved more effectively when the tenant determines the conditions under which to participate. Tenants should have a right to treatment and a right to refuse treatment.
4. The Assertive Community Treatment (ACT) team model serves as an excellent clinical support for the CPSH program.
5. Staff composition should include approximately 50% consumer representation (peer counselors, people in recovery, etc.) to serve as role

models and embody the empowerment model espoused by the program.
6. Vocational rehabilitation is an essential program component, if independence and community integration are the long-term goals. Immediately after moving into an apartment, tenants are more likely to seek paid employment rather than treatment.
7. Harm reduction and other substance treatment models that allow for prevention are effective treatment strategies for dually diagnosed individuals.

Housing

1. Housing and treatment must be regarded as separate domains.
2. It is useful to have several transitional apartments (or the local YMCA) in order to provide immediate access to safe and comfortable housing for eligible tenants while they await a place of their own.
3. The scattered-site model has several important advantages: (a) landlords are surprisingly welcoming of program tenants because they are assured of regular rent payments; (b) there is no required bureaucracy, that is, no community board approval, zoning, Not in My Back Yard (NIMBY), etc.; and (c) it is most effective at community integration when no more than 15% of the units in any building are rented by program tenants.

Financial

1. The program accounting department must be flexibly structured in order to be able to issue checks for emergency housing and other urgent client needs as necessary.
2. The money management component should operate like a bank, including providing tenants with monthly statements.

In summary, the Pathways program has provided a unique opportunity for tenants and staff to participate in an exciting and courageous program with results that demonstrate that when we look beyond psychopathology and focus on person remarkable accomplishments are possible.

> They took me around and showed me some apartments. It was wonderful coming out of the jungle and into success. This is a successful program. They do want to help people get their lives together. They turned me around and made me see there is somebody that cares about another individual.
>
> *R. G., East Harlem ACT Team tenant*

REFERENCES

Anthony, W.A., & Blanch, A. (1989). Research on community support services: What have we learned? *Psychosocial Rehabilitation Journal, 12,* 55-81.

Asmussen, S.M., Romano, J., Beatty, P., Gasarch, L., & Shaughnessey, S. (1994). Old answers for today's problems: Helping integrate individuals who are homeless with mental illnesses into existing community-based programs. *Psychosocial Rehab Journal,* 17, 17-34.

Barrow, S.M., Hellman, F., Lovell, A.M., Plapinger, J.D., & Struening, E.L. (1989). Effectiveness of programs for the mentally ill homeless. Final report submitted by the NYS Psychiatric Institute Community Support Systems Evaluation Program.

Bassuk, A.K. & Lamb, H.R. (1986). Homelessness and the implementation of deinstutionalization. *New Directions for Mental Health Service,* 30, 7-14.

Brown, M.A., Ridgway, P., & Anthony, W.A. (1991). Comparison of outcomes for clients seeking and assigned to supported housing services. *Hospital and Community Psychiatry,* 42, 1150-1153.

Carling, P.J. (1993). Housing and supports for persons with mental illness: Emerging approaches to research and practice. *Hospital and Community Psychiatry,* 44, 439-449.

Cometa, M.S., Morrison, J.K., & Ziskoven, M. (1979). Halfway to where? A critique of research on psychiatric halfway houses. *Journal of Community Psychology,* 7, 23-27.

Elizur J. & Minuchin, S. (ND). *Institutionalizing madness: Families, therapy, and society.* New York: Basic Books Publishing.

Erickson, J.R., Stevens, S., McKnight, P., & Figueredo, A.J. (1995). Willingness for treatment as a predictor of retention and outcomes. *Journal of Addictive Diseases,* 14, 135-150.

Goldfinger, S.M., Schutt, R.K., Tolomicenko, G.S, Tuner, W.M. et al. (1997). Housing persons who are homeless and mentally ill: Evolving consumer households In W.R. Breakley & J.W. Thompson (Eds.) *Mentally ill and homeless: Special programs for special needs.* Amsterdam: Harwood Academic Publishers.

Goldfinger, S.M. (1994). The Boston project: Promoting housing stability and consumer empowerment. In *Making a difference: Interim status report of the McKinney research demonstration program for mentally ill adults.* Washington, DC: Center for Mental Health Services, Substance Abuse and Mental Health Services Administration, US Department of HHS.

Grunberg, J. & Eagle, P. (1990). Shelterization: How the homeless adapt to shelter living. *Hospital and Community Psychiatry,* 41, 521-525.

Hough, R. L., Harmon, S., Tarke, H., Yamashiro, S. et al. (1997). Supported independent housing: Implementation issues and solutions in the San Diego project. In W.R. Breakley & J.W. Thompson (Eds.) *Mentally ill and homeless: Special programs for special needs.* Amsterdam: Harwood Academic Publishers.

Howie the Harp (1990). Independent living with support services: The goals and future for mental health consumers. *Psychosocial Rehabilitation Journal,* 13, 85-89.

Katz, S.E., Sabatini, A., & Codd, C. (1993). The homeless initiative and project HELP: Historical perspectives and program description. In S.E. Katz, D. Nardacci, & A. Sabatini (Eds.) *Intensive treatment of the homeless mentally ill.* Washington, DC: American Psychiatric Press, Inc.

Livingston, J.A., Srebnik, D., & King, D.A. (1992). Approaches to providing housing and flexible supports for people with psychiatric disabilities. *Psychosocial Rehabilitation Journal*, 16, 27-43.

Livingston, J.A., Srebnik, D., King, D.A., & Gordon, L. (1992). Approaches to providing housing and flexible supports for people with psychiatric disabilities. *Psychosocial Rehabilitation Journal*, 16, 27-43.

Oakley, D. & Dennis, D.L. (1996). Responding to the needs of homeless people with alcohol, drug, and/or mental disorders. In J. Baumohls (Ed.) *Homelessness in America* (pp. 179-186). Washington, DC: Oryx Press.

Osher, F.C., & Drake, R.R. (1996). Reversing a history of unmet needs: Approaches to care for persons with co-occurring addictive and mental disorders. *American Journal of Orthopsychiatry*, 66, 4-11.

Owen, C., Rutherford, V., Jones, M., Wright, C., Tennant, C., & Smallmann, A. (1996). Housing accommodation preferences of people with psychiatric disabilities. *Psychiatric Services*, 47, 628-632.

Plapinger, J., Gounis, K., & Dennis, D.L. (1988). The development of the residential placement management program: Issues and implications for housing mentally ill homeless persons. Final report submitted in accordance with the Office of Mental Health, contract #C001917 with the Research Institute, Philadelphia, PA.

Ridgway, P., & Zipple, A.M. (1990). The paradigm shift in residential services: From the linear continuum to supported housing approaches. *Psychosocial Rehabilitation Journal*, 13, 20-31.

Schutt, R.K., & Goldfinger, S.M. (1996). Housing preferences and perceptions among homeless mentally ill persons. *Psychiatric Services*, 47, 381-386.

Srebnik, D., Livingston, J., Gordon, L., & King, D. (1995). Housing choice and community success for individuals with serious and persistent mental illness. *Community Mental Health Journal*, 31, 139-152.

Stein, L.I., & Test, M.A. (1980). Alternative to mental hospital treatment: I. Conceptual model, treatment program, and clinical evaluation. *Archives of General Psychiatry*, 37, 392-397.

Struening, E.L. (1987). A study of residents of the New York City shelter system. Reported supported by contracts #85206/86206 with the NYC DMHMRAS.

Susser, E., Struening, E.L., & Conover, S. (1988). Psychiatric problems of homeless men in NYC shelters. Epidemiology of Mental Disorders Research Department. CSS Evaluation Program, NYS Psychiatric Institute.

Tanzman, B. (1993). An overview of surveys on mental health consumers preferences for housing and support services. *Hospital and Community Psychiatry*, 44, 450-455.

Teague, G.B., Bond, G.R,. & Drake, R.E. (1998). Program fidelity in assertive community treatment: Development and use of a measure. *American Journal of Orthopsychiatry*, 68, 2, 216-232.

Telson, H.W. & Cuoco, L.F. (1993). Innovative community living: The continuing treatment program. In S.E. Katz, D. Narducci, & A. Sabatini (Eds.) *Intensive treatment of the homeless mentally ill.* Washington, DC: American Psychiatric Press, Inc.

Trochim, W. (1989). Outcome pattern matching and program theory. *Evaluation and Program Planning*, 4, 355-366.

Tsemberis, S (1996). From outcasts to community: A support group for homeless men. In M. Adronico (Ed.) *Working with men in groups* (pp. 39-45). Washington, DC: APA Press.

Tsemberis, S., Cohen, N. L., & Jones, R. (1993). Conducting emergency psychiatric evaluations on the street. In S. Katz, D. Nardacci, & A. Sabatini (Eds.) *Intensive Treatment of the Homeless Mentally Ill* (pp. 71-89). Washington, DC: American Psychiatric Press, Inc.

U.S. Department of Health and Human Services (1994). *CMHS making a difference: Interim status report of the McKinney demonstration program for homeless adults with serious mental illness.* Washington, DC: DHHS Publication No. (SMA) 94-3014 SAMHSA.

Project H.O.M.E.: A Comprehensive Program for Homeless Individuals with Mental Illness and Substance Use Disorders

Kathleen Coughey, PhD
Kelly Feighan, BA
Karlene Lavelle, MPA, RN
Kristen Olson, MA
Maureen DeCarlo, MSW
Monica Medina

SUMMARY. Project H.O.M.E. (Housing Opportunities, Medical Care and Education) is an innovative, multi-faceted homelessness prevention program in Philadelphia, PA, designed to reduce individual, community/neighborhood and societal risk factors for the recurrence of homelessness among individuals with severe mental illness and/or substance use disorders. Tailored to the needs and abilities of each individual,

---

Kathleen Coughey is Senior Research Associate, Kelly Feighan is Research Assistant and Karlene Lavelle is Research Associate, all at the Philadelphia Health Management Corporation, 260 S. Broad Street, Philadelphia, PA 19102. Kristen Olson is Project Manager Analyst with the Rehabilitation Institute of Chicago, 345 E. Superior, Chicago, IL 60611. Maureen DeCarlo, Co-Director of Residential Services and Monica Medina, Director of Development are with Project H.O.M.E., 1515 Fairmont Avenue, Philadelphia, PA 19130.

[Haworth co-indexing entry note]: "Project H.O.M.E.: A Comprehensive Program for Homeless Individuals with Mental Illness and Substance Use Disorders." Coughey, Kathleen et al. Co-published simultaneously in *Alcoholism Treatment Quarterly* (The Haworth Press, Inc.) Vol. 17, No. 1/2, 1999, pp. 133-148; and: *Homelessness Prevention in Treatment of Substance Abuse and Mental Illness: Logic Models and Implementation of Eight American Projects* (ed: Kendon J. Conrad et al.) The Haworth Press, Inc., 1999, pp. 133-148. Single or multiple copies of this article are available for a fee from The Haworth Document Delivery Service [1-800-342-9678, 9:00 a.m. - 5:00 p.m. (EST). E-mail address: getinfo@haworthpressinc.com].

© 1999 by The Haworth Press, Inc. All rights reserved.

Project H.O.M.E. uses a combination of prevention strategies that includes street outreach, three levels of housing, extensive on-site services (education, employment, health care, addictions counseling, and social activities) and linkages to other services. Project H.O.M.E. also advocates for the homeless population through political activism. *[Article copies available for a fee from The Haworth Document Delivery Service: 1-800-342-9678. E-mail address: getinfo@haworthpressinc.com]*

KEYWORDS. Strength-based treatment, client-based case management, comprehensive program, housing continuum model, "housing as treatment"

INTRODUCTION

During the 1980s, a complex set of social, political and economic factors led to a widespread and significant increase in homelessness across the country. At the same time, these factors created a dramatic change in the composition of the homeless population, which shifted from a generally homogenous group of elderly, alcoholic males to a heterogeneous mix of individuals and families confronting poverty, substance use, and mental illness. Homelessness, for many, became an unbreakable cycle. As the social services system began to address the issue, it became clear that short-term, symptomatic treatment of homelessness would not provide a solution to such a large and complex social problem. Moreover, conventional approaches to ameliorating the plight of homelessness proved inadequate for individuals with severe mental illness and/or substance use disorders.

In the past 15 years, information accumulated through epidemiologic and social science research has increased our understanding of the unique characteristics, as well as the health and social service needs of the mentally ill and substance-using homeless population. Researchers have also begun to document the types and combinations of strategies effective in treating the causes and consequences of homelessness. One promising program is Project H.O.M.E. (Housing, Opportunities, Medical Care and Education), a not-for-profit organization that uses a combination of prevention strategies to combat the problem of homelessness. As a model of homelessness prevention, Project H.O.M.E. uses a client-centered approach to provide a range of housing and services that are tailored to each person's needs and abilities. This paper describes in detail the theory, structure, and implementation of this multi-faceted program so that this information can be used by policymakers, program planners and service providers in their efforts to break the cycle of homelessness.

REVIEW OF THE LITERATURE

Homelessness prevention can be understood as facilitating the recovery and retention of stable housing by reducing individual, community/neighborhood, and structural or societal risk factors for homelessness as well as increasing protective factors (Lezak and Edgar, 1996). Approaches that address individual risk factors of homelessness include the development of permanent and transitional housing, employment opportunities, health care, education and training, social services, prevention programs, advocacy and self-help (Stoner, 1989; Johnson and Cnaan, 1995; Lezak and Edgar, 1996). Furthermore, long-range case management services, in conjunction with service brokerage and resource allocation are essential to the amelioration of individual risk factors associated with mental illness (Johnson and Cnaan, 1995).

Programs designed to reduce community/neighborhood risk factors for homeless mentally ill and dually-diagnosed persons are often directed toward improving the system of service delivery (Lezak and Edgar, 1996). Strategies to improve the delivery of services include planning for discharge from psychiatric facilities, preparing for post-incarceration release, combining drug and mental health treatment for dually-diagnosed persons, assigning specialists in dual diagnosis to psychiatric emergency rooms, and providing substance use expertise to mental health teams (Fischer and Breakey, 1991). Strategies to reduce community/neighborhood risk factors for homelessness also focus on the surrounding areas in which at-risk, precariously-housed persons live. Programs that revitalize neighborhoods by rehabilitating houses, assisting residents with home ownership and financial management, and providing employment and educational opportunities can be effective in preventing homelessness. Other programs that target community/neighborhood risk factors focus on enhancing community support systems to reduce the stigma of mental illness and substance use disorders by providing family supports and integrating the individual into a community. Community integration can address personal needs while also creating interest groups that foster collective power (Cohen et al., 1991).

Prevention programs developed to address structural or societal risk factors for homelessness are often aimed at increasing affordable housing options (Lezak and Edgar, 1996; Stoner, 1989). Some initiatives have involved the financing of new housing through bond sales and encouraging the creation of new housing by private developers. Other strategies have provided loans to developers for the construction of supportive housing for individuals with mental illness, recognizing that many homeless people need treatment, support services and rehabilitation (Ridgway et al., 1994).

The number of comprehensive homelessness prevention programs that address all three levels of risk among individuals with mental illness has increased over the past 15 years, and researchers have found that many of these programs have enabled individuals to meet housing, treatment and service needs more conveniently (Auerbach, Beckerman, and Levitt, 1990). Programs that adopt a holistic approach to meet the diverse needs of homeless individuals have been found to be more successful in preventing homelessness and its recurrence (Stoner, 1989). By providing a wide range of housing options along with support and services, these needs can be better met, particularly among the mentally-ill homeless population (Dennis et al., 1991).

Project H.O.M.E. addresses individual risk factors by providing street outreach, three levels of housing, extensive services (case management, education, employment and advocacy programs) and linkages to health care, mental health treatment, and drug and alcohol treatment. At the community/neighborhood level, Project H.O.M.E. staff work to establish close working relationships with neighbors, local businesses and community-based organizations in order to revitalize neighborhoods, a critical component of homelessness prevention. At the structural, or societal, level, the organization constructs new housing units for future occupancy and advocates for changes in public policies that effect low income persons and those who are homeless.

HISTORY OF PROJECT H.O.M.E.

Homeless advocate, Sister Mary Scullion, began conducting street outreach in the late 1970s when homelessness was increasing rapidly in Philadelphia and other major metropolitan areas. She and a team of activists compiled lists of homeless persons they encountered on the street, many of whom were mentally ill and had "fallen through the cracks" of the social services system. Scullion found that many previously non-compliant individuals could be engaged and brought indoors when treated with dignity, prompting her to open Women of Hope, a low-demand residence for homeless women with mental illness. Scullion also opened a temporary men's winter shelter and found that many of the residents obtained stable housing and enrolled in mental health and drug treatment programs during their shelter stay. The organizational groundwork for Project H.O.M.E. was forged during this time, and Scullion turned her focus to creating permanent supportive housing for chronically homeless persons with special needs.

In 1990, Project H.O.M.E. opened a transitional residence for men seeking recovery from substance use disorders, providing residents with educational and employment programs. That same year, the organization began coordinating street outreach for the City of Philadelphia and was awarded a grant from the Department of Housing and Urban Development (HUD) to open 48 units of permanent supportive housing. Despite receiving this substantial grant and raising development funds, Project H.O.M.E. became embroiled in a highly-publicized political and legal battle that impeded development of this residence until 1994. A citywide media debate ensued over the fair housing rights of people with disabilities; however, Project H.O.M.E. ultimately maintained the legal right to open the residence. Occupancy at this controversial facility began in 1996.

During the 1990s, Project H.O.M.E. opened a total of ten sites with 242 units of supportive housing, two community centers, and three businesses that provide residents with hands-on job training and long-term employment. A variety of educational and recreational programs were also instituted. In early 1992, Project H.O.M.E. recognized the need to work with surrounding communities to prevent homelessness and responded by first opening an after-school program for neighborhood youth. Later, staff, volunteers and neighbors collaborated to rehabilitate abandoned houses and to beautify vacant open areas; staff also provided home ownership consultation and money management advice. In 1994, Project H.O.M.E. expanded and formalized its commitment to neighborhood development by participating in *The Philadelphia Plan,* a ongoing citywide partnership of low-income residents, nonprofit organizations, government, and corporations whose mission is to revitalize impoverished communities. The organization's latest innovative endeavor is the construction of housing units for women and children scheduled to open in the Fall of 1998.

PROJECT H.O.M.E. ELIGIBILITY CRITERIA

Project H.O.M.E. defines their target population using HUD's definition of homelessness. According to HUD's criteria, an individual is considered homeless if he/she (1) lacks a fixed, regular, and adequate nighttime residence or (2) resides in a publicly- or privately-operated shelter or any other facility designated to provide temporary living situations. In addition to these criteria, individuals must also have a diagnosis of severe mental illness or substance use disorder to be considered eligible for residency at Project H.O.M.E. Eligibility may be established during street outreach and intake assessments, however, many residents are referred through local mental health agencies where individuals with a history of homelessness and mental illness or substance use disorders are undergoing treatment.

CHARACTERISTICS OF PROJECT H.O.M.E. RESIDENTS

Socio-demographic and clinical characteristics of Project H.O.M.E. residents are presented for the seven month period between July 1, 1997 and January 31, 1998 (see Table 1). Data indicate that over two-thirds (72%) of

TABLE 1. Demographic and Clinical Characteristics of Project H.O.M.E. Residents, July 1, 1997–January 31, 1998

Race	Number	Percent	Income Sources*	Number	Percent
African American	232	72%	Employment**	57	18%
White	89	27%	SSI/SSDI	184	57%
Hispanic	3	1%	DPA	49	15%
Gender			Other Income	25	8%
Male	202	63%	No Income	51	16%
Female	118	36%	Unknown	8	1%
Unknown	4	1%	*Diagnosis*		
Age			Drug and Alcohol Addiction	56	17%
18-34	50	15%	Mental Illness	134	41%
35-59	212	66%	Dual Diagnosis	132	41%
60+	58	18%	Unknown	2	1%
Unknown	4	1%	*Unduplicated Residents*	324	

* Categories are not mutually exclusive
** Includes full and part-time employment

the population are African American and just over one-quarter (27%) are White. Only 1% of the residents are of Hispanic origin and there are no Asian residents. Over one-half of the residents (63%) are men. Two-thirds of the men and women are between 35 and 59 years old and 15% are over 60 years of age. About two-thirds (57%) of Project H.O.M.E. residents receive income from Social Security or Disability and 15% from public assistance. Eighteen percent receive income from either part-time or full-time employment, while 16% receive no income. Staff report that 41% of the residents have severe mental illness, 41% have substance use disorders in conjunction with severe mental illness and 17% have substance use disorders only.

LOGIC MODEL DESCRIPTION

The program logic model (see Figure 1) illustrates how Project H.O.M.E. addresses individual, community/neighborhood and societal risks of homelessness. The complex model is intended to elucidate the organization's social context, mission and philosophy by highlighting its: (1) social environ-

FIGURE 1. Project H.O.M.E. Program Logic Model

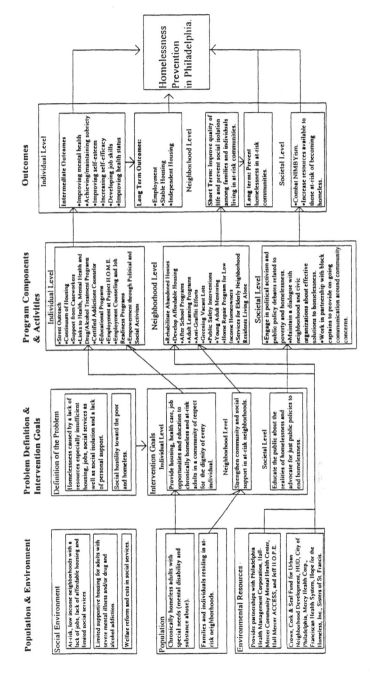

ment, population and resources; (2) definition of the problem, or root causes, of homelessness; (3) intervention goals; (4) program components and activities; and (5) desired outcomes. The remainder of this paper describes Project H.O.M.E. using the logic model as outlined.

POPULATION AND SOCIAL ENVIRONMENT

Project H.O.M.E. residences are located in at-risk, low income neighborhoods that lack jobs, affordable housing and services. A majority of the facilities are located in Lower North Philadelphia neighborhoods, where poverty is endemic. A recent report (Philadelphia Health Management Corporation, 1994) provides a descriptive profile of the population and social environment in which Project H.O.M.E. operates. Over one-third (39%) of families in this community live in poverty, half of whom (53%) have children under 18 years of age. Nearly three-quarters of residents are African American (72%). The median household income ($18,300), is significantly lower than the City as a whole ($30,900). Unemployment among residents in Lower North Philadelphia (18%) is almost double the percentage for the city (9.7%) and the overall level of residential stability is low, with fewer stable housing units, fewer owner-occupied houses and almost double the amount of vacant or abandoned houses (21%) than in the City overall (11%). Not surprisingly, the depressed economic conditions in this community are also reflected in the poor health status of neighborhood residents. Low birth weight, infant mortality, and adolescent fertility rates are the highest in Philadelphia. In addition, this community has the highest annual mortality rate (1,145.4 deaths per residents) in the city, a rate which is significantly higher than Philadelphia as a whole (740.1), Pennsylvania (519.7) and the United States (515.1).

The severity of problems in this community is compounded by a lack of supportive housing specifically designed for adults with severe mental illness and/or substance use disorders. Numerous homeless shelters exist in this community, however few offer services to the mentally ill and substance-using populations Project H.O.M.E. was established to serve. Although resources for neighborhood residents are scarce, Project H.O.M.E. has been able to marshal a variety of resources from the community such as a strong volunteer base and partnerships with a number of organizations to bring services into their residences. Project H.O.M.E. works closely with medical professionals and clinicians from local mental health centers, not-for-profit organizations and health systems who provide regular on-site medical care, and physical and occupational therapy.

Project H.O.M.E. relies on a mix of funding from both private and public sources. Public sources include the U.S. Department of Housing and Urban

Development and the City of Philadelphia. Private monies come from Crown Cork & Seal, The Pew Charitable Trusts, Mercy Health Corporation, Franciscan Health System, Hope for the Homeless, Inc., the Sisters of St. Francis, Connolly Foundation, Independence Foundation, and numerous other local foundations.

Staff working in Philadelphia Health Management Corporation's (PHMC) Health Care for the Homeless Program have facilitated health care services for Project H.O.M.E. residents through many other community agencies. PHMC's community health nurse, funded through The Pew Charitable Trusts Vulnerable Adults program, has developed health promotion programs for Project H.O.M.E. residents with the help of agencies such as Weight Watchers Corporation, the American Cancer Society (Fresh Start Smoking Cessation Program) and the Restaurant School (food shopping and preparation). PHMC also provides special programs such as a Women's Health Day which offers mammograms and health screenings for women living in Project H.O.M.E. residences.

PROBLEM DEFINITION

Project H.O.M.E. defines homelessness as a complex problem caused by multiple overlapping social, economic and political influences such as insufficient low-income housing, employment opportunities, and social services, as well as social isolation and a lack of personal support. In addition, symptoms of serious mental illness and substance use disorder increase one's vulnerability to homelessness by causing or exacerbating problems with managing activities of daily living and placing a strain on family and social relationships. Mental health and drug treatment service systems also contribute to the problem of homelessness when service providers release individuals without adequately planning for the housing and social support that an individual will need upon discharge. Finally, Project H.O.M.E. also views the problem of homelessness as an outgrowth of social hostility towards low-income persons and the stigmatization of mental illness resulting in the formulation of punitive public policies.

INTERVENTION GOALS

Project H.O.M.E.'s homelessness prevention strategies address individual, community/neighborhood, and societal causes of homelessness. Project H.O.M.E. reduces individual risks among chronically homeless, mentally ill and/or addicted individuals by providing three levels of housing and multiple supportive services. Specifically, Project H.O.M.E.'s goals to reduce the risk of homelessness for individuals include providing appropriate, affordable housing, case management, health care, as well as educational and employment opportunities. At the community/neighborhood level, the goals are to strengthen the community and social supports in at-risk neighborhoods. Finally, societal-level intervention goals are to educate the public about the realities of homelessness and advocate for equitable legislation and social policies affecting homeless persons.

PROGRAM COMPONENTS AND ACTIVITIES

Individual Level

Street Outreach. Outreach is a cornerstone of Project H.O.M.E.'s intervention, as it opens the door to needed housing and services for those living on the street. The primary purpose of outreach is to establish a trusting relationship with homeless individuals by using a process of engagement characterized by active listening, sensitivity, and respect for individuals' rights and decisions. For persons with substance use disorders, outreach workers focus on motivations for recovery when appropriate.

Project H.O.M.E. manages the City of Philadelphia's Outreach Coordination Center (OCC). The OCC coordinates four outreach teams, one of which is comprised of Project H.O.M.E. staff, a resident peer outreach worker, and a nurse practitioner who identifies and responds to medical needs. The other teams consist of individuals with expertise in the areas of mental health and substance use as well as members from the Office of Emergency Shelter Services and the police who help transport individuals to shelters on "Code Blue" nights when the windchill is 10 degrees or less and homeless persons are urged to go inside.

Appropriate placements are key to the success of outreach efforts. Individuals who enter programs incompatible with their needs and abilities tend to return to the streets. These individuals will be less trusting of future contacts with outreach workers, which exacerbates the difficulty of performing effective outreach. Outreach staff assure appropriate placement by offering homeless individuals information about housing options, rules and regulations and providing introductions to on-site staff.

Continuum of Housing. Project H.O.M.E. has three levels of housing: safe havens (entry-level shelters), highly supportive residences (transitional housing), and minimally supportive residences (independent living facilities). The sequence of the intervention generally begins at safe havens and ends at independent living; however, residents can move from a more independent living situation to a more supportive one during periods of relapse. Residents are encouraged to move toward higher levels of independence, but progress through the program at their own pace, and may stay at any of the housing facilities for as long as necessary.

Safe havens are entry-level residential facilities designed for severely mentally ill or dually-diagnosed individuals who require intensive supervision, support and structure. Staff are available 24 hours a day. Residents are not required to be clean and sober, but must refrain from substance use on the premises or from exhibiting aggressive or disruptive behavior. Discussions about drug and alcohol issues are held, and residents are encouraged to attend recovery meetings. Residents receive weekly on-site primary medical care and are referred to specialized mental and physical health care services as needed. A major goal of the safe havens is to stabilize mentally ill residents and to educate them about the importance of taking their medications. Case workers meet with the residents and encourage them to progress to their highest potential.

Highly supportive residences are designed for individuals with stabilized psychiatric conditions and who require less structure and assistance with daily activities. These individuals have demonstrated progress towards achieving personal goals and generally function at a higher level than residents of safe havens. Residents meet regularly with case workers and 24-hour staffing is provided. Residents receive psychiatric care from nearby community mental health centers. At the two recovery facilities for men, residents with substance use disorders or dual diagnoses are provided with addictions counseling and education. All residents attend outpatient drug and alcohol treatment programs and are encouraged to take part in daily activities. These residents must attend recovery group meetings such as Alcoholics Anonymous or Narcotics Anonymous. Random urine screens are conducted to monitor substance use activity.

Minimally supportive, permanent residences are designed for those individuals with high-level functioning who are ready for more independent living. No drug or alcohol use is permitted. A certified addictions counselor provides counseling services and workshops for all recovering residents and conducts random urine screens. Residents who relapse are not asked to leave if they have an interest in recovery and/or re-entry into a treatment program.

In minimally-supportive facilities, residents do their own cooking, laundry, cleaning and other daily chores. Most residents maintain their own budgets, although some individuals are assigned to representative payees. Case workers regularly meet with residents and assistance is available for emergencies. The residents utilize community-based services for mental health care and drug and alcohol treatment, and a nurse practitioner provides primary health care that includes vaccinations, blood pressure screenings and health education.

Case Management Services. Project H.O.M.E. staff offer comprehensive case management services to all residents using a strengths-based and client-centered approach. Case workers have frequent contact with residents to assist them with establishing and achieving goals that are personally salient in the areas of mental health, recovery, health care, activities of daily living, employment and education. Case workers in safe havens or highly supportive residences also oversee medication procurement and distribution, and provide social support to residents as needed. Case workers accompany residents to mental health services, participate in social and recreational activities, and maintain contact with residents' external social workers (ICMs) assigned by the City's mental health system. All Project H.O.M.E. case workers make referrals to appropriate medical, psychiatric, and social services and orient new residents to house rules and regulations.

Linkages to Physical Health, Mental Health and Drug/Alcohol Treatment Programs. Since its inception, Project H.O.M.E. has worked in partnership with community agencies that provide specialized professional services to homeless persons. PHMC, through its Health Care for the Homeless Program, is the primary provider of physical health services and Hall-Mercer Community Mental Health Center is the primary provider of mental health services to Project H.O.M.E. residents. As Project H.O.M.E. does not provide formal drug and alcohol treatment services, residents in recovery are referred to outside treatment programs.

On-Site Certified Addictions Counselor. Project H.O.M.E. case workers strongly encourage all residents with substance use disorders to take responsibility for their addictions and follow a 12-step recovery program. To assist with this process, drug and alcohol counseling and consultative services are the primary responsibility of Project H.O.M.E.'s Certified Addictions Counselor (CAC). In addition, the CAC works closely with external ICMs and on-site case workers to monitor recovery progress of each resident.

Educational Programs. Project H.O.M.E. provides a range of educational programs and activities to its residents. GED classes, study groups, and beginner and advanced computer classes give participants valuable experience that can be applied outside Project H.O.M.E. Computer laboratories at three locations allow students to gain hands-on experience and expand their knowledge. Adult literacy tutoring is also available to all Project H.O.M.E. residents, neighborhood residents, and other adults who have been referred to the program. Ceramics, art and sewing classes give participants from Project H.O.M.E. and the surrounding communities an opportunity to socialize, learn and express their creativity. A creative writing group affords residents an opportunity to develop writing skills and to share ideas with one another in a positive and creative manner. Residents also publish written material in Project H.O.M.E.'s monthly newsletter, *The Dwelling Place*. Finally, aerobics classes and social outings offer residents and neighbors the opportunity to increase their mobility while enjoying themselves.

Residential Employment Program. Project H.O.M.E.'s employment program offers various opportunities for residents to be employed, depending upon their skill level and interests. Specifically, the program offers residents employment training opportunities, volunteer stipend activities, casual labor, and full- and part-time positions inside and outside of Project H.O.M.E. The primary objective of this program is to empower residents and build self-confidence while preparing them for meaningful employment. A volunteer stipend program provides employment experiences to residents not yet ready for full- or part-time work. Volunteers work a limited number of hours each week and receive a small stipend to cover travel expenses. Volunteers may work as mail couriers, cashiers, clerks, or perform a variety of other tasks. This work often serves as a stepping stone for future employment and allows a resident to sharpen his or her interpersonal and organizational skills.

Typically, individuals who express a desire and commitment to work are placed in a six- to eight-week internship/training position at Project H.O.M.E.'s Back Home Café. A supervisor assumes the role of mentor, guiding and training resident-employees through the interim period. Once a resident has completed this training and is ready to work part-time or full-time, the employment program coordinator places him or her in a position that is available.

Residents may work in a variety of positions at Project H.O.M.E that include the bookstore, thrift shop, café, and reception area as well as custodial and other service positions. Occasionally, Project H.O.M.E. staff hire residents through the casual labor program to perform these short-term tasks. They are paid no less than minimum wage and may earn more than minimum wage, depending on the difficulty of the work task.

Political and Social Activism. Project H.O.M.E. invites residents to help educate the public about homelessness and speak to interested groups about their experiences. Residents are also involved in advocating for equitable public policies to end homelessness, which can take many forms including letter writing and telephone calls to elected officials, public rallies, political marches, press conferences, and, at times, civil disobedience. Project H.O.M.E. also offers introductory workshops on political science and civics so that staff and residents can gain a better understanding of the judicial and legislative system. Involvement in political activism and advocacy promotes a sense of empowerment and provides an opportunity for residents to be part of a movement to change the attitudes, laws, funding and other social impediments which negatively impact their lives.

Community/Neighborhood Level

Project H.O.M.E. provides a number of services to North Philadelphia neighborhoods. Staff are presently converting abandoned, deteriorated row homes into housing for families who are at-risk for homelessness or who are currently living in shelters or transitional living.

Project H.O.M.E. also conducts an after-school program for neighborhood children at three North Philadelphia facilities. The after-school programs are part of an effort to reach out to the community in which Project H.O.M.E. residences are located, to "adopt" the local neighborhood. The after-school programs serve elementary school students from kindergarten through seventh grade and are open from three to six o'clock in the afternoon five days a week. Games, toys, a computer lab and a kitchen are available, and once a month, Junior League volunteers come to prepare meals and teach students to cook.

Project H.O.M.E.'s adult education program for neighborhood residents offers classes in computers, ceramics, aerobics and GED preparation. Project H.O.M.E. sponsors efforts to "green," or landscape, vacant lots and remove graffiti. They also provide home repair assistance for low-income homeowners and services for elderly residents living alone.

Societal Level

Project H.O.M.E.'s engagement in political advocacy and social education includes a variety of activities. Project H.O.M.E. staff work in collaboration with the Mental Health Association of Southeastern Pennsylvania on a range of homeless advocacy and public education issues, as well as participate in a coalition of homeless advocates called the Open Door Coalition. Project H.O.M.E. staff maintain a dialogue with neighborhood and civic organizations about effective answers to the problem of homelessness. There is a concerted effort to listen and respond to community concerns in neighborhoods where Project H.O.M.E. facilities are located. These dialogues help maintain a friendly, working relationship between Project H.O.M.E. and the communities in which they are located. For example, prior to the opening of a safe haven for women, Project H.O.M.E. met several times with the Logan Square Neighborhood Association to address their members' quality-of-life concerns. The neighborhood association and Project H.O.M.E. subsequently formed an advisory committee to discuss and resolve these issues.

Project H.O.M.E. residents and staff take part in the public debate on homelessness, poverty and welfare reform. In the Fall of 1996, Project H.O.M.E. residents and staff traveled to the state capital, Harrisburg, to advocate for the restoration of funds which would allow the city shelters to reopen for the Winter of 1996-97. In the Spring of 1997, a group of Project

H.O.M.E. residents and staff traveled back to Harrisburg, to speak out about the need to create jobs for individuals no longer eligible for welfare benefits. In addition, Project H.O.M.E. residents and staff wrote letters to the editor that were published in the *Philadelphia Inquirer* expressing personal views on proposed Philadelphia City Council legislation which would ban aggressive panhandling and sleeping on the streets. Recently, Project H.O.M.E.'s Executive Director and Director of Education and Advocacy traveled to Georgia to participate in a conference about the impact of Atlanta's new "anti-homeless/anti-panhandling" legislation.

OUTCOMES

Project H.O.M.E. has three sets of desired outcomes that correspond with its three-tiered approach to preventing homelessness. First, there are intermediate and long-term outcomes established specifically for the mentally ill and dually-diagnosed individuals who live at Project H.O.M.E. Intermediate outcomes include improving mental health, increasing self-esteem and self-efficacy, and improving health status, as well as achieving and/or maintaining sobriety and developing/improving job skills. Long-term individual outcomes include obtaining employment and stable, independent housing. To achieve both intermediate and long term outcomes, Project H.O.M.E. works in partnership with the individual to address the issues that place him/her at risk for homelessness.

At the community/neighborhood level, short-term outcomes are to prevent social isolation among families and individuals living in at-risk communities and to improve their quality of life. The long-term outcome is to prevent homelessness in these impoverished areas. Project H.O.M.E.'s staff believe that revitalizing low-income neighborhoods is paramount to preventing homelessness.

Finally, at the societal level, Project H.O.M.E.'s outcome is to combat the NIMBY (Not-in-My-Back-Yard) syndrome by educating the public about answers to the problem of homelessness and to encourage everyone to participate in the struggle against homelessness. Additionally, Project H.O.M.E. aims to increase resources available to individuals at-risk of becoming homeless.

CONCLUSION

At both the national and local level, Project H.O.M.E. has been recognized by service providers and social policymakers as a model program committed to working in partnership with homeless persons and communities. As part of a cooperative agreement funded by the Substance Abuse and Mental Health Services Administration (SAMHSA), PHMC is currently conducting an evaluation to determine the efficacy of Project H.O.M.E.'s intervention in preventing the recurrence of homelessness among persons with severe mental illness and/or substance use disorders. The project's outcome evaluation involves a longitudinal study design to collect quantitative and qualitative data from individuals in an intervention group (Project H.O.M.E. residents) and matched comparison group (non-Project H.O.M.E. residents) at three six-month intervals. In addition to site-specific analyses, quantitative data will be pooled for analysis with the seven other Homelessness Prevention Program sites that are employing similar data collection methods. The findings will be used to inform, replicate and refine future programs designed to prevent homelessness among individuals with severe mental illness and substance use disorders.

REFERENCES

Auerbach, C., Beckerman, A. &Levitt, L. (1990). Can Homelessness be Prevented? An Evaluation of a Homelessness Prevention Program. *Jewish Social Work Forum, 26*, 31-37.

Cohen, E., Mowbray, C.T., Gillett, V. & Thompson, E. (1991). Preventing Homelessness: Religious Organizations and Housing Development. *Prevention in Human Services, 19*(1), 169-185.

Dennis, D.L., Levine, I.S. & Osher, F.C. (1991). The Physical and Mental Health Status of Homeless Adults. *Housing Policy Debate, 2*(3), 815-834.

Fischer, P.J. & Breakey, W.R. (1991). The Epidemiology of Alcohol, Drug, and Mental Disorders among Homeless Persons. *American Psychologist, 46*(11), 1115-1128.

Johnson, A.K. & Cnaan, R.A. (1995). Social Work Practice with Homeless Persons: The State of the Art. *Research on Social Work Practice, 5*(3), 340-382.

Lezak, A. & Edgar, E. (1996). *Preventing Homelessness Among People with Serious Mental Illnesses: A Guide for States.* Rockville, MD: Center for Mental Health Services, Substance Abuse and Mental Health Services Administration and the U.S. Department of Health and Human Services.

Philadelphia Health Management Corporation. (1994). *Neighborhood Health Profiles Volume 5: Lower North Philadelphia.* Philadelphia: Philadelphia Health Management Corporation (PHMC).

Ridgway, P., Simpson, A., Wittman, F.D. & Wheeler, G. (1994). Home-Making and Community Building: Notes on Empowerment and Place. *The Journal of Mental Health Administration, 21*(4), 407-418.

Stoner, M.R. (1989). Beyond Shelter: Policy Directions for the Prevention of Homelessness. *Social Work Research & Abstracts*, December, pp. 7-11.

A Home-Based Family Intervention for Ethnic Minorities with a Mentally Ill Member

Linda Connery, LCSW, MPA
John Brekke, PhD

SUMMARY. This article presents the background, development, and content of a manualized home-based family intervention for ethnic minority families with a seriously mentally ill member. The development of this homelessness prevention intervention is based on the premise that the client's home can be one of the most effective venues for achieving long-term positive outcomes from mental health services. By observing the patient within the context of the home environment, staff can more accurately assess the family dynamics and encourage family members to fulfill more effective roles as caregivers.

The agency within which this manualized intervention is implemented is an Integrated Services Agency (ISA) which serves the highest utilizers of the most costly mental health services in the public sector. Through effective case management and other interventions, the agency has been able to change the service utilization pattern from inpatient care, homelessness, and incarceration to community treatment within the framework of integrated comprehensive services. Ten salient points which have been significant to this agency's positive outcomes are discussed. We also provide a model for conceptualizing the strengths and burdens of the study population of low-SES African Americans and Latinos. We identified the strengths as the extended

---

Linda Connery is Director of Research and Evaluation, Barbour and Floyd ISA, 3221 N. Alameda, Compton, CA 90222. John Brekke is Associate Professor, USC School of Social Work.

[Haworth co-indexing entry note]: "A Home-Based Family Intervention for Ethnic Minorities with a Mentally Ill Member." Connery, Linda and John Brekke. Co-published simultaneously in *Alcoholism Treatment Quarterly* (The Haworth Press, Inc.) Vol. 17, No. 1/2, 1999, pp. 149-167; and: *Homelessness Prevention in Treatment of Substance Abuse and Mental Illness: Logic Models and Implementation of Eight American Projects* (ed: Kendon J. Conrad et al.) The Haworth Press, Inc., 1999, pp. 149-167. Single or multiple copies of this article are available for a fee from The Haworth Document Delivery Service [1-800-342-9678, 9:00 a.m. - 5:00 p.m. (EST). E-mail address: getinfo@haworthpressinc.com].

© 1999 by The Haworth Press, Inc. All rights reserved.

family, the kinship network, the church and spirituality, and strong education and work ethics. The burdens for this population include racism, discrimination, and poverty which co-occur in a poor inner-city community.

The main element of the family intervention is the home visit. Case managers make home visits on a semi-weekly basis. While the components of the home visit are not all innovative, the delivery of the services is designed to take into consideration the cultural values, beliefs, and behaviors of the minority groups that receive the services. The services provided are engagement, assessment, and development of the service plan, monitoring, strategies for coping with mental illness, the extended provider role, and family skill development. Other family support services are family groups and family respite. *[Article copies available for a fee from The Haworth Document Delivery Service: 1-800-342-9678. E-mail address: getinfo@ haworthpressinc.com]*

KEYWORDS. Family support, supported respite model, *in vivo*

This paper presents the background, development, and content of a manualized home-based family intervention for ethnic minority families with a seriously mentally ill member. The development of his homelessness prevention intervention is based on the premise that the client's home is the most effective venue for achieving long-term positive outcomes from mental health service.

The agency within which this manualized intervention is implemented is an Integrated Services Agency (ISA) which serves the highest utilizers of the most costly services in the public sector. Through effective case management and other interventions, the agency has been able to change the service utilization pattern from inpatient care, homelessness, and incarceration.

As part of our intervention we conceptualize the strengths and burdens of the study population of low-SES African Americans. We identified the strengths of the extended family, the kinship network, the church and spirituality, and strong education and work ethics. The burdens for this population include racism, discrimination and poverty co-occurring in a poor inner-city community.

The main element of the family intervention is the home visit. Case managers make home visits on a weekly basis. While the components of the home visit are not all innovative, the delivery of the services is designed to take into consideration the cultural values, belief and behaviors of the minority groups that access the services. The services provided are engagement, assessment, development of the service plan, and ongoing monitoring. The service plan consist of strategies for coping with mental illness, the extended provider role, family skill development, family support services, family groups, and family respite.

Conceptual Framework for the Intervention. This agency's philosophy toward the treatment of severely and persistently mentally ill adults and their families is rooted in several fundamental beliefs: the importance of a partnership; client-driven services; the empowerment of families and their mentally ill family members; the creation of culturally congruent and relevant services; cultural consistency between case coordinators and members; and member and family involvement in the development of services specifically designed to meet their needs. The agency recognizes that the day-to-day reality of many of these families is characterized by significant burden and stress as they attempt to care for mentally ill family members within the context of a hostile and often dangerous inner-city setting. They require all of the services and support which we provide in order to maintain their mentally ill family member in the home, to improve the quantity and quality of family contacts if the member is not residing with the family, and to diminish the risk of homelessness.

The solution for this agency has been the development of "in vivo" interventions in the family's home. The literature supports the contention that the client's home can be an effective locus of treatment (Dixon & Lehman, 1995; Penn & Mueser, 1996). "In vivo" services can also be an important aspect of certain community-based models of care (Test, 1992; Scott & Dixon, 1995). This is particularly true of skills training as all too often learning which takes place in a foreign setting has poor generalization to a more natural environment (Dilk & Bond, 1996). This, coupled with cultural consistency between service provider and families, the family as the unit of treatment and the home as the locus of treatment has resulted in a unique provider relationship.

Principles of the Intervention. Several principles are integral to the "in vivo" intervention: (1) home visits must address the convenience of the family rather than that of the service provider; (2) "in vivo" interventions are more effective and more likely to work over time than are services delivered in a clinical setting; (3) home visits break down barriers between staff, family members and consumers; (4) home visits made by staff members who share the ethnicity, culture and values of the family provide better opportunities for bonding to take place; (5) by making the home the major locus of treatment, a better assessment can be made of family functioning, how family members relate to their mentally ill family member and how family members interact with each other (this assessment must take into account cultural patterns of interaction and cultural values); (6) by addressing the family as the locus of treatment interventions, the stigma attached to the mentally ill family member is reduced and family members are encouraged to begin to see the profound impact their interactions with their family member can have; (7) families are more open to learning new ways of coping with difficulties when they understand that they can change their behavior in ways which will be beneficial to the member and the family system; and (8) all family interventions must take into account the cultural context in which they take place. They must be culturally sensitive and consistent within the cultural context.

Agency Setting: The Environmental Context. Los Angeles has the dubious distinction of being known as the "homeless capital" of the nation. Of the approximately 84,300 homeless individuals in Los Angeles County, 16,950 are located in South Central Los Angeles. This represents 20 percent of the total homeless population. This is significant as South Central is the geographically smallest planning area of the eight planning areas used by governmental agencies; however, it is second only to the downtown Skid Row in the size of its homeless population. According to a county-wide needs assessment conducted by the Los Angeles Homeless Services Authority 36 percent, or 6,102 of these homeless individuals suffer from a mental disorder and half of these–3,051 individuals–have been conservatively identified as having co-occurring disorders of mental illness and substance abuse. In a study conducted by the Rand Corporation, they estimated that 50% of the homeless population are mentally ill and that 65 percent of homeless persons with mental illness also have a substance use disorder.

Our agency–Barbour and Floyd Integrated Services Agency–is located in the heart of South Central Los Angeles, an inner-city network of communities including Watts, Compton, Florence, and Willowbrook. South Central Los Angeles is infamous for a number of reasons. Seriously impacted by the 1965 Watts civil uprising, from which the community never fully recovered, the area was further devastated by the 1992 civil unrest resulting from the Rodney King beating and its aftermath. The 1994 Northridge earthquake also took its toll on local housing–much of it old and unable to meet present earthquake building standards. This was perceived as yet another blow to the community and its ability to cope with life on a day-to-day basis.

The Agency. Barbour and Floyd Integrated Services Agency was in its third year of operation at the beginning of this project. Funded through a contract with the Los Angeles County Department of Mental Health (DMH), it represents DMH's first foray into the area of managed care. Enrollees into this program were identified by DMH as the highest utilizers of the most costly services in the public sector, costing DMH between $30,000 to $80,000 annually for at least two years of the five years prior to enrollment in this program.. The average cost for the comprehensive services provided has been decreased to approximately $15,000 annually. The family intervention costs $150 per week, or $7,800 per year.

REVIEW OF THE LITERATURE

Homelessness and Mental Illness. In developing this family intervention for individuals at high risk for homelessness due to mental illness and substance abuse, we reviewed literature on homelessness and severe mental illness; families with mentally ill members; African American families and their strengths and burdens, including African American families with a mentally ill family member relative to utilization of mental health services. The literature on homelessness among this population emphasized such characteristics as longer periods of homelessness, more limited contact with friends or family, more barriers to employment, poorer physical health and considerably more contact with the legal system (Atkinson et al., 1992; Drake et al., 1991; Koegel et al., 1988; Tessler, 1986). In another study (Lehman and Dixon, 1995) these individuals were found to have more problems with daily activities, safety, law, employment and familial or social relationships, and were less likely to be receiving federal disability entitlements. Suggestions for improving the quality of life included helping them to develop a social support network and improving access to disability entitlements as well as to treatment services.

Families with Mentally Ill Members. The literature on families with a mentally ill member was most helpful in identifying the needs of families which, if addressed, would enable them to cope more successfully: (1) inexpensive housing programs when relatives are unable to care for members at home; (2) a psychiatric crisis system during periods of acute symptom exacerbation; (3) financial support to help find a family member an independent housing situation and (4) respite services which would give caregivers an opportunity to recoup and the mentally ill member the opportunity to "practice" independent living for a brief period of time (USICHTFH, 1992).

Family Interventions and Ethnic Minorities. While there are data to indicate that ethnic minority groups are involved in a wide range of community-based psychosocial interventions (Atkinson et al., 1992), there are several reasons to believe that family interventions hold particular promise for these groups. First, ethnic minority groups are more family and socially oriented in their orientation than non-minorities (Gaines, 1994; Lefley, 1985; Marin & Triandis, 1985; Baldwin & Hopkins, 1990). Second, it has been suggested that the family plays a notable role in the lives of ethnic minority individuals (Lin & Kleinman, 1988; Kleinman, 1988). Third, ethnic minorities diagnosed with a chronic mental illness are more likely to live with their families and to maintain family involvement than non-minorities (Lefley, 1987, 1990; Rodriguez, 1986). Therefore, family intervention is particularly relevant to ethnic minorities diagnosed with a chronic mental illness.

The literature on family intervention has found that structured, problem-solving family-based interventions can reduce relapse and rehospitalization rates for individuals with schizophrenia (Penn & Mueser, 1996; Scott & Dixon, 1995). In at least one study, aspects of family functioning were also improved (McFarlane et al., 1995). Concerning ethnic minorities, however, the findings are equivocal. In a study that included over 40% African Americans in their study sample, McFarlane et al. (1995) found that multifamily group was more effective than individual family intervention. On a less optimistic note, Telles et al. (1995) found that a behavioral family intervention was not effective for Latino families in the U.S. that were not well acculturated. Penn and Mueser (1996) concluded that generalizing effective family intervention across ethnic groups is sorely needed, and it is also clear that it requires sensitivity to the unique cultural context that each ethnic minority group represents (Guarnaccia & Parra, 1996; Plummer, 1996).

African American Families. The literature on African American families consistently recognizes their strengths, including kinship networks, the extended family, strong religious bonds, and firmly held education and work ethics (Alston and Turner, 1994) These assets have alternately been described as "strong kinship bonds, strong work orientation, adaptability of family roles, high achievement orientation and religious orientation" (Hurd, Moore & Rogers, 1995). In terms of family bonds, African Americans are more likely to live in an extended family situation consisting of grandparents, unmarried adults and other relatives in addition to the nuclear family (Raley, 1995). Benefits of the extended family include the sharing of financial burdens (Tienda & Angel, 1992); role flexibility (Alston & Turner, 1994); care and support for children, older people, and needy adult members; and role modeling (Anderson, 1992).

The role of spirituality in the African American community has historically been a strong, primary one (McAdoo & Crawford, 1990). Throughout its history, African American religious practice has relied on an ideology that stresses belonging, a sense of community, the provision of role models, the teaching of effective coping strategies for everyday problems, and a network of social relationships (Moore, 1991). Even when African American families are not involved with a church, their spirituality, as enacted through such beliefs as "life is a testing ground" and one can cope effectively "to endure what you have to endure" are a strong force in dealing with the burdens of everyday life (Hurd, Moore, Rogers, 1995). Consequently, African Americans are more likely to view spiritual factors as important in the treatment of mental illness than are Caucasians (Miller et al., 1990).

The African American community places a high valuation on formal education, with a tradition of looking to schools to provide avenues for economic and social advancement (Anderson, 1992). However, the ubiquitous misconception that African Americans lack a strong work or education ethic persists (Turner & Alston, 1992).

Although African American families are resilient in the face of adversity, their burdens are many. Poverty, racism, and discrimination are three major factors that generate stress (Werner & Smith, 1989). Other potential risk factors include a physical handicap or chronic illness; early disruption of the attachment relationship; parental dysfunction in the form of chronic and serious psychopathology or substance abuse; loss of a parent through divorce, imprisonment, or death; and living under conditions of chronic violence, community disasters, or homelessness (Barbarin, 1993).

While these risk factors have a cumulative effect, poverty stands out as one of the most frequently identified agents (Barbarin, 1993). Urban poverty is typically associated with the neighborhood violence. Crime is a fact of life with which inner-city African American families have to contend on a daily basis (Furstenberg, 1990). It leads to instability in such basic aspects of life as residence, marriage, and family relations. Lack of consistency in these areas has been identified with an increased risk of impaired psychosocial functioning (Masten, 1992). Poverty is a multifaceted situation diminishing an individual's capacity for supportive, consistent and involved family relationships, leaving family members more vulnerable to the debilitating effects of negative life events (McLoyd, 1990). Protective environmental factors countering the effects of poverty and its corollaries include positive aspects of family life, including warmth, cohesion, culture and ethnic identification, supportive extrafamilial relationships and the church (Barbarin, 1993).

The utilization of mental health services by African Americans and the kinds of services they are more likely to receive as compared to their Caucasian cohorts is revealing. The literature documents an overrepresentation of African Americans using in-patient services and psychiatric emergency rooms (Snowden & Holschuh, 1992; Sue, Mckinney, Allen & Hall, 1974; Bulhan, 1985). African Americans have consistently been more likely to receive chemotherapy in most studies (Segal, Bola, & Watson, 1996; and Snowden & Holschuh, 1992). Another constant throughout the mental health literature is the decreased likelihood that African Americans will participate in "talk" therapy and other modes of treatment such as residential services, day treatment, and vocational rehabilitation. While African Americans are willing to enter the system, they are not willing to stay. As Pernell-Arnold (1983) notes, traditional mental health treatment models are inconsistent with the experience of poor African Americans.

Several articles address the role of the African American family with a disabled family member. These studies provide information to conceptualize the process African American families undergo with their mentally ill family members. Alston and Turner (1994) emphasize the importance of psychosocial adjustment for African Americans with disabilities, examining the personal resources that expedite the adjustment process. They believe the family system is a primary resource for this adjustment, although the onset of a disability and its resulting complications can affect the functioning of any family. The quality of the functioning preceding the onset of a disability-including the type of support demonstrated among family members and the amount of cooperation during crisis events-can determine how family members will cope with the stress brought on by a disability (Power & Dell Orto, 1980). Each family's unique style of interaction also plays a role in adjusting to the disability, including methods of conflict resolution and problem solving, processes of decision making, and role expectations for the members (Roberts & Magrab, 1991).

A family strengths model of adjustment for African Americans with disabilities draws on three principles: many African Americans share a deep concern for the members of the community; the African American family structure often consists of both the nuclear and extended family; and the strengths of the African American family-including kinship bonds, role flexibility, active religious orientation, and strong education and work ethics-are assets that can assist individual and family adaptation when a member becomes disabled (Hines & Boyd, 1982). These family assets interact in a manner enhancing the strength of each in dealing with disability. Role flexibility allows other family members to assume a "head of household" or mothering role when necessary. This allows a family member other than the parents to handle the day-to-day crises, often circumventing the stress of role overload (Alston & Turner, 1994). Some authors (Staples, 1985; Belgrade, 1991) encourage professionals to understand and utilize these cultural strengths to enhance their interventions with disabled African Americans and their families.

In summary, the literature review reinforces the effectiveness of both the home visit intervention and the family as the unit of treatment. Strengths of the African American family were consistently identified as the extended family, kinship networks, strong religious beliefs, and substantial work and education ethics. Poverty, coupled with racism and discrimination, have the most devastating effects on families, with neighborhood danger and violence serving as major contributors to family dysfunction. Inappropriate treatment and lack of access to suitable treatment interventions characterize the literature on service utilization. Research specific to families living with disabled family members emphasized the inclusion of the family, the extended family, kinship networks and spirituality in the therapeutic process as paramount to successful rehabilitation.

Description of the Client Population. This agency serves 110 adults with severe and persistent mental illness who have been enrolled in this ISA due to their histories of overutilization of the most costly services in the mental health system. Their adult lives have been characterized by hospitalizations, homelessness, and incarcerations with little connectedness with ongoing mental health treatment and rehabilitation. Of these 110 individuals, 65 percent–or 66 individuals–have histories of substance abuse or are currently abusing substances. They are considered to be at risk of homelessness because of their residential instability, frequent hospitalizations, inability to utilize community-based services, dual-diagnosis status, incarcerations due to offenses related to their mental illness and/or substance abuse, and histories of episodic homelessness interspersed with hospitalizations and/or incarcerations.

Diagnostically, this population falls into the following DSM IV categories: schizophrenia–68%; bipolar disorder–20%; and schizoaffective disorder–12%. Some 52 percent of clients are male, with 48 percent female. They are 89 percent African American, 10 percent Hispanic, and one percent other. By age, the majority are approaching their middle years: 4% are between the ages if 18-24; 24% are between the ages of 26-35; 50% are between the ages of 36-45; 18% are between the ages 46-55; and 4% are between the ages of 56-69.

Description of the Homelessness Prevention Intervention. The goals of the home visit intervention are specific and multifaceted: (1) to provide needed support to the family and decrease stress within the family system, enabling the family to have its mentally ill member continue to reside at home and to improve the quantity and quality of contacts when the mentally ill member is not residing with the family; (2) to increase the family's participation in the member's rehabilitation; (3) to improve the functional level of the family member who is mentally ill by enabling the family to be more supportive and less overly protective or rejecting; (4) to strengthen the family by improving family functioning in the following areas–daily living skills (budgeting and money management, meal planning and nutrition, shopping, and hygiene and grooming), parenting skills, communication skills, problem-solving and decision-making skills, crisis management skills, substance abuse knowledge, self-esteem development, and grief/mourning skills; (5) to level the playing field by removing institutional intimidation; (6) to use the home environment to increase the comfort level of family members, allowing them to begin talking about family secrets when they realize they are not being judged; and (7) to ensure all services and interactions are consistent with the cultural context of the family and that family values are respected.

Logic Model of the Intervention. Please see the logic model on the following page. (Figure 1) The logic model was developed based on the agency's philosophy and the literature review.

Staffing and Staff Training. The ISA is staffed by psychiatrists, social workers, licenced psychiatric technicians (LPT), substance abuse counselors, and case coordinators–who are paraprofessionals. While our paraprofession-

FIGURE 1. Barbour and Floyd Integrated Services Agency Logic Model for Family Interventions

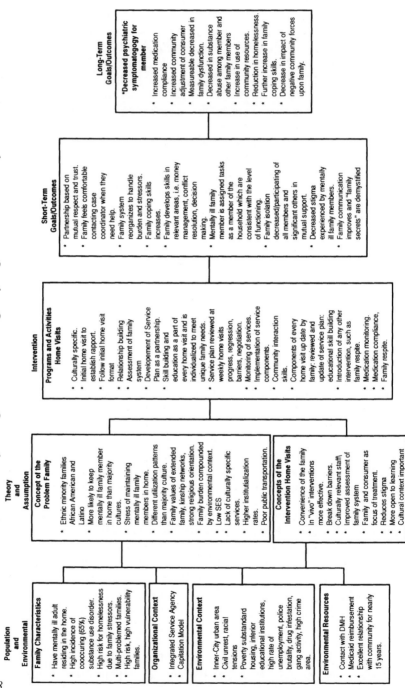

als may not all have a bachelor's degree, they have been selected for the varied experience and cultural compatibility they bring to our project. In general, when choosing staff, we rate energy and enthusiasm highly. We have discovered that to be effective with the target population, staff members must lend their enthusiasm and energy to members and their families within the framework of the rehabilitation model. While the families have contact with all staff categories, the case coordinators are the mainstay of the services provided. Having a 1:10 ratio of case coordinators to members has provided the opportunity for relationships to congeal.

Much of the agency's training is done through role modeling. When case coordinators are first hired, they spend their initial two weeks with an experienced case coordinator and the agency's assistant program director, making home visits, providing linkages to community agencies, and working with members and families in the area of skills development. Ongoing in-service training is provided twice monthly for one-and-one-half hours. Teaching approaches include didactic presentations, handouts, role playing, and "in vivo" observation during home visits. This observation of the staffs' implementation of the manual ensures fidelity to the model.

Cultural, Ethnic, and Gender Relevance and Sensitivity. Cultural and ethnic relevance and sensitivity are seminal to the success of this project, and they are addressed at all levels of the intervention. In searching for an operational identification of cultural competence, we selected one developed by Milstrey (1994). She states, "Cultural competence is nothing more than recognizing and accepting individual differences, and nothing less than a fundamental shift in the current paradigm of mental health treatment." This includes accepting differences, recognizing strengths, and respecting choices-all of which are critical to this program. Milstrey describes a five-step process to developing cultural competence: (1) awareness and acceptance that people are different; (2) self-awareness enabling one to step outside of cultural assumptions to meet others with different beliefs as a way to learn more about oneself; (3) understanding the dynamics of difference-how learned expectations about another's culture may cause individuals to misjudge each other; (4) developing cultural knowledge-learning about different groups' communication styles, kinship patterns, and values; and (5) adapting treatment to fit the cultural context of consumers.

The Homelessness Prevention Intervention-Home Visits. The five major elements to our agency's home visit intervention are: engagement; assessment; development and implementation of the service plan; monitoring, and provider role.

Engagement. This involves individualization to suit the particular family and the use of intuition and observation to decide how to proceed with the initial interview. Major issues to be considered include how to increase the family members' comfort level, how to involve them in a discussion of their situation, how to quickly identify and reinforce similarities between the case coordinator and one or more family members, and how to gauge the degree of intimacy or formality that will be most effective in the intervention. Cultural relevance is an important aspect of engagement. Cultural relevance appears to be especially important to multi-problem families who have never had a mental health worker visit their home before. Throughout the initial and subsequent home visits, it is essential to show respect for the family's integrity and not to overstep boundaries. Additionally, consistent, clear, and persistent messages verbalized in a manner with which the family can identify must be the salient feature of all interaction with the mentally ill client and the family. It is important to spend as much time as necessary on the engagement phase, for the success of all future interventions will be based on the strength of the relationship between the family and the case coordinator.

Assessment. Using an assessment instrument the following information is obtained on the member: psychiatric history, medical history, medications, substance abuse, psychosocial history, including current living and support situation, education, employment history and legal history; mental status examination; diagnostic summary, a five-axis diagnosis and Global Assessment Functioning (GAF); and disposition/recommendation/plan. The family assessment utilizes a culturally determined family strengths/family burden model–this includes gathering information on: the extended family; the kinship network; role flexibility; religious bonds and spirituality; work and education ethics. After assessing the strengths of the family the case coordinator addresses the family burden: employment/economic status; adequacy of housing; the neighborhood in terms of degree of safety, level of comfort traveling into the neighborhood, the presence of gang activity, the extent of crime, etc., both from the perspective of the family and the observations of the case coordinator; the community in terms of resources and accessibility; the availability of transportation; family dysfunction; denial/acceptance of the presence of mental illness; knowledge of mental illness; and pre-morbid family adjustment.

Service Plan Development. Utilizing an established Service Plan form, which includes sections for member and family participation, family-driven service planning is initiated. Working with the family and the member within the context of partnership, the Service Plan consists of the following steps: (1) deciding upon the desired outcome(s)–also known as long-term goals; (2) identifying barriers–both functional and skills deficits–which interfere with the member and family reaching their desired outcome; (3) frequency and duration of services–weekly contacts of approximately one hour is the standard for the agency but are negotiable with the family; (4) the establishment of short-term concrete goals which will enable the family unit to ultimately reach the desired outcome(s); (5) the specific tasks which the member, family members, and staff will carry out which are designed to further goal attainment; and (6) on a six-month basis, the progress made toward the desired outcome(s). Once again, it is essential that the Service Plan is individualized and that it is the product of a consensual effort.

Monitoring. This is the ongoing process of ensuring that all of the key constituents remain committed to the Service Plan and are carrying out the activities they agreed upon when the plan was first developed. To ensure this, the case coordinator reviews the Service Plan during the weekly home visits. This is an ongoing, self-monitoring process and provides the opportunity to revise the plan if it is no longer relevant, if other priorities have come to the forefront, or if it is not realistic in terms of outcomes and the time required to achieve them. This provides a feedback mechanism for the plan and keeps staff, family and their mentally ill member focused in their weekly contacts.

Provider Role. An interesting phenomenon often takes place when case coordinators utilize the home visit model. They frequently assume a functional and instrumental role within the family. This may happen early in the relationship, take place over time, or not occur at all. The operative factor appears to be the "neediness" of the family and the case coordinator's ability to respond to this need. Often the case coordinator takes on the role of a quasi-family member, as the family views the case coordinator as a partner-someone who will take on functions usually handled by a family member in a more traditional family. This phenomenon is more likely to happen if only one family member has assumed the caregiver role for the mentally ill individual. This family member frequently assumes that problems related to the client as well as any other family concerns will be handled together with the case coordinator.

In the service plan implementation, there are two domains which are addressed–*coping with mental illness* and *skills development*. We have built upon the works of Fallon, Leberman, and Mueser and Glynn in developing our interventions.

Strategies for Coping with Mental Illness. In view of the target population being served, the need for assistance from the case coordinator in helping members and their families cope with mental illness will almost universally be an identified goal of the Service Plan. Several strategies are integral to this process.

Family Psychoeducation. It has been our experience that family members have very little knowledge about the mental illness from which their family member suffers, the prognosis of the disorder or actions that can be taken to decrease discomfort and symptomatology. Because of this, it is essential that an educational approach be incorporated into home visits.

The psychoeducational format used in the family visit relies on discussion and questions, with less emphasis on a didactic approach. Prior to beginning this format, the case coordinator attempts to gather information which will indicate the family's level of sophistication in understanding mental illness–alleviating the risk of alienating the family if it already has a fair degree of basic knowledge. Concise one-page handouts are used as a basis for family discussion and for eradicating many commonly held misconceptions about mental illness.

Family Support. Family support is provided primarily by our program's case coordinators. The focus of the home visits is largely directed toward communicating to family members that they are not alone, the case coordinator is always accessible, the whole agency is a source of support for them, and we have a real concern for them with a genuine desire to assist them in improving the quality of their lives.

Case coordinators also help family members better utilize existing potential helpers. Often members have not fully actualized their extended family, kinship networks, fictive kin (such as a "play aunt"), and community resources such as the church. Often dormant resources can be revived, and the case coordinator can assist in this endeavor.

Family Respite. Families with a mentally ill family member living in the home face enormous stress and the sense of being overwhelmed on a frequent basis. The cyclical nature of the member's psychiatric disorders places even greater pressure on the family system. Not knowing when a member is going to cycle into an acute episode of mental illness places the family at a high risk of experiencing a constant state of anxiety and anticipatory malfunction. This is particularly true when a mentally ill family member is a high-rate cycler and when there are few warning signs of an impending decompensation. Consequently, many of these households have enmeshed systems, perpetual activity, and a high level of emotionality which results in episodes of "burn-out." A "vacation" for both family members and the mentally ill member from each other is often indicated, and we have arranged for this. We utilize our Day Rehabilitation Services for a five-hour respite on a daily basis, and we arrange for longer periods on a regular basis by placing the member in a residential facility with which we have a close working relationship with and which has staff skilled in working with this population. The family is able to enjoy this respite, knowing that their family member is being well cared for in their absence.

Family Skill Development. Many of the families in this project have difficulty dealing with the stress of daily life as they do not have the skills necessary to carry out their respective roles within the family. Therefore, we have developed skill building modules in essential areas based on cognitive and behavioral intervention strategies. These modules include: daily living skills (budgeting and money management, meal planning and nutrition, shopping, and hygiene and grooming), parenting skills, communication skills, problem-solving and decision-making skills, crisis management, substance abuse education, self-esteem development and grief/mourning skills. The decision to focus on the development of a particular skill is the result of the assessment, the service planning that has taken place, and the use of a decision tree.

Community Interface. While many families receive relief and solace from their community contacts, others remain isolated. There are a number of reasons why this occurs: a high level of crime, gang activity, drug infestation–especially crack cocaine–and the general deterioration of the neighborhood. Many families have been victims of crimes, ranging from harassment while traveling in the community to having their homes broken into and robbed to being physically assaulted.

However, the community also offers a potential source of support for these families. The literature indicates that African Americans in inner-city areas move less often than African Americans of solid middle class backgrounds (Alston & Turner, 1994). According to the literature, inner-city African American families more often have relatives living nearby. Taking into account kinship systems–including fictive kin who live in close proximity–these community members can be a powerful source of support which all too often is not tapped into by these overwhelmed families and mental health service providers.

In order to increase community interaction with all possible community resources, the families will be introduced to and enabled to utilize community resources by their case coordinators. These sources of support within the community include: the church; church members and elders; long-standing neighbors; members of their kinship networks, including fictive kin; community centers; senior citizen centers, Alano (Alcoholics Anonymous) clubs; political affiliations; social service agencies, and entitlement services.

Significance. The effectiveness of the home-visit intervention is being assessed over an 18-month period using both experimental and quasi-experimental methods. Consumers and family members are interviewed every six months in a face-to-face semi-structured format by trained interviewers. This project is particularly significant to the field in four ways (Penn & Mueser, 1996; Dixon & Lehman, 1995). First, most research on family interventions for this population have involved samples during an inpatient episode, or upon discharge from an inpatient facility. Very importantly, this study uses a sample that is being treated in the community. Second, there have been very few attempts to test family intervention methods with ethnic minority populations of individuals with chronic mental illness. It is hoped that this project will have relevance to other inner-city ethnic minority populations in the U.S. Third, this intervention is unique in its comprehensiveness. It treats the whole family as the unit of intervention, and attends to a wide range of family functioning issues. Fourth, most family intervention research in this area has focused on the clinical outcomes of the consumer, and there has been a very limited focus on the functioning of the family. This research project is gathering data on the clinical and psychosocial functioning of the consumer, but also on an array of family functioning variables that reflects the scope of the intervention. As such, we will have a comprehensive assessment of the impact of the intervention on both the consumer and the family unit.

REFERENCES

Alston, R.J. & Turner, W.L. (1994). A family strengths model of adjustment to disability for African American clients. *Journal of Counseling and Development*, 72, 378-382.

Anderson, P.D. (1992). Extended kin networks in Black families. *Generations*, 16(3), 29-32.

Atkinson, C., Cook, J., Karno, M. et al. (1992). Clinical services research. *Schizophrenia Bulletin*, 18 (4), 561-626.

Baldwin, J.A. & Hopkins, R. (1990). African-American and European-American cultural differences as assessed by the world-views paradigm: An empirical analysis. *The Western Journal of African-American Studies*, 14(1), 38-52.

Barbarin, O.A. (1993). Coping and resilience: exploring the inner lives of African-American children. *Journal of Black Psychology*, 19(4), 478-492.

Belgrade, F.Z. (1991). Psychosocial predictors of adjustment to disability in African Americans. *Journal of Rehabilitation*, 57, 37-40.

Bulhan, H.A. (1985). Black Americans and psychopathology: An overview of research and theory. *Psychotherapy*, 22, 370-378.

Dilk, M.N. & Bond G.R. (1996). Meta analytic evaluation of skills training research for individuals with severe mental illness. *Journal of Consulting and Clinical Psychology*, 64: 1337-1346.

Dixon, L.B. & Lehman, A.F. (1995). Family interventions for schizophrenia. *Schizophrenia Bulletin*, 21(4), 631-643.

Drake, R.E., Antosca, L.M., Noordsy, D.L., Bartels, S.F., and Osher, F.C. (1991). New Hampshire's specialized services for the dually diagnosed. In K. Minkoff and R.E. Drake (Eds.), *Dual diagnosis of major mental illness and substance disorders: Vol 50. New directions for mental health services* (pp. 57-67). San Francisco, CA: Jossey-Bass.

Furstenberg, F. (1990). *How do families manage risk and opportunity in dangerous neighborhoods*. Paper presented at the 85th Annual Meeting of the Association, Washington, DC.

Gaines, S.O. (1994). Generic, stereotypic, and collective models for interpersonal resource exchange among African American couples. *Journal of African-American Psychology*, 20(3), 294-304.

Glynn S.M. & Mueser, K.T. (1997). Commentary on "Applying research on family education about mental illness to development of a relatives' group consultation model." *Community Mental Health Journal*, 33(6) 571-574.

Guarnaccia, P. & Parra, P. (1996). Ethnicity, social status, and families' experiences of caring for a mentally ill family member. *Community Mental Health Journal, 32(3)*, 243-260.

Hines, P.M., Boyd-Franklin, N. (1982). Black families. In McGoldrich, J., Pierce, J. & J. Giordano (Eds). 84-107. New York: Guildford Press.

Hurd, E.P., Moore, C., & Rogers, R. (1995). Quiet Success: parenting strengths among African American families in society. *Journal of Contemporary Human Services*, 434-443.

Kleinman, A. (1988). *Rethinking psychiatry: From cultural category to personal experience.* New York: Free Press.

Koegel, P.M., Burnam, A., & Farr, R.K. (1988). The prevalence of specific psychiatric disorders among homeless individuals in the inner city of Los Angeles. *Archives of General Psychiatry, 45*, 1085-1109.

Lefley, H.P. (1990). Culture and chronic mental illness. *Hospital and Community Psychiatry, 41(3)*, 277-286.

Lefley, H.P. (1987). Culture and mental illness: The family role. In Hatfield, A.B. & Lefley, H.P. (Eds). *Families of the mentally ill: Coping and adaptation.* 30-59. New York: The Guildford Press.

Lefley, H.P. (1985). Families of the mentally ill in cross-cultural perspective. *Psychosocial Rehabilitation Journal, 8*, 57-75.

Lehman, A.F., & Dixon, L.B. (1995). *Double jeopardy: Chronic mental illness and substance use disorders.* Chur, Switzerland: Harwood Academic.

Lin, K.M. & Kleinman, A.M. (1988). Psychotherapy and clinical course of schizophrenia: A cross-cultural perspective. *Schizophrenia Bulletin, 21(4)*, 669-675.

Marin, G. & Triandis, H.C. (1985). Allocentrism as an important characteristic of the behavior of Latin Americans and Hispanics. In R. Diaz Guerrero (Ed.), *Cross-cultural and national studies in social psychology*, 85-104. North Holland: Elsevier Science Publishers.

Masten, A. (1992). Resilience in development: Implications of the study of successful adaptation for developmental psychopathology: In A. Sameroff (Ed.), *Developmental psychopathology*, 261-294. New York.

McAdoo, H. & Crawford, V. (1990). The Black church and family support programs. In *Families as Nurturing Systems.* 193-203. New York: Hawthorne Press.

McAdoo, H.P. (1991). The ethics of research and intervention with ethnic minority parents and their children. In Fisher & Tyron (Eds.), *Ethics in Applied Developmental Psychology*, 273-283. Norwood, NJ.

McFarlane, W.R., Lukens, E., Link, B. et al. (1995). Multiple-family groups and psychoeducation in the treatment of schizophrenia. *Schizophrenia Bulletin, 20*, 519-536.

McLoyd, V.C. (1990a). Minority children: Introduction to the special issue. *Child development, 61*, 263-266.

Miller, F., Dworkin, J., Ward, M., Barone, D. (1990). A preliminary study of unresolved grief in families of seriously mentally ill patients. *Hospital and community Psychiatry, 41*, 1321-1325.

Milstrey, S. (1994). Response to homelessness requires cultural competence. *Access-*

Information from the National Resource Center on Homelessness and Mental Illness, 6, 1-6.
Moore, T. (1991). The African-American church: A source of empowerment, mutual help, and social change. *Religion and Prevention in Mental Health, 10,* 147-167.
Penn, D.L., Mueser, K.T. (1996). Research update on the psychosocial rehabilitative programs for African-Americans. *Psychosocial Rehabilitation Journal, 19(4),* 37-43.
Pernell-Arnold, A. (1983). Agency perspective in proceedings of the Aftercare Mosaic: A symposium on community services to discharged psychiatric patients. Federation for Community Planning, Ohio, April 26, 1983, 25-28.
Plummer, D.L. (1996). Developing culturally responsive psychosocial rehabilitative programs for African-Americans. *Psychosocial Rehabilitation Journal, 19(4),* 37-43.
Power, P.W. & Dell Orto, A.E. (1980). *Role of the family in the rehabilitation of the physically disabled,* Baltimore, MD. University Part Press.
Raley, R.K. (1995). Black-White differences in kin contact and exchange among never married adults. *Journal of Marriage and Family, 47,* 1005-1013.
Roberts, R.N. & Magrab, P.R. (1991). Psychologists' role in a family-centered approach to practice, training, and research with young children. *American Psychologist, 46,* 144-148.
Rodriguez, O. (1986). Overcoming barriers to clinical services among chronically mentally ill Hispanics: Lessons from the evaluation of Project COPA. *Fordham University Hispanic Research Center Research Bullentin,* vol. 9.
Segal, S.P., Bola J.R., & Watson, M.A. (1996). Race, quality of care, and antipsychotic prescribing practices in psychiatric emergency services. *Psychiatric Services, 47(3),* 282-285.
Scott, S. E. & Dixon, L.B. (1995). Assertive community treatment and case management for schizophrenia. *Schizophrenia Bulletin, 21(4),* 657-667.
Snowden, L.R., & Holschuh, J. (1992). Ethnic differences in emergency psychiatric care and hospitalization in a program for the severely mentally ill. *Community Mental Health Journal 28(4),* 281-291.
Staples, R. (1985). Changes in Black family structure: The conflict between family ideology and structural conditions. *Journal of Marriage and Family, 47,* 1005-1013.
Sue, S., McKinney, H., Allen, D., & Hall, J. (1974). Delivery of community mental health services to black and white clients. *Journal of Consulting & Clinical Psychology, 42,* 794-801.
Telles, C., Karno, M., Mintz, J., Paz, G. et al. (1985). Immigrant families coping with schizophrenia: Behavioral family intervention v. case management with a low-income Spanish-speaking population. *British Journal of Psychiatry, 165,* 239-257.
Tessler, R.C., Willis, G., & Gubman, G.D. (1986). Defining and measuring continuity of care. *Psychosocial Rehabilitation Journal, 10,* 27-38.
Test, M.A. (1992). Training in community. In Liberman, R.P (Ed.). *Handbook of Psychiatric Rehabilitation,* New York, NY: Macmillan Press.
Tienda, M., & Angel, R. (1992). Headship and household composition among Blacks, and Hispanics, and other Whites. *Social Forces, 61,* 508-531.

Turner, W.L., & Alston, R.J. (1992). The role of the family in psychosocial adaptation to physical disabilities for African Americans. *Journal of the National Medical Association, 86 (12),* 915-921.

United States Interagency Council on the Homeless Task Force on Homelessness and Severe Mental Illness (USTICHTFH) (1992). *Outcasts on the street: Report of the Federal Task Force on Homelessness and Severe Mental Illness.* Washington, DC: USICHTFHSMI.

Versluys, H.P. (1980). Physical rehabilitation and family dynamics. In R.H. Marinelli & A.E. DellOrto, (Eds.) *The Psychological and Social Impact of Physical Disability* 102-106.

Werner, E., & Smith, R. (1989). *Vulnerable but invincible: A longitudinal study of resident children and youth.* New York: Adams, Bannister & Cox.

Representative Payee for Individuals with Severe Mental Illness at Community Counseling Centers of Chicago

Kendon J. Conrad, PhD
Michael D. Matters, PhD
Patricia Hanrahan, PhD
Daniel J. Luchins, MD
Courtenay Savage, MA
Betty Daugherty, RN
Marc Shinderman, MD

Kendon J. Conrad is affiliated with Health Policy and Administration, University of Illinois at Chicago, Chicago, IL and Midwest Center for Health Services and Policy Research, Hines Veterans Administration Hospital, Hines, IL. Michael D. Matters is affiliated with Health Policy and Administration, University of Illinois at Chicago, Chicago, IL 60612. Patricia Hanrahan and Daniel J. Luchins are affiliated with the Illinois Department of Human Services, Chicago, IL and the Department of Psychiatry, University of Chicago, Chicago, IL. Courtenay Savage is affiliated with the Department of Psychiatry, University of Chicago, Chicago, IL. Betty Daugherty is affiliated with the Community Counseling Centers of Chicago, Chicago, IL. Marc Shinderman is affiliated with the Center for Addictive Problems, Chicago, IL.

Address correspondence to: Kendon J. Conrad, Health Policy and Administration, University of Illinois at Chicago, 2035 W. Taylor Street, Chicago, IL 60612 (E-mail: KJConrad@uic.edu).

Funding for this work was provided by the Substance Abuse and Mental Health Services Administration (SAMHSA) Project number G5B749 through the Illinois Department of Human Services, the University of Illinois at Chicago, and the University of Chicago. The authors would also like to acknowledge the valuable contributions of Danielle Quasius, Research Assistant.

[Haworth co-indexing entry note]: "Representative Payee for Individuals with Severe Mental Illness at Community Counseling Centers of Chicago." Conrad, Kendon J. et al. Co-published simultaneously in *Alcoholism Treatment Quarterly* (The Haworth Press, Inc.) Vol. 17, No. 1/2, 1999, pp. 169-186; and: *Homelessness Prevention in Treatment of Substance Abuse and Mental Illness: Logic Models and Implementation of Eight American Projects* (ed: Kendon J. Conrad et al.) The Haworth Press, Inc., 1999, pp. 169-186. Single or multiple copies of this article are available for a fee from The Haworth Document Delivery Service [1-800-342-9678, 9:00 a.m. - 5:00 p.m. (EST). E-mail address: getinfo@haworthpressinc.com].

© 1999 by The Haworth Press, Inc. All rights reserved.

SUMMARY. This paper describes a representative payee (RP) program at Community Counseling Centers of Chicago (C4). This program features a mental health agency bank that works with clients and case managers (CMs) to ensure the financial stability of clients. After reviewing the literature on money management services, the chapter discusses the history, context, and target population of the program. It then describes the logic and functioning of representative payeeship and concludes with a discussion of the advantages and challenges involved in implementing an agency RP program with a central banking system. *[Article copies available for a fee from The Haworth Document Delivery Service: 1-800-342-9678. E-mail address: getinfo@haworthpressinc. com]*

KEYWORDS. Representative payee, money management, financial stability, central banking system

INTRODUCTION

Many persons with severe mental illness and/or substance abuse issues have difficulty managing the money they need to care for themselves. They have multiple problem areas such as financial instability, vulnerability to financial victimization, heavy hospital use, and homelessness. Various types of representative payee have been tried for years, but the payees have often been relatives or friends who have their own problems and may use their RP status for their own benefit to the detriment of clients. Some agency RPs have also taken advantage of RP clients. This is regrettable since effective money management can, theoretically, provide a linchpin service that makes the entire service system more effective.

When an agency develops a banking system to serve as the RP in cooperation with case managers, this has the advantage of linking therapeutic services with clients' basic needs, such as payment of rent and other bills. It also relieves the CM of monetary demands from clients that can distort the clinical relationship. The division of responsibilities can also provide a system of checks and balances. The CM stays aware of the clients' financial status while the bank is aware of their program status. It is best when clients have access to banking statements and are trained to develop their own money management skills so that they may begin to take responsibility for themselves. This is the nature of the RP system at C4.

REVIEW OF REPRESENTATIVE PAYEE LITERATURE

Historically, RP programs have been developed, e.g., by the Social Security Administration (SSA), principally to facilitate the responsible management of the funds of children and the elderly by caring family members. This program was extended to provide RPs to help adults with disabilities to live in the community. The program has been generally successful when the RPs are the family members of children and older persons. However, problems have occurred when family members are not involved. This is especially the case for disabled adults, who are more likely to be living on their own without a responsible spouse, parent or adult child to assist in managing financial affairs. In these cases, the SSA has often been forced to turn to individual payees in the form of more distant relatives and acquaintances who do not live with the beneficiary and may have only sporadic contact. Studies by the Office of Inspector General suggest that this kind of payee poses a greater risk to the beneficiary. Therefore, in the last few years the SSA and Congress have attempted to increase the availability of qualified, non-custodial organizations to serve as payee (Social Security Administration, 1996).

Relationship of Social Security Payments and Drug Abuse

Policymakers and care providers are concerned that public financial support may help maintain or exacerbate substance abuse among the population with severe mental illness, a group in which substance abuse and dependence are prevalent. Research findings from a study of 105 people with schizophrenia suggested a temporal relationship between receipt of disability income at the first of the month, and increased substance abuse (Shaner et al., 1995). This increase was accompanied by an exacerbation of psychiatric symptoms and re-hospitalization, prompting the authors to question whether disability income is a "government-sponsored revolving door." More recently, a study of 143 veterans (Grossman et al., 1997) assessed temporal patterns of psychiatric service utilization, disability payments, and recent cocaine use over each of the four weeks of the month. Supportive of Shaner et al., this study found that cocaine users have the most emergency room visits during the first week of the month following receipt of benefits.

However, evidence that public assistance supports or exacerbates substance abuse remains controversial. This issue was examined in a study of 665 homeless veterans with a history of substance abuse problems (Rosenheck & Frisman, 1994). The authors concluded that "it is the addictive disorders that drive substance use, not the availability of one or another type of funds. . . . It would be more efficient to target intensive RP services at selected clients, rather than providing hit-or-miss services to all those whose substance abuse appears to contribute to their disability. The practicality and value of this approach would depend ultimately on the procedure developed for identifying beneficiaries who are most in need of such a program."

Need for Representative Payee Services

No previous studies exist on the criteria used to target clients to receive organizational RP. Although Ries and Dyck (1997) and Luchins et al. (1998) have observed that dual diagnosis is common in persons assigned RPs, we know very little else about which clients in actual practice are assigned payees, or why.

Conrad et al. (1998) conducted a study to describe clients using an agency RP. They were compared to non-RP clients using variables developed from the literature, clinical and expert input, and retrospective data analysis. Based on data from 56 RP compared to 54 non-RP participants over two years, the best descriptors were: (1) indicators of financial distress or disability such as schizophrenia, homelessness, no rent money, and lacking financial skills; (2) those indicating long-term dependence on Social Security and the mental health system, such as receiving SSI and frequent hospitalizations; and (3) indicators of independence such as work history, employment income, and family support.

Effectiveness of Representative Payee

Very little evaluative research has been conducted on RP programs for mentally ill persons with substance abuse problems. If RP is a linchpin treatment that makes all other treatments more effective, then substance abuse should be affected as well. In methadone maintenance treatment, Herbst, Batki, Manfredi, and Jones (1996) found that clients without RP missed significantly more clinic days than those with a payee. Clients without a payee also had more drug positive urine tests (37% vs. 18%). In a pre/postassessment of 61 "treatment-unresponsive alcoholics" in New Zealand, Spittle (1991) found an 86% reduction in alcohol-related hospitalization for a posttest period averaging 1,056 days. Rosenheck, Lam, and Randolph (1997) found a reduction in homelessness for person with RP. In another pre/poststudy without a comparison group Stoner (1989) found reductions in victimization and arrests with improvement in cooperation with treatment. In a pre/postanalysis of retrospective hospitalization data, Luchins et al. (1998) found significant reductions in hospital days from the year before having an RP to the year after. However, more rigorous evaluations of agency-provided RP programs are needed.

COMMUNITY CONTEXT

Located on the north side of Chicago near the lake shore, the Edgewater-Uptown area has served as an entry point to mainstream society for thousands of individuals with psychiatric disabilities when they were discharged from hospitals. It is estimated that 10,000 to 20,000 patients have been discharged to the Uptown area since 1968. In the 1970s and '80s, the community became a repository for hundreds of homeless people, many of whom had a mental illness and/or a substance abuse disorder. This interaction between severe disability, homelessness, and substance abuse resulted in high rates of psychiatric rehospitalization among this population.

AGENCY CONTEXT

In 1969, concerned citizens from every segment of the community gathered with agency representatives to incorporate the Edgewater-Uptown Community Mental Health Council. In the decades that followed, the agency expanded greatly. It significantly enlarged its geographic service area and broadened the spectrum of persons eligible for comprehensive behavioral health and social services.

To reflect the evolution of agency operations, the agency changed its name to Community Counseling Centers of Chicago (C4) in 1992. Today, C4 has over 300 employees and over 20 different services available to the more than 7,000 clients it serves each year. The C4 team works closely with Chicago Read Mental Health Center, the local, state psychiatric hospital. Staff are on site there for several weekly staff meetings in order to facilitate smooth transitions from the hospital into the community. C4's mission is to deliver needs-based, comprehensive mental health and substance abuse treatment and support services to community residents.

DEVELOPMENT OF REPRESENTATIVE PAYEE AT C4

In 1981, the first case management program was established within the Edgewater-Uptown Community Mental Health Center. Three staff members assisted clients in managing their money, with only six participating that year.

In 1984, the agency was the recipient of an Illinois Department of Mental Health and Developmental Disabilities New Initiatives grant. This funding allowed for a housing specialist to serve as a banker and maintain all client funds using manual accounting procedures.

In 1985, the agency opened an account with the Uptown National Bank of Chicago and deposited all monies there. The agency kept sub-accounts for each client in the individual ledger. By 1992, the program had grown to 151 clients. A part-time accounting clerk was hired to set up a business bookkeeping system, and monthly reconciliation of the ledger was conducted in conjunction with the agency's business office.

In 1994, the agency and its RP program received a Special Recognition Award from the Social Security Administration in appreciation of their willingness, over the years, to undertake this difficult and time-consuming task. The original system, where clients dealt only with case managers, was eliminated that year when the first over-the-counter banking service was offered to case managers and clients.

In 1995, the agency entered into a contract with the SSA to become the mandated payee for a large number of clients who qualified for benefits due to drug and alcohol disabilities. The operation converted into a simulated bank environment and included three teller windows for faster service.

A financial coordinator was hired and worked with the agency's business office to convert the manual record-keeping system into a sophisticated computerized program. Using the Quickbooks system, checks were generated to pay clients' rent and other bills. Clients had access to a monthly report showing the status of their accounts. Additionally, staff performed monthly reconciliation of accounts and produced reports.

As client numbers grew, so did the staffing pattern. As of mid-year 1997, there were 464 RP clients and 7.5 full-time equivalent RP staff members. Positions now include: RP liaison, financial coordinator, data entry person, cashier, clerk, receptionist and security guard. Agencies that do not have RP services make referrals to the C4 RP program, and a brochure is being created to further market these services.

LOGIC MODELS

Two logic models are provided here. Figure 1 is a graphic, one-page summary of C4's entire array of services. Figure 2 describes the C4 RP program.

DESCRIPTION OF REPRESENTATIVE PAYEE CLIENTS

The largest racial/ethnic groups within the RP group are Caucasian (66%), African-American (18%), and Latino (11%). The RP group is 68% male. Sixty-three percent of the RP group is between 25 and 44 years of age. These clients have a moderate level of education: 32% are high school graduates; another 25% had one to three years of schooling after high school; and 2% completed college.

The primary psychiatric diagnoses of RP clients can be divided into three categories: schizophrenia (37%); schizoaffective disorder (29%); and bipolar disorder (18%). The remaining diagnoses (16%) consisted of depressive, impulse control, and personality disorders. Fifty-five percent of RP clients

FIGURE 1. Logic Model of Community Counseling Centers of Chicago

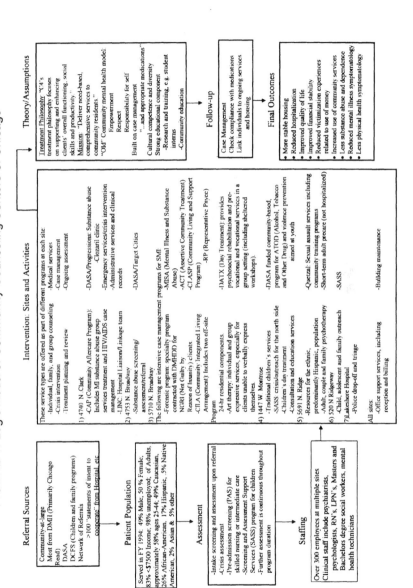

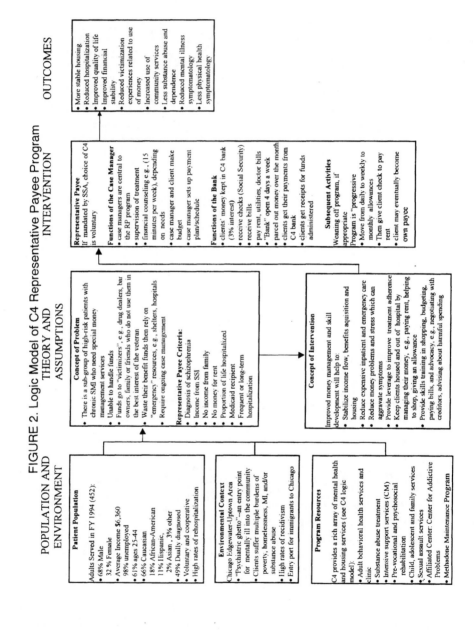

FIGURE 2. Logic Model of C4 Representative Payee Program

had a secondary diagnosis, with forty-nine percent of the RP group being dually diagnosed with both severe mental illness and some form of substance abuse disorder.

CLIENT NEEDS AND RESOURCES

Representative payee clients relied heavily on government resources to meet their needs for housing, food, clothing, and other necessities with 52% receiving SSI. The remainder received Social Security Disability Insurance (SSDI), or both. A review of C4's May, 1997 bank records of 44 clients indicated that for most, employment and family cash contributions accounted for negligible amounts of their yearly income, though some clients periodically received food, clothing, and other goods from family members. In the retrospective study sample, only 2% of RP clients listed employment as a source of income and none of those in the study listed family members as regular sources of funds.

Some banking clients received additional income from miscellaneous government sources, such as transitional assistance, yearly rent rebates from the State of Illinois, and Veterans Administration benefits. In the study sample, 27% of RP clients received food stamps, and 21% received Transitional or General Assistance. For 44 RP clients that were studied, income ranged from $250 to $847 for a person who received SSDI, with a mean of $529.10. A large proportion of clients studied lived at or below the federal poverty threshold which was $8,163 for a one-person household in 1996.

Our study showed that clients had several types of insurance. Fifty-nine percent received Medicaid only, 9% received Medicare only, and 21% had access to both. Two percent had access to private insurance. None of the RP clients lived with family members, and a large majority routinely paid their own rent.

THE REPRESENTATIVE PAYEE PROGRAM AT C4

In the C4 RP program, arrangements are made to provide rent directly to landlords, ensuring housing stability. Case managers and banking staff work together as a team although their responsibilities are distinct. CMs use their clinical skills to assist clients in developing budgets that meet their needs. Banking staff use their financial expertise to ensure careful handling of clients' funds and individual accounts. Special accounting software is used to maintain and update the clients' accounts daily. This combination of clinical and financial expertise appears to be unique, at least in Illinois, and our preliminary findings suggest it is effective (Luchins et al., 1998).

The RP program provides the following four general types of services: protection; maintenance in the community; skills training; and advocacy.

Protection. Many individuals with severe mental illness have difficulty managing the money they need to care for themselves. Daily allowances are often provided in the initial phase of the RP program. For many clients, receipt of the allowance is contingent on meeting with their case manager for treatment. The RP program assists clients with treatment needs. The CM performs crucial roles for the client, such as medication monitoring and on-going assessment of whether the service plan is meeting their needs.

When Social Security checks are deposited directly into the C4 RP bank and allowances are regularly dispersed through agency RPs, victimization and mismanagement are reduced and clients are able to spend their funds on their basic needs.

For example, one C4 client believed that God required her to give away everything she had. She typically gave away all her spending money and, unless her CM went with her for groceries, she would give away all her food on the way home. Now this client receives a daily allowance. Over time, she has learned to keep and handle a larger amount of her money appropriately.

Maintenance in the Community. Many individuals with severe mental illness who are in need of RP services have a history of homelessness and frequent hospitalizations. Persons with severe mental illnesses, such as schizophrenia, have a 25% to 50% risk of homelessness. This is 10 to 20 times the risk of homelessness for the general population (Susser et al., 1997), and is due in part, to their difficulties managing money well enough to pay rent on a timely basis.

Agency RPs facilitate maintenance in the community by paying clients' rent and bills every month and serving as liaisons to landlords. The C4 RP program has established relationships with board and care homes by ensuring regular rent payments. Also, the increased likelihood of compliance with treatment makes behavioral problems and endangerment to others in the client's residence less likely. For example, one client would impulsively spend his whole Social Security check at the start of the month without paying his rent. Although his landlord was sympathetic to his problems, over time she could not afford to keep him as a tenant. To make matters worse, he was not receiving any treatment for his schizophrenia, became delusional, and eventually set a fire in the apartment. This led to a psychiatric hospitalization. His discharge plan included using C4 as his RP, and he has steadily improved since then. Because of this client's enrollment in the RP program, a case manager was able to help him find housing–something that would otherwise have been very difficult due to his history.

Skills Training. Some individuals with severe mental illness need skills training; particularly those who have had long hospitalizations, frequent hospitalizations, or nursing home placements. During periods of institutional care, there is no opportunity to perform tasks such as securing an apartment, paying rent and buying groceries. Upon discharge these tasks can be quite daunting given the relatively small amount of money available to those who depend on Social Security payments for their basic needs.

For example, one client, who was referred to the C4 RP program from a nursing home, had to pay rent and buy groceries with $484 a month. Developing a budget with his case manager was an important first step toward learning to reside in the community. Within the first month, a financial crisis arose because the client needed new glasses. He was very concerned about how much the doctor was going to charge. Did he have to bring all the money with him to his appointment? Would she accept time payments? The CM role-played phoning the doctor with him, and helped him develop a payment schedule.

This case is typical of C4's individualized approach to improving money management skills. Because the range of skill deficits and problems is quite broad, skills training is tailored to the needs of each client. In every case, however, a specific budget is developed jointly with the client and modified as needed.

Advocacy. Securing and maintaining clients' benefits is a very important role of the RP program. Even when clients receive SSI/SSDI and have been residing in a nursing home, the transition to community living can require advocacy. It is not unusual for SSI/SSDI checks to continue being sent to the nursing home after the client has been discharged. When C4 is the RP, however, this situation is quickly uncovered and remedied. When this situation arose in a past case, a CM accompanied the client to the nursing home to get the check and then to the currency exchange to obtain a money order for rent. The CM commented that without the RP program, clients often forget to mention not having received their first check until problems arise with living arrangements and basic needs.

PROGRAM STRUCTURE AND PROCESS

Program Structure

Staffing. Though the case manager has gatekeeper responsibilities for each client's funds, the RP banking staff actually manages, distributes and handles the money. This separation of responsibilities is designed to ensure the therapeutic relationship between CM and client is not compromised. Banking staff and CMs communicate regularly about each client's status, progress and any problems that arise. With the client, the CM develops a monthly budget and may also issue vouchers for clients to redeem at the bank for cash. The ultimate goal of the RP program is for clients to develop the skills to manage their financial affairs independently.

C4's RP program involves banking staff and CMs from the adult clinical programs. Case managers evaluate clients' needs for banking services, explain the C4 banking program and answer questions. They formally enroll clients in the program and help them develop monthly budgets. They work with banking staff to locate housing for clients as needed. They inform banking staff about special requests for clients' funds and work to solve any account problems.

Cost of Operating the Program. The total direct cost of the program in 1997 was $206,645. Most of this budget was for salaries and personnel related expenses.

Client Fees

Throughout the years that C4 has provided RP services to its client population, service fees have never been assessed for clients who have a primary diagnosis of mental illness. Under the SSA fee structure a 10% fee (not to exceed $25) could be assessed. C4 has assessed a fee for banking clients who receive disability benefits through The SSA's drug abuse and alcoholism category. The SSA has allowed up to 20% of a person's monthly check (not to exceed $50) for those receiving benefits under this disability category. However, due to the termination of this category, this revenue source no longer exists.

As of July, 1, 1997, the RP program began to assess clients' fees on a sliding scale. Depending on an individual's circumstances, one might pay the full 10% or be assessed $10, $5, or $3. This decision is not popular with clients, nor with some staff, but it has become necessary due to increasing costs and losses in revenue. However, this is still a lower fee than clients would pay if they had to use currency exchanges. Also, paying for C4 banking services is similar to what clients will have to do if they have accounts at commercial banks in the future. In that regard, the new fee structure represents normalization of lifestyle.

THE BANKING FACILITY

The bank is part of a three-story facility operated by C4. It occupies about 20% of the building's first floor and consists of six rooms and offices. After entering, the client registers in the reception area. The waiting area holds 15 people and is equipped with a television to entertain clients while they wait. Access to the cashier windows is gained through a long, narrow hall that equally divides four administrative offices. Three of these offices have actual banking windows to serve clients, including the coordinator's office. This office stands directly behind the reception room and contains the bank's safe, and clients' files. The banking system has the following rules or policies:

1. The bank is open Monday, Tuesday, Thursday, and Friday. The hours for case managers are from 9 a.m. to 10 a.m.; for C4 clients from 1 p.m. to 3 p.m.; and for other clients from 10 a.m. to 12 p.m. and 1 p.m. to 3 p.m.
2. As a general rule, clients are required to provide receipts for 80% of the money given to them by the bank. For example, if a client receives $100 per month, s/he must prove purchase of $80 in necessities such as groceries, in order to receive that full amount again. If the 80% level is not achieved, the bank is authorized to give only $50 for that month. The maximum amount of cash given to one client on any particular day is $200. Intoxicated and unruly clients will not receive any services and will be escorted out of the bank.
3. Special requests require 24-hour notification, and money will only be allocated on the date noted on the slip. This rule is flexible in verifiable emergencies.

PROGRAM PROCESS

Determination of Need. The first step in the process is to determine whether a client needs RP. Case managers have internalized the criteria for RP services and offer the program when it is believed to be needed. Initially, the CM informs the client that s/he has determined the client's need to participate in the program. Before asking if the client is willing, the CM should first explain the program enables clients to get money management assistance through C4. Since clients can be fearful or reticent to participate, it is important to: (1) explain the benefits of the program; (2) explain that C4's financial backing will help pay their debts, and reassure them that they and their creditors will be paid; (3) refer them to or introduce them to other clients in RP who can provide testimonials about the effectiveness and reliability of the program; and (4) take them on a tour of the banking facilities and explain how the system works.

If a client is unwilling to enroll and the CM firmly believes they need the program, s/he will enlist the help of other people, such as family members and the psychiatrist. The CM can urge the physician to write or go to the Social Security Administration and ask them to mandate RP for the person on SSI or SSDI. In a case where a client is already enrolled, but the CM believes the payee is abusing their responsibility, s/he will try to work with the payee and the client to have payeeship transferred to the agency. The DONReP form (Conrad et al., 1998) is being used to assist in determining whether a particular client is eligible for the program.

Managing Clients' Money. Once a client is in RP, the case manager works with him or her to develop a budget, obtain benefits, set up automatic payments from the bank to the landlord, utility companies, etc., and to conduct an ongoing assessment of needs for skill development. The budget outlines basic income vs. needs and tabulates the monthly expenditures and special allotments needed. The budget includes rent, utilities, transportation, laundry, cigarettes, medications, and a weekly allowance. Case managers work with clients to develop practical money management skills, such as shopping and paying bills. Some CMs hold the monthly supply of bus tokens and cigarettes, and hand out only a set amount per day. For some C4 programs, cigarettes are bought in bulk to save clients money.

Follow-Up Activities. Follow-up is addressed in the clinical record using a Data Assessment Plan (DAP). The case manager records all client contacts on the DAP. This record includes an assessment of how the client is doing in regard to their RP. If problems are observed, the treatment plan is revised to address the problem.

Every six months the CM is required to write a follow-up review on the treatment plan where every item is evaluated in terms of its achievement. The CM coordinates this evaluation with everyone involved. In the case of RP, the CM works with the banking staff and any other significant persons involved with the client to assess how well the RP process is going. This necessarily includes feedback from landlords, restaurants, and other agencies.

Because most RP clients have long term severe mental illnesses, there is no specified length of time for them to be in the program. For many, it is unrealistic to leave RP and become financially independent. For others, this is a realistic goal, but may take years to achieve. The goal of financial independence is one of many treatment goals that are worked on concurrently. Ideally, RP services will enhance and facilitate attainment of substance abuse and mental health treatment goals. As improvement is observed in these areas, financial independence becomes attainable.

SIGNS OF IMPROVEMENT

The administrative staff noted that a marker of improvement is when clients come in less often, but get more money–a weekly, rather than a daily stipend. This indicates greater independence.

Another area of improvement–indicated by staff observation–is that clients in some programs were hospitalized much less often since enrolling in RP. Prior to admission in the program, some clients would spend all of their money in the first two weeks of the month, then they would look for ways to get back into the hospital.

The staff also noted that some clients have achieved financial independence from the RP program. Whereas these clients were previously rejected by banks because of bad credit histories, inability to maintain a minimum balance, and inability to understand paperwork, accounts, and procedures, they now have command over their financial skills and the ability to successfully maintain themselves in the community.

LESSONS LEARNED AND RECOMMENDATIONS

Abuses of Representative Payee. In a focus group, representatives from outside agencies such as the SSA, the VA, and local health care and housing providers, thought that the most problematic issue of RP programs in general, is the dishonest RP. Three versions were described:

1. The payee who works with the client to cheat the SSA. One of the health centers noted cases where two or more SSA recipients serve as RP for each other. The SSA noted they had found cases like this among drug and alcohol recipients, who were mandated to have an RP. They felt that more people need RP than organizations can manage.
2. The payee who works against the client to cheat him or her. For example, the VA hospital and the SSA described situations where agency RPs charged drug and alcohol clients $50 per month, the maximum allowed by law, and did nothing more than cash their checks. One medical center staff member said they knew of situations where clients with relatives as RPs were found homeless.
3. The payee who would like to help the client, but is incapable. The Social Security Administration representatives cited the case of a man who beat-up his payee (elderly mother), when she did not want to give him money for drugs. These SSA representatives indicated they have no policing powers to crack down on, or retrieve money from, dishonest payees.

The foregoing problems highlight the need for guidelines and accountability in representative payeeship.

Representative Payee as Treatment Incentive

There was a continuum of opinion about using RP as an incentive to engage clients in treatment. A health center representative said she felt this approach might not be ethical and that it was important to separate treatment from RP. Another health center representative felt RP is a good incentive that gets people to attend treatment. Her clients have a very long history of homelessness and are very independent. Agencies often establish RP allowances so it is convenient for the organization to see the client for treatment at certain times, especially for medication. "They'll come for the money . . . so we're very strategic about the disbursement of the check." As to RP's effect, the health center representative said, "I really do think rep' payeeship helps us keep some people out of the hospital."

THE RATIONALE FOR A CENTRALIZED BANKING SYSTEM

An important incentive for centralizing the RP program with a banking system has been the benefits to case managers and clients:

1. It greatly decreases the amount of time CMs need to spend on administrative work related to RP. This is particularly true for CMs in programs where most of the clients have C4 as payee (e.g., Assertive Community Treatment). This allows more time for work with all clients.
2. Separating responsibility for cash disbursement and money management counseling decreases the power differential perceived by clients. As a result, clients can feel comfortable in their relationships with case managers.
3. RP helps ensure that time between client and CM will not be completely usurped by disputes over money. It also limits the possibilities of touchy situations that could lead to threats of violence, or actual aggression. Thus, CMs and clients spend time more constructively; focusing directly on treatment-plan goals.
4. Disbursement funds are located in a single, secure location within the agency. This decreases any security risk and lessens the possibility that clients' money will be lost or temporarily misplaced. It also relieves clinical staff of the fear of personal liability, and diminishes the possibility that a client will accuse them of stealing money or of "holding it back."

ADVANTAGES OF AGENCY RP

Though the Social Security Administration has historically preferred for family members to be RPs, relatives are not automatically selected. The SSA representatives felt organizational RP helped remove issues of misuse/abuse between relatives and claimants. The SSA often reassigns recipients to organizational RPs if they discover misuses of the type discussed above.

The administrative staff generally agree that the RP program works well for the majority of clients. The rigid structure is necessary for many clients because they simply are unable to handle money independently. Once clients begin to reap the benefits of the program–with rent paid, enough to eat, and possibly some extra spending money–they become more comfortable with the structure.

The program is also reassuring to landlords, utility companies, and other vendors. Without the backing of C4 and the RP program, many clients are unable to obtain leases or maintain the use of utilities. They are often unwelcome in stores and restaurants. Therefore, case managers use RP and the status of C4 to ensure rent payment. They also empower clients to obtain their credit histories, contest their credit reports, and re-establish credit. They arrange for bill payments, train clients in shopping, and general money management. Lessons include practice in comparison shopping and discussions about how to make money last for a full month.

With stable housing and finances, case managers help clients achieve a better quality of life by teaching the basic activities of living, such as doing laundry, getting haircuts, glasses, medical and dental care, and so on. The program also helps promote improved treatment adherence by providing clients with positive consequences associated with treatment participation.

ONGOING CHALLENGES

Although the RP system at C4 has become quite sophisticated, there are still several ongoing challenges for RP in general. Significantly, some RPs are abusing the responsibility. The examples given earlier indicate that the case manager needs to set criteria for RPs.

The RP administrative staff stated that their jobs are very stressful, because money is a big issue in people's lives. The money belongs to the clients, and they feel they have a right to it. There is a great deal of legitimate pressure placed on the RP when a client requests money. Refusing to give them their money may lead clients to panhandle, steal, or prostitute themselves in order to get the money they want anyway. Additionally, the clients can become very insistent, manipulative and even indignant with staff members. Despite good teamwork and a very capable security guard, significant stress exists as a result of bad behavior, or the threat of bad behavior, exhibited by some clients.

EXPANDING THE KNOWLEDGE BASE

Until now there has been no in-depth study of a sophisticated RP program such as the one at C4. With the evaluation that is to be done, our study will provide previously unavailable, but sorely needed information on the effectiveness of RP. Additionally, we will provide instrumentation and documentation that will enable replication of this project as well as the ability to develop future studies of different aspects of RP.

REFERENCES

Conrad, K.J., Matters, M.D., Hanrahan, P., Luchins, D., Savage, C., & Daugherty, B. (1998). Describing patients with mental illness in representative payeeship. *Psychiatric Services, 9*, 1223-1225.

Grossman, L.S., Willer, J.K., Miller, N.S., Stovall, J.G., McRae, S.G., & Maxwell, S. (1997). Temporal patterns of veterans' psychiatric service utilization, disability payments, and cocaine use. *Journal of Psychoactive Drugs, 29*(3), 285-290.

Herbst, M.D., Batki, S.L., Manfredi, L.B., & Jones, T. (1996). Treatment outcomes for methadone clients receiving lump-sum payments at initiation of disability benefits. *Psychiatric Services, 47*(2), 119-120.

Luchins, D., Hanrahan, P., Conrad, K., Savage, C., Matters, M.D., & Shinderman, M. (1998). Agency-based representative payee program: Improved community tenure among persons with severe mental illness. *Psychiatric Services, 9*, 1218-1222.

Ries, R.K. & Dyck, D.G. (1997). Representative payee practices of community mental health centers in Washington State. *Psychiatric Services, 48*(6), 811-814.

Rosenheck, R.E., & Frisman, L. (1994). Do public support payments encourage substance abuse? New Haven, CT: Yale University School of Medicine.

Rosenheck, R., Lam, J., & Randolph, F. (1997). Impact of representative payees on substance use among homeless persons with serious mental illness. *Psychiatric Services, 48*(6), 800-806.

Shaner, A., Eckman, T.A., Roberts, L.J., Wilkins, J.N., Tucker, D., Tsuang, J.W., & Mintz, J. (1995). Disability income, cocaine use and repeated hospitalization among schizophrenic cocaine abusers: A government sponsored revolving door? *New England Journal of Medicine 333*, 777-783.

Social Security Administration, Office of the Inspector General. (1996). Monitoring representative payee performance: Roll-up report (SSA/OIG Publication No. A-09-96-64201). San Francisco: Office of Audit.

Spittle, B. (1991). The effect of financial management on alcohol-related hospitalization. *American Journal of Psychiatry, 148*, 221-223.

Stoner, MR. (1989). Money management services for the homeless mentally ill. *Hospital and Community Psychiatry, 40*(7), 751-753.

Susser, E., Valencia, E., Conover, S., Felix, A., Tsai, W.Y., & Wyatt, R.J. (1997). Preventing recurrent homelessness among mentally ill men: A "critical time" intervention after discharge from a shelter. *American Journal of Public Health 87*(2), 256-263.

Cross-Site Issues in the Collaborative Program to Prevent Homelessness: Conclusion

Patricia Hanrahan, PhD
Deirdre Oakley, MA
Lawrence D. Rickards, PhD
Daniel J. Luchins, MD
James M. Herrell, PhD, MPH
Kendon J. Conrad, PhD
Michael D. Matters, PhD
Cheryl Gallagher, MA

INTRODUCTION

This paper shifts from the site-specific focus of the previous papers to a cross-site focus that explores similarities and contrasts between projects and

---

Patricia Hanrahan is Associate Professor, Department of Psychiatry, University of Chicago. Deidre Oakley is Research Associate II/Prevention Policy Coordinator, Policy Research Associates, Inc. Lawrence D. Rickards is Project Officer, Homeless Programs Branch, Center for Mental Health Services, JAMHSA. Daniel J. Luchins is Associate Director for Clinical Services, Illinois Department of Human Services. James M. Herrell is affiliated with the Division of Practice and Systems Development at CSAT. Kendon J. Conrad is Professor, School of Public Health, University of Illinois at Chicago. Michael D. Matters is Research Assistant Professor, School of Public Health, University of Illinois at Chicago. Cheryl Gallagher is Project Officer, Division of Practice and Systems Development, Center for Substance Abuse Treatment, SAMHSA.

[Haworth co-indexing entry note]: "Cross-Site Issues in the Collaborative Program to Prevent Homelessness: Conclusion." Hanrahan, Patricia et al. Co-published simultaneously in *Alcoholism Treatment Quarterly* (The Haworth Press, Inc.) Vol. 17, No. 1/2, 1999, pp. 187-208; and: *Homelessness Prevention in Treatment of Substance Abuse and Mental Illness: Logic Models and Implementation of Eight American Projects* (ed: Kendon J. Conrad et al.) The Haworth Press, Inc., 1999, pp. 187-208. Single or multiple copies of this article are available for a fee from The Haworth Document Delivery Service [1-800-342-9678, 9:00 a.m. - 5:00 p.m. (EST). E-mail address: getinfo@haworthpressinc.com].

© 1999 by The Haworth Press, Inc. All rights reserved.

describes activities being conducted conjointly. The cooperative agreement between the federal government (CMHS & CSAT) and the grantees specified that projects not only must provide unique site-specific interventions and conduct fidelity and outcome evaluations, but that providers must also establish standard processes to allow cross-site data collection and analysis. As described in earlier papers, a steering committee comprising the principal investigators from each project and the lead agency government project officer, developed the key domains, measurement instruments, data intervals, and analytic methods that will be used by each project for the cross-site evaluation. This collaborative effort provided the basis for examining program results collectively, and for revealing the diversity inherent in locality, subpopulations, philosophies, and intervention approaches. Fortunately, while there is cohesiveness to the program, the collective effort has not artificially homogenized the projects; they remain eight distinct approaches to preventing homelessness among a population with psychiatric and/or substance use disorders who are at high risk for homelessness.

In this paper, the similarities and differences between the project sites will be described on the dimensions of: logic models, populations, outreach and enrollment procedures, theoretical perspectives, intervention components, stages of treatment and recovery, approaches to harm reduction, use of case management models, policies regarding relapse and retention, and goals and anticipated outcomes.

Homelessness Prevention Program Logic Model

The Collaborative Program to Prevent Homelessness (CPPH) logic model incorporates features of the logic model described for the Homeless Programs Branch (Rickards, Leginski, Randolph, Oakley, Herrell, & Gallagher, 1999) and the logic models presented by each of homelessness prevention program project sites in the preceding chapters. The CPPH logic model provides a linkage between the broad prevention goals of the Branch, the narrower pragmatic goals of a single prevention program, and the preventive interventions implemented by local program sites. These interventions are imbedded within an array of agency/provider services, goals, and objectives which vary somewhat across sites and are described in previous chapters.

The linkage, organizing, and guidance functions of the CPPH logic model become evident in a review of Figure 1. The first column, "Populations and Environment," provides a definition of the target population for the study that is consistent with the definition used in Homeless Programs Branch (HPB) logic model: *Adults with psychiatric and/or substance use disorders who are formerly homeless or at-risk for homelessness and who are engaged with the mental health and/or substance abuse treatment system.*

FIGURE 1. Homelessness Prevention Program: Logic Model

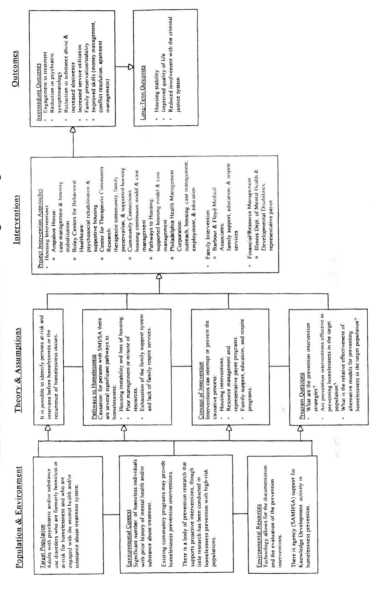

No one project site could embrace all the potential adult subpopulations that might be included in the target definition. Each site selected a subpopulation for inclusion in its study that was consistent with the defined target population and appropriate for its environmental context, resources, and specific intervention. For example, Barbour and Floyd's Family Intervention (Connery and Brekke, 1999) is studying services to multi-problem African American and Latino families who have an adult with mental illness (and often co-occurring disorders) living in the home. Boley Centers (Clark, Teague, & Henry, 1999) selected a study population with mental illnesses or dual disorders with backgrounds fraught with poverty, few job skills, lack of a support system, and a high level of fear and distrust. The Center for Therapeutic Community Research (Sacks et al., 1999) focused its attention on minority, single, and unemployed mothers who have a substance abuse history. Likewise, each of the other project sites has identified a study population of persons at-risk and has developed an intervention to intercede prior to homelessness or the recurrence of homelessness. And although the identified populations are dissimilar from one another, they are all within the scope of the HPB and CPPH logic models.

The common baseline data protocol will allow a description of the similarities and differences of the target populations across project sites, and an analysis of population characteristics based on consistent demographic questions and consistent assessment measures. The set of common outcome measures may ultimately provide information on the diversity of responses to prevention approaches.

In the second column of the CPPH logic model, "Theory and Assumptions," several risk factors are identified as pathways to homelessness, including: (1) housing instability and loss of housing; (2) poor management or misuse of financial resources; and (3) exhaustion of the family support system and the lack of family respite services. Closely related to these risk factors are inappropriate and insufficient services which may leave the individual vulnerable to relapse and homelessness. The logic model posits that appropriate interventions can interrupt or prevent the causative process; that housing interventions, resource management, and family-directed approaches can operate as protective factors for homelessness. Each project developed a logic model that contains its underlying theory(ies) and assumptions for the pathways to and interventions that prevent homelessness. For example, Community Connections (Bebout, 1999) identifies poor service coordination and system fragmentation as systems level problems that lead to service attrition, attenuated treatment gains, and housing instability. At the individual level, Community Connections identify multiple untreated impairments and the erosion of social supports, poor money management, and treatment disengagement as leading to residential instability. Although the basic philosophies, values, theories, and assumptions differ as to specifics of subpopulation, context, and prevention intervention concept, the underlying themes across projects are consistent with the HPB and CPPH logic models.

Three key program questions have been posed: (1) What are the prevention intervention strategies? (2) Are prevention interventions effective in preventing homelessness in the identified target populations? (3) What is the relative effectiveness of alternative models for preventing homelessness in the target population? Only the first question can be addressed prior to the completion of data collection and analysis.

The "Interventions" column in the CPPH logic model categorizes the eight homelessness prevention projects into three intervention approaches: housing, family support, and financial/resource management interventions. Six of the projects address housing interventions, and one project each has a primary focus on family interventions and financial/resource management interventions. The logic model does not convey the mixed approaches used by some project sites. For example, Pathways to Housing (Tsemberis & Asmussen, 1999) is primarily a supported housing intervention that also uses Assertive Community Treatment (ACT) teams, a harm reduction approach to substance abuse, and a representative payee model. Similarly, the Center for Therapeutic Community Research (Sacks et al., 1999) has, as part of its treatment and supportive housing approach, components that address and support family preservation.

The final column of the logic model, "Outcomes," provides intermediate and long-term goals and outcomes that are consistent across the eight project sites. They are the anticipated consequences to be derived from the interventions. The logic model enumerates only the common outcomes, such as: housing stability, reduction in substance abuse and increased abstinence, and reduction in psychiatric symptoms, and improved skills. Each of the project sites also has unique goals and projected outcomes that are consistent with its study population, theory and assumptions, and homelessness prevention intervention.

Finally, the CPPH logic model provides guidance in helping projects maintain fidelity to their evaluation designs. By providing the linkage between research questions, populations, interventions, and goals and outcomes, the logic model helps prevent drift and distraction that can arise in multi-year projects. Likewise, under the cooperative agreement, the logic model provides the Government Project Officers with a useful tool to help assess project progress and ongoing compatibility with program goals.

POPULATIONS

Substance Abuse and Mental Illness. All of the homelessness prevention projects serve some persons with substance abuse problems; however, two projects are designed to serve *only* persons with substance abuse problems: Arapahoe House and the Center for Therapeutic Community Research (Kirby et al., Sacks et al., 1999; Table 1). Both serve a high proportion of individuals who also have mental illnesses, e.g., depression, 70%, at Arapahoe House. Although 60% of the Therapeutic Community group have mental disorders, persons with severe mental illness such as schizophrenia are screened out.

One program, Project H.O.M.E., serves clients with a mix of primary disorders (Coughey et al., 1999; Table 2). The majority of these clients have a mental disorder, others have substance abuse problems or are dually diagnosed. The remaining five projects serve clients whose primary diagnosis is a mental illness, although a substantial proportion of their clients also have problems involving substance use (Clark, Teague and Henry; Bebout; Tsemberis and Asmussen; Connery et al.; Conrad et al., 1999). Psychotic disorders predominate, with schizophrenia or schizoaffective disorder affecting half or more of their clients. Mood disorders are also frequent. These diagnoses, together with high rates of substance abuse, suggest that the clients are severely mentally impaired.

Race and Ethnicity. A high proportion of racial and ethnic minorities are served by these programs with African-Americans being the majority in four projects (Sacks et al; Bebout; Coughey et al.; Connery and Brekke, 1999), while a fifth project has a fairly even split between African-Americans (38%) and Caucasians (41%, Tsemberis and Asmussen, 1999). Caucasians compose the majority in the remaining three projects with about a fifth being African-

TABLE 1. Demographics: Projects serving persons with a primary diagnosis of substance abuse.

PROJECT AND CITY	TYPE DISORDER	RACE AND ETHNICITY GENDER
Arapahoe House PROUD: Project to Reduce Over-utilization of Detoxification Services Thornton & Denver, CO Kirby et al., 1999	Substance abuse, all Alcohol, 75% Drugs, 25%, mostly Cocaine Mental illness, high proportion Depression, 70%	Caucasian, 60% African-American, 20% Hispanic, 20% Men, 87% Women, 13%
Center for Therapeutic Community Research Philadelphia & Westchester, PA Sacks et al., 1999	Substance abuse, all Crack cocaine, 72% Heroin, 19% Alcohol, 13% Other cocaine, 3% Mental illness, 60% Serious MI screened out	African-American, 75% Hispanic, 15% Caucasian, 10% Women, 100%

TABLE 2. Demographics: Projects serving persons with a primary diagnosis of mental illness.

PROJECT AND CITY	TYPE DISORDER	RACE AND ETHNICITY GENDER
Boley Centers for Behavioral Health Care St. Petersburg, Florida Clark, Teague and Henry, 1999	Mental illness, all Schizophrenia or other psychotic disorder, 48% Mood disorder, 45% Anxiety and other, 2% Substance abuse, 43%	Caucasian, 79% African-American, 18% Other 2% Men, 70%; Women, 30%
Community Connections Washington, DC Bebout, 1999	Mental Illness, all Psychotic, 95% Schizophrenia and Schizoaffective, 75% Mood Disorders, 20% Personality Disorder, 5% Substance abuse Lifetime hist., 70% Last 12 months, 35-40%	African-American, 75% Caucasian, 20% Other, 5% Women, 55-60% Men, 40-45%
Pathways to Housing NYC, NY Tsemberis and Asmussen, 1999	Mental Illness, all Schizophrenia, 52% Mood Disorders, 27% Other Psychoses, 9% Other Disorder, 13% Substance abuse Within past year, 60%	Caucasian, 41% African-American, 38% Hispanic, 13% Asian, Native American or Other, 8% Men, 64%; Women, 36%
Philadelphia Health Management Corp. Phil., PA, Project H.O.M.E. Coughey et al. 1999	Mental Illness, 41% Substance abuse, 17% Both MI and SA, 41%	African-American, 72% Caucasian, 27% Hispanic, 1% Men, 63%; Women, 37%
Barbour and Floyd Medical Associates Los Angeles, CA Connery, 1999	Mental Illness, all Schizophrenia, 68% Schizoaffective, 12% Bipolar, 20% Substance Abuse, 65%	African-American, 89% Hispanic, 10% Other, 1% Men, 52%; Women, 48%
Illinois Dept. of Human Services Representative Payee Chicago, IL Conrad et al., 1999	Mental Illness, All Schizophrenia, 37% Schizoaffective, 39% Bipolar, 18% Other, 16% Substance abuse, 49%	Caucasian, 66% African-American, 18% Hispanic, 11% Other, 5% Men, 68%; Women, 32%

Americans (Kirby et al.; Clark, Teague and Henry; Conrad et al., 1999). Hispanics are present in six of the projects, although the proportion ranges widely from 1% to 20% (Kirby et al.; Sacks et al.; Tsemberis and Asmussen; Coughey et al.; Connery and Brekke; Conrad et al., 1999). Two projects located in the largest urban areas also serve small proportions of Asians and native Americans (Tsemberis and Asmussen; Conrad et al., 1999).

Gender. Two programs that emphasize the family served either all women in the Therapeutic Community, or a high proportion of women in the Barbour and Floyd project (Connery and Brekke; Sacks et al., 1999). Women were the majority in the Community Connections project (Bebout, 1999), with men being the majority in the remainder (60% to 87%).

OUTREACH/ENROLLMENT PROCEDURES

A wide range of outreach and enrollment procedures are used across the eight interventions (Table 3). The places in which outreach and recruitment are conducted, and the enrollment procedures used, span various points of entry into the service system from street outreach to community mental health agencies. Some of the interventions use more than one point of entry in the system for recruitment. For example, Boley Centers recruits from street outreach, emergency shelter settings, and state and community mental health agencies (Clark, Teague and Henry, 1999).

Three important implications can be drawn from reviewing these varying settings. First, the clients recruited into the intervention settings are at different stages along the homeless continuum. Some are literally homeless at the time of recruitment, while others may be housed but lacking the appropriate

TABLE 3. Engagement/enrollment into interventions: Identifying at-risk populations.

PROJECT	Street Outreach Emergency Shelters	Safe Havens or Other Low-Demand Transitional Residences	Emergency Detox. Facilities	Community Mental Health Centers CMHCs	Mental Health Authority (State, Municipal, County)	County Dept. of Social Services	County Criminal Justice System
Arapahoe House			----				
Barbour and Floyd Medical Associates					----		
Boley Center for Behavioral Health Care	----	----		----	----	----	
Center for Therapeutic Community Research						----	----
Community Connections	----	----			----		
Illinois Dept. of Human Services, RP	----			----			
Pathways to Housing	----	----					
Philadelphia Health Management Corp. Project H.O.M.E.	----	----		----			

supports needed to maintain stable housing. These supports include services such as various doses and methods of case management, linkages to treatment, money management, and family respite. Second, identification of persons at-risk of homelessness may productively occur at multiple points along the treatment continuum rather than at a singular portal of entry. Third, these points of entry mirror the risk factors that have been identified as pathways to homelessness. For example, recruitment from the identified pathway of housing instability or eviction from housing precipitated by illness would most likely occur in a street outreach or emergency shelter setting. On the other hand, recruitment from the poor management or misuse of financial resources pathway would be more likely to occur in a community mental health organization than in an emergency shelter.

THEORETICAL PERSPECTIVES/INTERVENTION COMPONENTS

Critical Components. The critical components across interventions are intended to fill in the gaps in support that form the identified pathways to homelessness. These components fall into five categories (Table 4). They include: (1) connection or provision of a range of affordable, safe housing options; (2) flexible case management services with varying degree of intensity; (3) linkages to mental health and/or substance abuse treatment; (4) money management; and (5) a range of community support services. The "dose" of each critical component varies depending on the configuration of the individual intervention, but some degree of each of these five categories is present in all of the homelessness prevention projects. For example, those interventions focused on housing loss, such as Project H.O.M.E., are linked to treatment rather than being integrated within the treatment system (Coughey et al., 1999). Interventions such as Barbour and Floyd's family support model do not include permanent or transitional housing because the clients are likely to live with family members (Connery and Brekke, 1999). Critical to this intervention then, are respite care and a variety of family supports targeted to ensuring that the clients remain housed within the family setting.

Commonalties

Ensuring Residential Stability. The provision of a range of housing alternatives is central to most of the interventions, although the type of housing available varies across projects. Two approaches to providing housing predominate: the housing continuum approach and supportive housing. Even in the two programs with alternative interventions, Representative Payee and Barbour and Floyd in-home family treatment, residential stability is still

TABLE 4. Critical components to prevention interventions.

PROJECT	INTERVENTIONS	Connection/Provision: Range of Housing Options					Flexible Case Management Services with Low Case Loads				Linkage to MH and Treatment for Substance Abuse			Money Management			Range of Community Support Services				
		Transitional	Permanent	Advocacy	Respite	ACT/CCT	Dyadic CM	Intensive CM	Integrated Tx	Linkages to Tx	Rep Payee	Money Management	ADL Training	Employment Services	Social Services	Support Skills	Char Int Cng/Skills
Arapahoe House Thornton, CO	Dyadic Case Management	-	-	-			-	-	-			-		-	-	-	-	
Barbour and Floyd Medical Associates Los Angeles, CA	In-Home Family CM		-	-				-				-		-	-	-	-	
Boley Center for Behavioral Healthcare St. Petersburg, FL	Housing and Housing-Related Supports	-	-	-	-				-			-		-	-			
Center for Therapeutic Community Research (Gaudenzia, Inc.) Philadelphia, PA	Five Stage Residential Recovery Model (SA women w/children).	-	-					-		-				-	-	-	-	-
Community Connections Washington, DC	Clinical Housing Continuum	-	-	-	-	-			-		-		-		-	-	-	
Illinois Department of Human Services (C4) Chicago, IL	Representative Payee (RP)					-	-	-		-								
Pathways to Housing New York, NY	Consumer Preference Independent Living (CPIL)	-	-	-	-				-			-						
Philadelphia Health Management (Projest H.O.M.E.) Philadelphia, PA	Housing Continuum Model.	-	-	-	-			-			-		-	-	-			

addressed directly (Conrad et al.; Connery and Brekke, 1999). The representative payee program includes help with locating housing and provides direct payment of rent. The in-home family treatment program supports residential stability by helping families maintain their mentally ill relatives at home and by providing periodic residential respite care.

Housing Continuum Model. In the continuum model, housing is an extension of treatment and clients are matched to various types of housing according to clinical considerations. This model is discussed extensively by Bebout (1999). Living arrangements often include group living with staff on site, especially early in the intervention. Independent housing is reserved for those persons with substantial improvements in functioning. However, the decision as to which housing arrangement is appropriate is *individualized* for each client, with a *broad range* of housing options available.

Housing options typically include crisis housing and specialized treatment houses (e.g., for persons who are dually diagnosed). These arrangements provide an alternative to institutional placement and are usually staffed around the clock. Clients who are more functional but still in need of treatment may be placed in transitional living arrangements which offer treatment for specific behavior patterns that have contributed to residential instability. These programs are usually less heavily staffed, but are likely to have some staff on site around the clock. Clients who are functioning fairly well are placed in supported independent living, where they are seen periodically by case managers. Clients who are expected to need supervision and assistance for a long time receive more intensive support with staff on-site for most of the day, e.g., until midnight.

There is not necessarily a linear progression through the various types of housing. *Responsiveness* to individual needs continues to be important throughout treatment. Housing decisions are made *collaboratively*; client preferences are followed as much as possible given the clinical context. Housing and clinical staff are co-located in the same agency to facilitate this goal. Housing supports and mental health services are *integrated.* From the clinician's perspective, many clients are seen as continuing to need structured and supervised living arrangements to maintain their treatment gains and remain in stable housing. The attainment of stabilized housing arrangements is a *longitudinal* process.

For the most part, projects that provide housing follow the "housing as treatment" approach, viewing the preferred type of living arrangement as a clinical decision (Kirby et al.; Sacks et al.; Clark, Teague and Henry; Bebout; Coughey et al., 1999). There are variations within this approach, for example, several projects use a combination of housing provided by the agency and referrals to other programs, rather than relying solely on housing provided by their own agency. The degree to which clients have progressed towards recovery also plays an important role in the type of living arrangement recommended.

Stages of Treatment. Although all CPPH programs address the need to individualize service plans, several of the housing continuum models do so within the context of theories concerning the stages of treatment. In the Community Connections model for dually diagnosed persons, the four stages of treatment are: *engagement*-forming an alliance between the individual and the treatment staff; *persuasion*-stressing the need to address the negative consequences of substance abuse; *active treatment*-developing a commitment to reducing and eliminating substance abuse; and *relapse prevention*-developing the skills to maintain recovery (Osher and Kofoed, 1989; Bebout, 1999). Housing arrangements in this model reflect the individual's stage of treatment. For instance, independent living is not advised during the initial stage of engagement. Similarly, in Project H.O.M.E., initial living arrangements provided in Safe Havens are fully staffed, low-demand residences in which abstinence is not required (Coughey, Feighan, Lavelle and Olson, 1999). Further progress towards sobriety leads to more independent housing. The PROUD program at Arapahoe house also uses a stages of change model (Prochaska, DiClemente and Norcross, 1992; Kirby et al., 1999). Using dyadic case management, staff match client needs to housing options both within Arapahoe House and within the larger network of housing programs in Denver. The Boley Homelessness Prevention Project also recognizes the importance of an initial engagement stage in which low-demand services are offered (Clark, Teague and Henry, 1999). Movement towards readiness for change is encouraged with treatment goals gradually increasing in difficulty.

The Therapeutic Community program, designed for substance abusing women with children, also provides a structured group living arrangement in the initial phase of treatment (Sacks et al., 1999). The first stage, called Foundation for Recovery, is similar to the engagement stage. The development of an alliance is stressed, followed by a commitment to recovery from substance abuse. Later stages prepare the client for independent living and focus on both pragmatic issues, such as applying for Section 8 housing, and a commitment to abstinence.

Supported Housing. The supported housing model aims to provide permanent homes in normal housing and is often referred to as "housing as housing" versus "housing as treatment." Clients are encouraged to select the mode of housing they prefer, with an emphasis on self-determination. Individualized rehabilitation plans are developed within this context. As developed by Pathways to Housing (Tsemberis and Asmussen, 1999), supported housing has the following tenets: (1) "Homeless individuals with psychiatric disabilities can maintain independent housing of their choice with the right supports; (2) the consumer selects his/her own housing (apartment); (3) apartments are rented from landlords in the community, and the agency providing housing is not the same agency that provides treatment or support services; (4) clinical crises such as relapse to substance abuse or psychotic episodes, do not place the tenant at risk for losing his/her housing; (5) services are offered by an ACT team, *in vivo,* in the community, and are available on an on-call basis 24 hours a day; (6) type, frequency, and sequence of services is determined by the tenant; and (7) sobriety, medication compliance, or any other form of treatment is not a requirement, the staff use a harm reduction model for drug and alcohol abuse."

Harm reduction provides an alternative conceptual framework for helping persons with substance abuse disorders and severe mental illness. "Harm reduction refers to attempts to minimize the damage from conditions that are unlikely to change in the short run. Recovery from substance abuse is a lengthy, stepwise process that begins with people who are not ready to be abstinent but who can benefit from services. Harm reduction techniques encourage substance abusers to cut down on their use, to switch substances, to use less dangerous modes of ingestion, or to adopt more healthful ways of living" (Oakley and Dennis, 1996, p. 184).

Pathways to Housing employs an approach that includes harm reduction for individuals who are dually diagnosed (Tsemberis and Asmussen, 1999). More than 60% of the clients have substance abuse disorders. Housing tenure and participation in treatment are considered separate domains. If tenants use drugs or alcohol in their apartment, their housing tenure is not threatened by the program. If drug use becomes excessive or out of control, other tenants in the building may call the police or the landlord may move to evict the client. The ACT team staff may address the behavior by stricter budgeting of clients' funds, recommending treatment, or escorting the tenant to meetings.

This approach attempts to improve the quality of life for people who are, at least temporarily, unwilling or unable to meet the demands of more traditional services. In the Pathways model, housing in independent living arrangements is provided with only two requirements. First clients must be willing to meet with Pathways staff at least twice a month. However, clients commonly accept the need for daily visits with Pathways staff, especially when first engaged. Second, clients must agree to use Pathways as an agency representative payee for social security funds in order to ensure that the rent is paid and basic needs are met. Exceptions to this rule are allowed, but are rarely made. Although medication compliance is encouraged, alternative solutions may be sought. For example, a client who was non-compliant with his medication disturbed his neighbors by pacing and talking to himself late into the night. Since he continued to refuse medication, a partial solution was to move him to an apartment in which his noise was less apparent to his neighbors.

Case management is another key component of all eight projects (Table 5). All of the interventions use a clinical case management model in which the case manager provides treatment and coordinates services directly, although some referrals are also provided. Case managers work closely with housing coordinators and/or landlords. Their case loads are usually small, and clients also have access to a multi-disciplinary team as needed. Several projects rely on one case manager who provides most of the treatment or counseling and service coordination (Connery and Brekke, 1999), often in conjunction with a

TABLE 5. Case management.

PROJECT AND CITY	SETTING	STAFF TO CLIENT RATIO	STAFFING PATTERN	CASE MANAGER CHARACTERISTICS
Barbour and Floyd Medical Associates Los Angeles, CA Connery and Brekke, 1999	Home and Community	1:10	Individual CM, Access to multi-disciplinary team	Paraprofessional
Arapahoe House Thornton & Denver, CO Kirby et al., 1999	Home and Community	1:12 or 2:12 Per team	Dyadic Team	Must have or be training for Addictions Counselor Certification
Community Connections Washington, DC Bebout, 1999	Home and Community Later stage: Office	1:15	Individual CM & Clinical Housing Coordinator, with Access to multi-disciplinary team	Master's level Clinicians
Pathways to Housing NYC, NY Tsemberis and Asmussen, 1999	Home and Community	1:10	Assertive Community Treatment Teams	Interdisciplinary team Psychiatrist, S.W., Nurse, Voc. Rehab., Service Coordinator
Center for Therapeutic Community Research Philadelphia, Pa. Sacks et al., 1999	Home and Community	Not Stated	Case Assistant	Not stated
IL. Dept. of Human Services Representative Payee Chicago, IL. Conrad et al., 1999	RP Bank Office, Home and Community	Varies with Type of Clinical Program	Case manager and Banking staff team	Paraprofessional. Most have BA in related field
Philadelphia Health Management Corp. Phil., PA., Project H.O.M.E. Coughey et al., 1999	Home and Community	Varies 1:12–18	Individual CM with access to multi-disciplinary team	Paraprofessional. Most have BA in related field
Boley Centers for Behavioral Health Care St. Petersburg, Fl. Clark, Teague and Henry, 1999	Home and Community	Not Stated	Individual CM/ Housing specialist and access to multi disciplinary team	Not stated

housing coordinator (Bebout, 1999), or banking staff (Conrad et al., 1999). Dyadic case management is used in the PROUD project at Arapahoe House (Kirby et al., 1999). In the Pathways to Housing project, case management is available around the clock on an on-call basis by an ACT team (Tsemberis and Asmussen, 1999).

Most projects provide case management in the client's home and community. In the later stages of treatment, the office may become the primary setting, e.g., the Community Connections program (Bebout, 1999). In the Representative Payee Program, case management often occurs in the office, while financial transactions take place in a bank run by the agency (Conrad et al., 1999).

All the interventions emphasize the importance of a collaboration between case manager and clients or a client-centered approach in which treatment goals, housing options and service linkages are strongly influenced by client preferences. Case managers use referral to substance abuse treatment in two of the projects, Barbour and Floyd and Project H.O.M.E. (Connery and Brekke, 1999; Coughey et al., 1999). Substance abuse treatment is integrated into the program in the remaining projects either by having a member of the team be an addictions specialist, as in Arapahoe House, or by having substance abuse programs within the agency, as in the Representative Payee Program (Kirby et al.; Conrad et al., 1999).

RELAPSE AND RETENTION POLICY

Relapse policies in the CPPH programs are directly related to their theoretical perspectives. Several approaches use a continuum model of housing and a stages model of substance abuse treatment (Bebout; Sacks et al.; Coughey et al.; Kirby et al., 1999). Progress toward housing stability parallels progress toward substance abuse recovery and mental health, occurring in stages. Substance abuse policies are often more flexible initially within more structured housing types and more restrictive in independent housing for clients who have made progress in their recovery from substance abuse (Bebout, 1999). For example, clients in Safe Havens are not required to be clean and sober; while, in independent living quarters, no drug or alcohol use is permitted (Coughey et al., 1999). In these programs, stage of recovery and individual factors play an important part in relapse considerations. Residents can move from a more independent living situation to a more supportive one during periods of relapse (Coughey et al., 1999).

One site combines the housing continuum model with both sensitivity to stages of recovery and a strength-based psychosocial rehabilitation perspective on substance abuse (Clark, Henry and Teague, 1999). Drugs and alcohol are not permitted in the more tightly controlled transitional housing, but in permanent housing clients can do as they want in their own private apartments. Relapses are viewed in terms of the problems they cause for the resident. Clients are often able to keep their apartments through brief hospital or detoxification stays.

In the Pathways to Housing approach, housing is seen as a basic right (Tsemberis and Asmussen, 1999). Clinical crises such as relapse to substance abuse or psychiatric episodes do not place the clients at risk for losing their housing unless it causes problems with the landlord or the police.

Two programs, Representative Payee and Barbour and Floyd's Home Visit Family Case Management model, are not primarily housing interventions. In the Representative Payee program housing is ensured through agency payment of rent, and the C4 bank can maintain housing during short hospitalizations if relapse occurs (Conrad et al., 1999). Barbour and Floyd provide in home services and did not discuss relapse policy (Connery and Brekke, 1999).

GOALS, OUTCOMES AND STAKE HOLDERS

To address the problem of homelessness in a dually diagnosed, mentally ill, chemical abusing population, the eight programs serve two, possibly disparate goals–preventing homelessness, and treating mental illness and substance abuse. The way these two goals are integrated into the programs ranges from the New York Pathways program that explicitly separates the provision of housing from any expectation of treatment, to the modified therapeutic community in which treatment and housing are by definition enmeshed (Tsemberis and Asmussen; Sacks et al., 1999).

In the absence of strong empirical evidence regarding the actual outcomes of these approaches, scientific argument regarding the relative merits of these approaches is premature. Nevertheless, in addition to the absence of compelling empirical evidence, there are issues of priority, policy and politics that confound the adoption of any single approach. First, there is the question of whether homelessness prevention or treatment should be the primary goal of the program. Is success judged by how many participants remain housed, or by how many become abstinent, or decrease psychiatric symptoms, become employed, etc.? If the goal is harm reduction, what type of harm are we to measure: the sequelae of homelessness, of mental illness, of substance abuse? Is the ultimate measure reduced costs, reduced illness, reduced criminality or reduced deviancy? These are not simply academic questions since the success or failure of a program will be judged by these often competing goals. For example, in our review of the representative payee and substance abuse literature, programs were often judged as not successful because they did not reduce substance abuse (Conrad et al., 1999). Reduction of hospitalization

(Luchins et al., 1998) or homelessness (Rosenheck, Lam and Randolph, 1997) were seen as secondary and less important outcomes.

It is possible that a particular approach yoking or separating housing and treatment will provide greater benefits both by preventing homelessness and by treating substance abuse and mental illness. From a scientific point of view this would simplify comparisons; if all outcomes are positive, it is not necessary to choose the most important outcome. It is also important to keep in mind that differences in target populations may require different interventions, and may also lead to different outcomes. Nevertheless, political decisions may make one approach, even if more successful, unpalatable. Free housing with few strings attached may provide better outcomes but may not pass the test of political acceptability.

THE COOPERATIVE AGREEMENT AND IMPLICATIONS FOR THE FUTURE

There has been general consensus among the grantees and the SAMHSA project staff that this cooperative agreement project has been particularly successful as of this writing, i.e., near the two-year mark of the three-year project. It is worthwhile to reflect on possible reasons why this is so. First, it could simply be good luck. This group seems to work well together, is willing to cooperate on the tasks involved in developing cross-site measures and analysis plans, and does not have hang-ups that get in the way of cooperation, e.g., overly competitive, or threatened by new and challenging ideas and tasks.

Second, the requirement during year one to develop a logic model and a program manual, followed by the need for a rigorous evaluation, may have fostered some unexpected benefits. The program staff and the researchers on each project had to work together closely in order to succeed. Clinical expertise and research expertise were both valued highly, and this may have helped both the clinicians and the researchers. For example, in developing the program manual, the researchers had to get deeply involved in the program and listen carefully to program staff in order to articulate the nature of the program. This probably helped them to be sensitive to programmatic issues that could be affected by the research procedures. In other words, the researchers were more sensitive to the program people and issues. Meanwhile, the program staff were learning about the research and participating in its development which improved their sense of ownership and facilitation of the research. Also, the program received a sophisticated description of their service model which was useful to them since it could facilitate program communication, implementation, and improvement.

Additionally, SAMHSA's principal agenda was to learn about the effectiveness of the programs in a scientifically rigorous way, but it was never at the expense of the program. For example, randomized experiments were not required for the evaluations. This probably avoided the problems of resentful demoralization, competition, and subversion of the design that often take place in experiments (see Conrad, 1994, for examples taken from actual studies).

Third, the organization of the cooperative agreement may have contributed to its success. Obviously, SAMHSA staff took the lead; but, at the first meeting of grantees in Washington, it was made clear that it would be a "steering committee" composed of representatives of the grantees and SAMHSA staff that would make decisions about the cross-site issues. Assisting SAMHSA staff and the steering committee was the contractor for research support, Policy Research Associates (PRA), which provided the plethora of services needed in carrying out the cooperative agreement.

The Collaborative Program to Prevent Homelessness is one of several coordinated, multiple-site evaluations (MSEs) currently underway within SAMHSA. The field continues to develop methodological and analytic approaches for MSEs (Orwin, Sonnefeld, Garrison-Mogren, and Smith, 1994 discuss evaluation issues from an earlier round of homelessness studies), and no approach to categorizing or defining MSEs has gained general acceptance.

MSEs are multidimensional. Some dimensions are integral–i.e., they define MSEs, whereas other dimensions are "optional"–i.e., some dimensions will apply, fully or partially, to a given MSE. Table 6 lists some dimensions that characterize MSEs, and the applicability of each to CPPH. Dimensions 1-3 are the integral, or defining dimensions; the remaining are optional. The dimensions can also be categorized as "program" and "structural." Program dimensions apply to services and recipients–that is, to the intervention and to the target population. Structural dimensions pertain to the organization of the evaluation–the design, the data instruments, etc.

"Multiple-site evaluation" may be used as a generic term that applies when two or more sites engage in a coordinated effort to address a core set of study questions. Sinacore and Turpin (1991) distinguished between those MSEs examining interventions that are implemented in the same way across all sites (e.g., multi-center clinical trials) and those that examine different implementation across sites. This distinction, while useful, does not reflect the multidimensionality of MSEs. The terms "multisite study" or "multisite clinical trial" seem usefully to describe MSEs in which all dimensions in Table 6 substantially apply. CSAT and CMHS support some multisite studies, but for many currently funded cooperative agreements, only some of the dimensions apply, and the term "cross-site study" may usefully distinguish such studies from multisite clinical trials.

Consistent with these definitions, CPPH is a cross-site study. It approaches

TABLE 6. Dimensions of multiple-site evaluations.

	Dimension	Type	Applies to CPPH?	Comment
1	Coordination	S	Fully	Coordination is mandated by SAMHSA. Project coordination implemented through steering committee.
2	Core Study Questions	S	Fully	All sites collect data addressing core questions defined by the steering committee. Each site may develop site-specific questions.
3	Simultaneous Implementation	S	Fully	Enrollment of participants into MSE began and will end at same time across all sites.
4	Intervention	P	No	Each site employs a unique intervention.
5	Target Population	P	Partially	Population is broadly defined across all sites, but each site sets more explicit requirements.
6	Design	S	Partially	All sites use pre-post-follow-up design. Comparison groups and procedures for group assignment differ across sites.
7	Measurement points	S	Fully	All sites collect data at same time points.
8	Instruments	S	Fully	Core set of measurement instruments sufficient to answer core study questions used by all sites.
9	Training	S	Fully	Interviewers are centrally trained.
10	QA	S	Fully	Procedural compliance of interviewers and of data are centrally managed.
11	Data analysis	S	Fully	All cross-site data are submitted to a central source. Analytic plans and reporting of findings are the responsibility of the steering committee. Sites may analyze and report on site-specific data.

Note: Type S = Structural; P = Program. See text for definitions.

the structural strength of a well-designed multisite clinical trial, in that all structural dimensions shown in Table 6 are fully applicable except for "design," which partially applies. In CPPH, well trained and supervised assessors gather data from hundreds of service recipients at established time points using standard instruments with established psychometric properties. However, program dimensions in Table 6 vary across sites, with particularly significant variation in the interventions, and target populations overlap only partially.

In this project, the steering committee directed the MSE. It began by forming subcommittees that split-up the measurement issues and developed the measures that were used in the cross-site data collection described earlier (Rickards et al., 1999). The steering committee and subcommittees were chaired by people selected from among the grantees. PRA facilitated ongoing conference calls to enable the committees to complete their work beyond the Washington meetings. Each project was still free to use its own project-specific measures and analysis plans tailored to the particular goals of each program. The cooperation is continuing as representatives of the projects have formed subcommittees to develop plans to analyze the cross-site data.

Cross-site analytic strategies present challenges beyond those presented by multisite clinical trials. The challenges for CPPH derive largely from the varieties of interventions and the varieties of target populations. It is possible to treat CPPH as eight independent studies and apply meta-analytic approaches to cross-site analysis, but such an approach would squander CPPH's structural strengths. A potential value of MSEs is the increase in power brought by an increase in sample size. In CPPH, the total sample will, of course, be several times larger than any single site's sample, but the variability in the interventions may render it unwise to pool clients across sites for analysis. Another potential benefit of MSEs is the opportunity to look at contextual effects (Mobray and Herman, 1991). Again, however, variability of interventions and of target populations will interact in a potentially confounding way with contextual effects. Despite these problems, the structural strengths of the project, combined with potential use of multivariate techniques, should yield benefits beyond those available through meta-analysis. It may be possible, for instance, to identify clusters of service recipients in several sites that share a core set of relevant demographic and clinical characteristics, then to compare cross-site outcomes within these clusters as a function of different approaches to service delivery. Conversely, it may be possible to identify service mix patterns applicable to several sites, and compare outcomes for different clients receiving similar services. Development of appropriate analysis plans continues as a focus of the steering committee.

This steering committee structure promoted empowerment of the grantees, an approach that is very different from a structure where "outside experts" would be hired to analyze the cross-site data. In the "outside expert" scenario, there is no gain involved for the grantees in developing cross-site measures, nor in helping to develop the analysis plans. The outside experts are usually at a disadvantage because they do not have the field-based experience using the measures that the grantees have. The grantees get to know the measures, their strengths and weaknesses, intimately because they are going to analyze them for their individual studies. They are heavily invested in their own individual projects and can often bring insights from the project that apply to the cross-site analyses. They usually bring interest in exploring these issues beyond their own sites. The prospect of developing a useful publication on a topic of interest provides greater incentive to invest. Additionally, they have the strength of numbers. If each project would do one cross-site paper, this would result in eight papers on diverse topics. Given the tremendous demands of doing one scientific paper well and the lack of funds to support the effort beyond the project, it is very unlikely that outside experts would be able to do more than one or two papers. In any case, the steering committee scenario does not preclude outside experts. Rather than being sole cross-site leaders, the outside experts act as consultants and can still work on or take the lead on papers. Meanwhile, SAMHSA project staff remain full partners in all discussions and decisions.

Fourth, SAMHSA staff remained very involved in each project by means of the site visits, steering committees meetings in Washington, and conference calls for both the steering committee and subcommittees. When problems arose, consultants were brought in to help resolve them. In this way, the problems were addressed before they became too difficult to solve.

Clearly, this volume reflects the spirit of collaboration that has pervaded the cooperative agreement. It promises to be one of the first products, among many yet to be created from this endeavor, that will inform and influence the crucial issue of prevention of homelessness in vulnerable populations.

REFERENCES

Bebout R. (1999). Housing solutions: The community connections housing program: Preventing homelessness by integrating housing and supports. *Alcoholism Treatment Quarterly*, 17(1/2), 93-112.

Clark C., Teague G.B., Henry R.M. (1999). Preventing homelessness in Florida. *Alcoholism Treatment Quarterly*, 17(1/2), 73-91.

Connery L. and Brekke J. (1999). A Home-based family intervention for ethnic minorities with a mentally ill member. *Alcoholism Treatment Quarterly*, 17(1/2), 149-167.

Conrad K.J. (Ed.) (1994). Critically Evaluating the Role of Experiments. *New Directions in Program Evaluation, no 63*. San Francisco: Jossey-Bass.

Conrad K.J., Matters M.D., Hanrahan P., Luchins D.J., Savage C., Daugherty B., Shinderman M. (1999). Representative payee for individuals with severe mental illness at Community Counseling Centers of Chicago. *Alcoholism Treatment Quarterly*, 17(1/2), 169-186.

Coughey K., Feighen K., Lavelle K., Olson K., DeCarlo M., Medina M. (1999). Project H.O.M.E.: A Comprehensive program for homeless individuals with mental illness and substance use disorders. *Alcoholism Treatment Quarterly*, 17(1/2), 133-148.

Kirby M.W., Braucht G.N., Brown E., Krane S., McCann M., VanDeMark N. (1999). Dyadic case management as a strategy for prevention of homelessness among chronically debilitated men and women with alcohol and drug dependence. *Alcoholism Treatment Quarterly*, 17(1/2), 53-71.

Luchins D.J., Hanrahan P., Conrad K.J., Savage C., Matters M., Shinderman M. An agency-based representative payee program and improved community tenure of persons with severe mental illness. *Psychiatric Services*, 49(9): 1218-1222.

Mobray, Carol T., & Herman, Sandra E. (1991). Using multiple sites in mental health evaluations: Focus on program theory and implementation issues. *New Directions in Program Evaluation*, 50, 45-57.

Oakley D., Dennis D. (1996). Responding to the needs of homeless people with alcohol, drug and or mental disorders. In Baumohl, J. Homelessness in America. Phoenix, AZ: Oryx Press.

Orwin, Robert G., Sonnefeld, Joseph L., Garrison-Mogren, Roberta, & Smith, Nancy G. (1994). Pitfalls in evaluating the effectiveness of case management programs for homeless persons. *Evaluation Review*, 18, 153-207.

Osher F.C., Kofoed L.L. (1989). Treatment of patients with psychiatric and psychoactive substance abuse disorders. *Hospital and Community Psychiatry*, 40, 1025-1030.

Prochaska J.O., DiClemente C.C., Norcrross J.C. (1992). In search of how people change: Applications to addictive behaviors. *American Psychologist*, 47, 1102-1114.

Rickards L.D., Leginski W., Randolph F.L., Oakley D., Herrell J.M., Gallagher C. (1999). Cooperative agreements for CMHS/CSAT collaborative program to prevent homelessness: An overview. *Alcoholism Treatment Quarterly*, 17(1/2), 1-15.

Sacks J.Y., Sacks S., Harle M., DeLeon G. (1999). Homelessness prevention therapeutic community (TC) for addicted mothers. *Alcoholism Treatment Quarterly*, 17(1/2), 33-51.

Rosenheck R., Lam J., Randolph F. (1997). Impact of representative payees on substance use among homeless persons with serious mental illness. *Psychiatric Services*, 48(6): 600-806.

Tsemberis S., Asmussen S. (1999). From Streets to Homes: The pathways to housing consumer preference supported housing model. *Alcoholism Treatment Quarterly*, 17(1/2), 113-131.

Sinacore, James M., & Turpin, Robin S. (1991). Multiple sites in evaluation research; A survey of organizational and methodological issues. *New Directions in Program Evaluation*, 50, 5-18.

Index

Access to Community Care and
  Effective Services and
  Supports (ACCESS), 3
Achievement orientation, of African
  Americans, 150
Addiction counselors, certified, 59,
  69-70, 144
Addiction Severity Index, 42,44,64
Adult Day Care Assessment
  Procedure, 24
African-American families
  adjustment to family member's
    disability, 155-156
  home-based homelessness
    prevention intervention for,
    149-167,190
    assessment component, 150,161
    case coordinator's role in,
      161-162
    community interface
      component, 163
    conceptual framework, 151
    coping strategies component,
      162
    cultural, ethnic, and gender
      relevance, 151-152,159-160
    description of client population,
      156-158
    description of intervention,
      157-158
    effectiveness assessment of,
      163-164
    engagement component of,
      150,159-160
    environmental context, 152,158
    family psychoeducation
      component, 151-152,
      162-163
    family respite component, 162

family skill development
  component, 162-163
family support component, 162
goals/outcomes, 157-158,
  160-161
intervention principles of,
  151-152
literature review for, 153-156
logic model, 157
monitoring of, 150,162
residential stability focus, 195,
  197
service plan development for,
  150,161-162
services provided by, 150
staffing and staff training for,
  157,159
African Americans
  attitudes toward education, 150,
    154,156
  coping strategies of, 150,161-163
  discrimination and racism toward,
    150,155-156
  as homelessness prevention project
    clients, 192-193
  of Boley Homeless Prevention
    Project, 76
  of Community Connections
    Housing Program, 99
  of Project H.O.M.E., 137-138,
    140
  of PROUD Project, 57
  of therapeutic community
    programs, 45
  kinship networks of, 150,154,156
  mental health services utilization
    by, 155
  as percentage of homeless
    population, 76

© 1999 by The Haworth Press, Inc. All rights reserved.   209

poverty of, 150,155-156
spirituality of, 150,154,156
stress experienced by, 155
Al Anon, 143
Alcohol abuse, relationship to housing stability, 94
Alcoholics
case management for, 59
representative payee systems for, 172
American Cancer Society, Fresh Start Smoking Cessation Program, 141
Arapahoe House, 9-10,191-192. *See also* PROUD (Project to Reduce Over-Utilization of Detoxification) Homelessness Prevention Project
case management by, 200-201
engagement/enrollment interventions of, 194
history of, 56-57
homelessness interventions of, 196
logic model of, 27-30
Assertive community treatment (ACT), 7,59, 114,117,121, 124-127

Barbour and Floyd Integrated Service Agency, 152
Home Visit Family Case Management program, 10-11,149-167,190,202
assessment component, 150,161
case management in, 200-201
community interface component, 163
conceptual framework, 151
coping strategies component, 162
cultural, ethnic, and gender relevance, 159
description of client population, 156-158

description of intervention, 157-158
effectiveness assessment of, 163-164
engagement/enrollment component, 150,159-160, 194
environmental context, 152, 158
family psychoeducation component, 151-152, 162-163
family respite component, 162
family skill development component, 162-163
family support component, 162
goals/outcomes, 157-158, 160-161
intervention principles, 151-152
logic model, 157
monitoring of, 150,162
residential stability focus of, 195,197
service plan development for, 150,161-162
services provided by, 150
staffing and staff training for, 157,159
Bipolar disorder, 174
Boley Centers for Behavioral Healthcare, Inc., 9-10
Boley Homelessness Prevention Project, 73-91,190,196
client population, 76-77,193
description, 82-87
engagement/enrollment component, 194,198
environmental context, 77-78
goals and outcomes of, 87-88
housing-related support services of, 84-87
intervention concept of
consumer-provider relationships, 79-81,86-87
integrated services, 80-82
organizational climate, 79-81
organizational structure, 79-82

Index

psychosocial rehabilitation approach, 80-82
logic model, 73-74
Supported Employment Program, 77
Supported Living Program, 83
theory of, 78-82
Boston McKinney Project, 94,96

Case management, 4,58-59,200-201
assertive community team (ACT) approach, 7,59,114,117, 121,124-127
"broker" v. clinical intensive, 59
of chronic alcoholics, 59
dyadic, 201. *See also* PROUD (Project to Reduce Over-Utilization of Detoxification) Homelessness Prevention Project
long-term, 135
as service-based intervention, 7
Case managers
as change catalysts, 61,63
home visits by, 150
housing issues training for, 69
in representative payee systems, 173-174,177,179-182, 184-185
Caucasians, as homelessness prevention project clients, 192-193
of Community Connections Housing Program, 99
of PROUD Project, 57
of representative payee programs, 174
of therapeutic community programs, 45
Center for Mental Health Services (CMHS) Interim Status Report of the McKinney Demonstration Program for Homeless Adults with Serious Mental Illness, 79
Center for Mental Health Services (CMHS)/Center for Substance Abuse Treatment (CSAT), Cooperative Agreements for Collaborative Program to Prevent Homelessness of, 8-14,20
cross-site evaluation issues of, 11-13, 187-208
case management, 200-201
client populations, 188-194
logic model, 188-191
goals and outcomes, 189,191, 202-203
interventions, 189,191,195-201
outreach/enrollment procedures, 194-195
relapse prevention policy, 201-202
government project officers (GPOs) of, 8-9
guidance for applicants (GFA) component, 8,11-12
harm reduction program, 199
program structure, 8-9
projects of, 9-11
stakeholders of, 202-203
Technical Assistance Coordinators (TACs) of, 12-13
Center for Therapeutic Community Research, 10-11,190-192, 194,196
case management by, 200
engagement/enrollment component, 194
study population of, 190
Centers for Mental Services, Homeless Programs Branch, 3-8
logic model of, 4-7,188,190-191
Checklist for Change, 64
Chicago Read Mental Health Center, 173
Children, homeless, 2-3
health and social problems of, 35

Cocaine users, disability payment use by, 171
Cognitive therapy, as service-based intervention, 7
Collaborative Program to Prevent Homelessness. *See* Center for Mental Health Services (CMHS)/Center for Substance Abuse Treatment (CSAT), Cooperative Agreements for Collaborative Program to Prevent Homelessness
Colorado Coalition for the Homeless, 66
Community-based care, continuum of, 4
Community Connections Housing Program, 9-10,93-112,196
  active treatment component, 99, 108,198
  case management in, 200-201
  client population, 99-100,193
  clinical housing coordinators of, 106-107
  clinical services, 98-99
  crisis services, 100,104
  effectiveness, 97
  engagement/enrollment component, 99,107-108, 194,198
  external housing resources, 99
  goals, 106-107
  housing continuum approach, 24-27,99,101-108
  integrated dual-diagnosis services of, 99,101
  logic model for, 102-103,190-191
  permanent staffed group homes, 106
  persuasion component, 99, 107-108,198
  relapse policy, 99,108-110,198
  stages of, 99,107-108
  supported independent living program, 105-106
  theoretical basis, 100-102
  transitional housing program, 104-105
  treatment stages of, 198
Community Counseling Center of Chicago, representative payee program of
  agency context, 173
  banking facility, 173,180-181,184
  client fees, 180
  client improvement, 182-183
  clients' needs and resources, 177
  community context, 172-173
  description of clients, 174,177
  development of, 173-174
  logic model for, 22-24,174-176
  operating costs, 180
  process of, 181-182
  program description, 177-182
  program structure, 179-180
  recommendations for, 183-184
  staffing, 174,179-180
Community integration, of the mentally-ill homeless, 135
Community mental health services
  federal funding of, 3
  use by the homeless, 79
Community/neighborhood risk factors, for homelessness, 135
Community resources, African Americans' use of, 163
Conflict resolution, by African-American families, 156
Consumer Preference Supported Housing (CPSH) Model, for homelessness prevention, 113-131
  administrative structure, 124
  assertive community treatment (ACT) teams of, 114,117, 121,124-127,191,198-199, 201
  case management in, 200-201
  client population, 114-115, 122-123,193

comparison with continuum of care housing model, 116-117
comprehensive service plan of, 126
concept mapping for, 118-121
critical components, 196
description, 121-127
development of, 115
eligibility criteria, 122
evaluation study of, 127
goals and outcomes, 121,202
harm reduction model of, 117-118,191,199
housing facilities of, 125-128
housing retention rate of, 118
logic model, 119-121
operating costs, 124
program structure, 121
recommendations for, 127-128
relapse policy, 202
representative payee program, 125-126,128,191
service coordinators of, 126
staff selection and training 123-124
tenets of, 117-118,198-199
Coping strategies, of African Americans, 150,161-163
Creative writing group, 144-145
Crisis systems, psychiatric, 153
Crown Cork and Seal, 141
Cultural competence, 159
Cultural relevance, of home-based interventions, 151-152, 159-160

Decision making, by African-American families, 156
Denver, Colorado, homeless population, 56-57
Depression, 174,192
Detoxification, over-utilization of *See* PROUD (Project to Reduce Over-Utilization of Detoxification) Homelessness Prevention Project

Diagnostic and Statistical Manual of Mental Disorders, Axis II disorders, 122
Discharge planning, 4,7,135
Discrimination
toward African Americans, 150, 155-156
toward homeless women, 35
toward Supplemental Social Security Income recipients, 79
District of Columbia
Commission on Mental Health Services, 99,104
Dual-Diagnosis Project, 97,108
Mobile Community Outreach Treatment Teams (MCOTT), 24-27
Dixon Class Action Suit, 97
Drug abuse
relationship to housing stability, 94
relationship to Social Security Disability income, 171
Drug abuse rates, of homeless women with children, 35
Dual diagnosis. *See* also Alcohol abuse; Alcoholics; Drug abuse; Substance abuse; specific types of mental illness
behavioral effects of, 78-79
as homelessness risk factor, 6-7,94
as poverty risk factor, 78-79
prevalence of, 2
Dual-Diagnosis Project, Washington, D.C., 97,108
Dual-diagnosis treatment, relationship to housing stability, 94
Dwelling Place, The, 145

Edgewater-Uptown Community Mental Health Council, 173
Education, African Americans' attitudes towards, 150,154, 156
Educational programs, of Project H.O.M.E., 144-146

Emergency rooms, dual-diagnosis specialists in, 135
Employment program, of Project H.O.M.E., 145
Ethnic-minority families, home-based homelessness prevention intervention for. *See* Home-visit intervention, for ethnic-minority families
Evaluation: Promise and Performance (Wholey), 18
Eviction, 35,78,88
"Eviction prevention," 84-85
Extended family, African-American, 150,154,156

Families, as percentage of homeless population, 34-35
Family-based intervention. *See* Home-visit intervention, for ethnic-minority families
Family mediation, 82
Family support, 162
Federal Interagency Council on the Homeless, 4
Financial Victimization Questionnaire (FVQ), 24
Florida
  Continuity of Care Case Management System of, 76
  homelessness prevention program in. *See* Boley Homelessness Prevention Project
Florida Mental Health Institute, 88
Foster care, 35
Fragmentation, of service systems, 117,190
Franciscan Health System, 141

Gaugenzia. *See also* Therapeutic community programs
  Kindred House, 38,45
  New Image program, 38,45

Gender distribution, of homelessness prevention projects' clients, 192-193
Gender sensitivity, of home-based interventions, 159
Goals, clarification of, 19
Group therapy, as service-based intervention, 7

Hall-Mercer Community Mental Health Center, 144
Hallucinations, 78
Harm reduction model, of substance abuse, 117-118,199
Health Care for the Homeless Program, 141,144,147-148
Hispanics. *See also* Latinos
  as homelessness prevention project clients, 45,138, 192-193
HIV-positive persons, residential treatment for, 104
"Homeless capital," of the United States, 152
Homeless Emergency Liaison Project (Project HELP), 115
Homelessness Prevention Program, logic model of, 18
Homelessness Programs Branch, 3-8
  logic model of, 4-7,188,190-191
Homeless persons. *See also* Homeless population
  definition of, 137
  mental illness prevalence in, 2
  number of, 2
Homeless population
  African-American, 76
  composition of, 134
  of Denver, Colorado, 56-57
  of New York City, 115-116
  of Washington, D.C., 97-98
Home-visit intervention, for ethnic-minority families, 149-167
  assessment component, 150,161
  case coordinator's role in, 161-162
  community interface component, 163

conceptual framework, 151
coping strategies component, 162
cultural, ethnic, and gender
    relevance, 151-152,159-160
description of client population,
    156-158
description of intervention, 157-158
effectiveness assessment of, 163-164
engagement component, 150,
    159-160
environmental context, 152,158
family psychoeducation
    component, 151-152,
    162-163
family respite component, 162
family skill development
    component, 162-163
family support component, 162
goals/outcomes, 157-158,160-161
intervention principles of, 151-152
logic model for, 157
monitoring of, 150, 162
service plan for, 150, 160-164
services provided by, 150
staffing and staff training for, 157,
    159
Hope for the Homeless, Inc., 141
Housing, 7
    comparative evaluation of, 24-27
    consumers' choice of, 81,117. *See also* Consumer Preference Supported Housing (CPSH) Model
    crisis, 197
    federally subsidized, 56-57
    financing programs for, 135
    logic model for, 24-27
    with specialized treatment, 197
    supported (independent/
        transitional), 135,142-144,
        197-199
    of Boley Homelessness Prevention
        Project, 83-84, 86
    of Community Connections
        Housing Program, 104-106
    consumers' preference for, 117

continuum housing versus, 24-27,
    95-96
definition of, 81
as longitudinal process, 101
of Pathways to Housing, Inc., 125
of Project H.O.M.E, 136-137,
    142-143
of PROUD Project, 65-66,69
respite services and, 153
scarcity of, 69
in Washington, D.C., 98
"Housing as housing". *See* Housing,
    supported (independent/
    transitional)
"Housing as treatment". *See* Housing
    continuum model
Housing continuum model, 95-97,
    197-198
    of Community Connections
        Housing Program, 99,
        101-110
    as dependency cause, 116
    lack of effectiveness of, 116-118
    of Project H.O.M.E, 196
    versus supported housing, 24-27,
        95-96
Housing Fidelity Scale, 26
Housing stability
    lack of income as barrier to, 117
    as longitudinal process, 110,197
    of the severely mentally ill, 117

Illinois Department of Human
    Services, representative
    payee program of, 10-11,
    193-194,200. *See also*
    Community Counseling
    Center of Chicago,
    representative payee
    program of
Illinois Department of Mental Health
    and Developmental
    Disabilities, New Initiatives
    Grant, 173
Impulse control, 174

Independent living. *See* Housing, supported (independent/transitional)
Interagency Workgroup on Improving Discharge Planning, 4
"In vivo" services, 151

Jail diversion programs, 7
Job training programs, 7

Kindred House, 38,45
Kinship networks, African-American, 150,154,156,163
Knowledge Exchange Network, 13-14

Landlord-tenant negotiations, 65,82, 125
Latinos
  home-based interventions for, 154
  homelessness prevention interventions for, 190
  as PROUD Project clients, 57
  as representative payee system clients, 174
Logan Square Neighborhood Association, 146
Logic models, of homelessness prevention, 4-8,17-31
  of Boley Homelessness Prevention Project, 73-74
  of Collaborative Project to Prevent Homelessness, 188-191
  of Community Connections Housing Program, 102-103, 190-191
  of Community Counseling Center of Chicago, 174-176
  of Consumer Preference Supported Housing, 119-121
  definition of, 18
  of home-based interventions, 157-158
  of Homelessness Program Branch, 4-7,188,190-191
  use in management, 27-30
  program goal clarification by, 19
  of Project H.O.M.E., 138-140
  in program evaluation, 18-21
    agency managers' perspective on, 27-30
    external evaluators' perspective on, 22-24
    funding agencies' perspective on, 21-22
    internal evaluators' perspective on, 24-27
  properties of, 18
Los Angeles, as "homeless capital of U.S.", 152
Los Angeles Department of Mental Health, 152

Management, logic model use in, 27-30
McKinney Act, 2-3
McKinney Research Demonstration Program for Homeless Mentally Ill Adults, 3,79
McKinney projects, 94
Medicaid, 177
Medicare, 177
Mental Health Association of Southeastern Pennsylvania, 146
Mental illness. *See also* specific types of mental illness
  as eviction cause, 78
  as homelessness risk factor, 178
  as primary diagnosis, 192-193
Mentally-ill persons, stigmatization of, 141
Mercy Health Corporation, 141
Methadone maintenance patients, representative payee systems for, 172
Metro Denver Homeless Initiative, 66-67
Mobile Community Outreach Treatment Teams (MCOTT), 24-27
Money management, skills training in, 178-179,182

Money Management Outcome Measure (MMOM), 24
Mood disorders, 76,100,122,192
Mother-child dyad, as therapeutic community program focus, 40-41
Motivation, of clients, 64-65

Narcotics Anonymous, 143
National Institute of Mental Health, Office of Programs for the Homeless Mentally Ill, 3
Native Americans, 57
Neighborhood development, by Project H.O.M.E, 137
New Hampshire-Dartmouth Psychiatric Research Center, 12
New Image program, 38,45
New York City, homeless population of, 115-116
NIMBY (Not-in-My-Back-Yard) syndrome, 147
Nuclear family, African-American, 156

Open Door Coalition, 146
Outcome evaluations, logic models for, 20
Outreach services, 194-195
  of Project H.O.M.E, 136,142
  of Supported Living Program, 83

Paranoia, 78
PATH (Projects for Assistance in Transition from Homelessness) grant program, 3-4
Pathways to Housing, Inc. 9-11,114. *See also* Consumer Preference Supported Housing (CPSH) Model, of homelessness prevention
Personality disorders, 76,94,100,174

Pew Charitable Trusts, Vulnerable Adults Program, 141
Philadelphia
  Outreach Coordination Center of, 142
  as Project H.O.M.E funding source?, 140-141
Philadelphia Health Management Corporation, 11,196 *See also* Project H.O.M.E
Health Care for the Homeless Program, 141,144,147-148
Philadelphia Inquirer, 147
Philadelphia Plan, 137
Piton Foundation, 56
Policy Research Associates, 204-205
Political activism, of Project H.O.M.E residents, 145-147
Polysubstance dependence, 76
Poverty
  of African-American families, 150,155-156
  as dual diagnosis risk factor, 78-79
Problem solving, by African-American families, 156
Program plans, 18
Program theory, 6
Project HELP (Homeless Emergency Liaison Project), 115
Project H.O.M.E. (Housing Opportunities, Medical Care and Education), 133-148, 195-196
  case management in, 144,200-201
  client-centered approach, 134
  client population, 192-193
  eligibility criteria of, 137
  evaluation of, 147-148
  funding sources, 140-141
  goals, 141-142
  history of, 136-137
  homelessness problem definition of, 141
  housing continuum approach, 196
  logic model of, 138-140
  outcomes, 147

outreach services, 136,142
population and social environment of, 140-141
program components and activities, 142-147
  community/neighborhood level, 146
  individual level, 142-145
  societal level, 146-147
residents' characteristics, 137-138
supportive housing sites, 136-137
Projects for Assistance in Transition from Homelessness (PATH) grant program, 3-4
Protective factors, against homelessness, 6-7
PROUD (Project to Reduce Over-Utilization of Detoxification) Homelessness Prevention Project, 27,30,53-71
  description, 61-67
  development of, 54,56-57,61-67
  dyadic case management model of, 58-60,69,198
  eligibility criteria, 57-58
  evaluation design for, 54,62,64,67
  homelessness prevention activities, 61-63
  implications of, 68-70
  logic model, 61,63
  multidisciplinary management team approach, 61
  objectives, 61
  outcomes, 54
  preliminary outcome data of, 68
  stages of change model of, 198
  target population, 53-54,57-58
  treatment theory of, 53-54,58-60
Psychoeducation, of family members, 161-162
Psychological disorders, 76
Psychopharmacologic therapy, 7
Psychotherapy, as service-based intervention, 7
Psychotic disorders, 122,192

Racism, towards African Americans, 150,155-156
Recovery, from substance abuse, 110
Relapse policies, 99,108-110,198, 201-202
Representative payee programs, 7, 169-186
  abuses of, 181-183,185
  administered by family, 170-171, 184-185
  case management in, 200-201
  client retention policies of, 202
  of Community Counseling Center of Chicago
    agency context, 173
    banking facility, 173,180-181, 184
    client fees, 180
    client improvement, 182-183
    clients' needs and resources, 177
    community context, 172-173
    description of clients, 174,177
    description of program, 177-182
    development, 173-174
    logic model, 174-176
    operating costs, 180
    process of, 181-182
    recommendations for, 183-184
    staffing, 174,179-180
    structure of program, 179-180
  of Consumer Preference Supported Housing (CPSH) Model, 125-126,128
  critical components, 196
  development of, 170-171
  effectiveness, 172
  of Illinois Department of Human Services, 10-11,193-194, 196,200
  logic models for, 22-24,174-176
  need for, 172
  residential stability focus of, 195, 197
  as treatment incentives, 183-184
Resource allocation, 135

Respite services, 7,153,162,190
Restaurant School, 141
Risk factor approach, to homelessness prevention, 135
Risk factors, for homelessness, 6,190
Role adaptability, of African Americans, 150
Role flexibility, of African Americans, 156
Role modeling, as staff training technique, 159

St. Elizabeth's Hospital, Washington, D.C., 97
SAMHSA. *See* Substance Abuse and Mental Health Services Administration
San Diego McKinney Project, 94
Schizoaffective disorder, 100,174, 192
Schizophrenia, 76,100,122,153-154, 171,174,178,192
Scullion, Sister Mary, 136
Section 8 housing, 65-66,69,198
Service-based interventions, for service delivery, improvement strategies for, 135
Service integration, 7
Sexual abuse, 94
Shelters, entry-level, 142-143
Single mothers, substance-abusing
  eviction rates of, 35
  therapeutic community program for, 33-39,196
    approach of, 40-42
    clients' characteristics, 45
    description of program, 38-47
    eligibility criteria, 42,44-45
    evaluation plan, 47
    homelessness prevention activities, 42-44
    implementation, 46-47
    logic model, 47-48
    peer hierarchy, 40-42
    perspective of, 40
    staff, 41
    stages, 41-42
Single parents, homeless, 2-3
Sister Mary Scullion, 136
Sisters of St. Francis, 141
Skills training, 7
  for family members, 162-163
  in home-based interventions, 151
  in money management, 178-179, 182
Socialization programs, 7
Social Security Administration, representative payee programs and, 170-171, 174,180,183-184
Social Security Disability Income (SSDI)
  relationship to drug abuse, 171
  as representative payee clients' income source, 177,179, 181
Social Security Income (SSI), 56
  as representative payee clients' income source, 177,179, 181
SOCRATES, 64-65
Spirituality, African-American, 150, 154,156
Stages of change model, of behavioral change, 59
Stewart B. McKinney Homeless Assistance Act (P.L. 100-77),2-3
Stigmatization
  of the mentally ill, 141
  of Supplemental Social Security Income recipients, 79
Stress, experienced by African-American families, 155
Substance abuse
  harm reduction model of, 117-118, 199
  as primary diagnosis, 191-192
Substance Abuse and Mental Health Service Administration (SAMHSA), 3,8-9,11, 13-14,127,147-148,204. *See also* Center for Mental

Health Services (CMHS)/
  Center for Substance Abuse
  Treatment (CSAT),
  Cooperative Agreements for
  Collaborative Program to
  Prevent Homelessness
Supplemental Social Security Income,
  78-79
Support services, 7
  for family members, 162
  fragmentation of, 117,190
  for homeless mothers, 35

Therapeutic community program, for
    addicted women with
    children, 33-49
  approach of, 40-42
  basic elements of, 42
  clients' characteristics, 45
  description of program, 38-48
  eligibility criteria, 42,44-45
  evaluation plan, 47
  goals, 38
  homelessness prevention activities,
    42-44
  implementation, 46-47
  logic model, 47-48
  peer hierarchy, 40-42
  perspective of, 40
  setting, 38
  staff, 38-41
  stages, 41-42

U. S. Department of Agriculture, 3
U. S. Department of Education, 3
U. S. Department of Health and
    Human Services, 3. *See also*
    Substance Abuse and Mental
    Health Service
    Administration (SAMHSA)
U. S. Department of Housing and
    Urban Development, 3,98,
    136
  homeless person definition of,
    137

  as Project H.O.M.E funding
    source, 140-141
  transitional housing funding by,
    106
U. S. Department of Labor, 3
U. S. Department of Veterans Affairs,
  3

Washington Homelessness Prevention
  Project, 24-27
Weight Watchers Corporation, 141
Welfare recipients, homeless mothers
  as, 35
Welfare reform, 146-147
Women of Hope, 136
Work orientation, of African
    Americans, 150,156